Common Sense
Solutions for a Better Government

By

James E. Razzino

Dedication

To Alicia and Scott, the joys of my life.

Acknowledgements

This book was made possible through the support of my family and friends who suggested I seek a professional to help me.
I want to thank Louise Harris, LAST Research and Editing for expertise in editing this book. I also want to thank Ellie D'Sa, dsa designs, for the great cover.

Table of Contents

Politics is the art of transferring wealth from one group to another for the purpose of acquiring more political power and wealth for the politician and their supporters.

Introduction

For several years, I have thought about writing a book. I made an outline, then filed it away. Years later, I would rediscover the folder with my outline and start again. None of the outlines seemed to be right. I could not seem to identify the core focus for the content. I had always been interested in politics and the various political "solutions" to social issues, such as education, welfare, housing and poverty.

Like most people, I had developed opinions based on television news, political speeches, interviews and print media articles. Intuitively, I knew these opinions were probably flawed because, in business, many of the preconceived ideas about problems prove to be wrong under the illumination of more extensive analysis. None of the media discussions (or what they passed off to the public as analysis) answered the questions I had. I wanted to do my own analysis to understand the data and to develop what I call an "informed opinion," rather than an opinion crafted for me by the media. As I approached my retirement, I finally had the time and decided that my research would be the core component of a book examining a selected group of issues facing the country today.

Both business and government continually face problems. I have found their approaches to solving them are very different. Politicians seem to demigod problems. They always attach some nefarious and unfair treatment of a constituency as the rationale to support their proposed program solution. The mantra always seems to highlight the disadvantaged groups mistreatment. Terms such as underserved community were used as descriptors to justify another round of benefits for the entitled group. The programs proposed are enacted as laws with no goals, no measurement of progress and of course no end. Once institutionalized, they have a constituency who benefits from even bad programs. Vendors are hired, and government workers are added to the payroll. These people do not want to lose their livelihood. It is one of the major reasons why government continues to expand.

The business approach is not so emotional. It can be very political as senior managers might have another agenda or many times, have a favored option even before they have assigned the project to analyze, much less viewed the data. However, most of the time, businesses take a rational approach to problems, are shown the data and follow it to the inevitable conclusion. If a plan is recommended, then the resources must be quantified. Capital is required. Staffing and equipment must be identified. Calculation of the Net Present Value or Internal Rate of Return is used to determine the Return on Investment. Measurements of success are important in business. Senior executives always ask, "What does success look like?". These measurements are non-existent in government. This is why business is successful at delivering products and services while making a profit. It is also why government programs rarely solve problems. In fact, many times, they perpetuate the problem.

My career in business has, for the most part, been one of a trouble-shooter. I was the person who received problems to analyze and create solutions. Successful problem-solving is mostly an unemotional, follow-the-data exercise. But don't think the good problem-solvers are just number crunchers. Much of the time, to solve problems, the analyst must consider soft and hard data, intuition, and sometimes trial and error. They needed to be creative in thinking when coming up with solutions.

In this book, I try to explain my rationale and provide examples to help the reader better understand how I reach a particular conclusion. Problems are complex and simple at the same time. This is a confusing statement, but what I mean here is that, many times, you can get an idea of the magnitude of the issue from some basic calculations. These can also help you to focus by eliminating non-essential investigations. Please be patient, and you will see several of these types of examples in various chapters.

Americans have become captive to the authority of

experts. Many times, these people are wrong. If their solutions were correct, America would have all the problems solved. Right? Experts are just people who have biases that color their analyses and conclusions. We have been taught to honor their education and experience. We are taught to accept their analyses and conclusions in lieu of our own beliefs. Witness their performance during the COVID-19 crisis. Many mistakes were made by the Centers for Disease Control and Prevention and scientists around the world. Felippa Lentzos, a social scientist who studies biological threats, was not ready to accept the conclusion that the virus originated in animals. Although the lab leak theory was more logical, it was refuted by the World Health Organization (WHO) and many scientists without much investigation because accepting the theory jeopardized their personal livelihood or career.

"She cautions us not to idealize scientists, but to see the scientific community as a place of normal conflicts of interest, agendas and human interaction of both good and bad actors". This is true in all areas of life and one of life's more important lessons.

Over the years, I have been involved in the preparation of numerous research projects. Each one has been a learning experience. Perhaps the most important lesson was how difficult it is to prepare a questionnaire that has no bias to a particular solution. This learning has made me extremely skeptical of studies conducted by experts. Recent "studies" of the studies themselves reveal many are sloppy, poorly constructed and have been paid for by companies or other interest groups to provide a specific conclusion. These studies are thrust out into the public domain as fact when they are virtual propaganda. I learned early to not rely on other peoples' data. I use my own whenever possible.

In business, people use the description "He's a smart guy" often. I have found that there is a distinctive difference between individuals who are intelligent and those who are smart. I define them as follows:

An intelligent person is one who knows a lot of things, has a large vocabulary and can think quickly on their feet. He or she usually takes a very theoretical approach to problems. This combination of skills makes him or her very persuasive.

A smart person is one who knows what to do, how to do it and when to do it. He or she is pragmatic, action- and results-oriented. He or she may not be as quick to provide the answer because he or she wants more time to get the right answer.

These two types of people come at problems from different perspectives and get different results. Government and academia have more of type No. 1 and business has more of type No. 2.

This book was written for the average American citizen, yes all of you deplorables, who are interested in politics and government but may feel intimidated by the experts and haven't the time to research the topics. My goal is to break down complex subjects into simpler pieces and to apply common sense to the problems. For over a thousand years, Catholic liturgy was presented to the people in Latin. The common people did not speak Latin, and so, the church set up a two-class system where they were the rulers, interpreting the Bible and passing along their interpretation to the people. In 21st century America, we have the same system in place. Replacing the church is the ruling class who are the architects and occupying office holders in government. Experts make recommendations, and politicians hire experts who support their point of view. One cannot argue with an expert as he or she has more credentials (more degrees) or better credentials (more prestigious degrees) than you and, therefore, they MUST be correct. Most people are intimidated and learn to stop disagreeing. After all, what does your puny opinion matter compared to that of a person with a doctorate from Harvard University. This is how we are controlled by the ruling class. I have endeavored to do the exact opposite to inform, to explain, to teach and mostly to provide readers with the confidence to analyze these issues for themselves. Always understand that, with a pen, a calculator and a yellow pad and very little additional information, you can outline the parameters of many issues yourself.

I take some positions in this book that are very controversial. Understand, as you read, that this is done completely to solve the problem at hand. Many of the most intractable problems cannot be resolved because constraints are set up that reduce the options to a few that really will not work in the real world. In fact, it is these constraints that maintain the status quo. Keep in mind that whatever rules are put in place by the government, many people benefit, and they do not want change. This is why once a law is passed to solve a problem, even though it is proved wrong, it cannot be changed. A good example is Head Start. Originally, sold as the solution to the minorities' early grade school education underperformance, it was later discovered that the kids not participating caught up by the 2nd grade. Those funds could be used more effectively to provide vouchers for Charter schools, but it will never happen because of the entrenched beneficiaries of Head Start funds.

Writing this book has enabled me to learn so much about the topics covered in the chapters and more ancillary information. I have enjoyed writing it immensely.

"Saber es poder." "Knowledge is power." This is one of the statements we had to memorize in my first-year Spanish class in high school. It is a truism that I hope every American believes. Our Democracy only works when its citizens support politicians who are making good decisions for the country and not enriching themselves financially or creating power blocks to milk the taxpayers.

Finally, a book is a bridge from the past to the future. The writer owes a debt of gratitude to all those who shared their thoughts and inspired him to research and write. Hopefully, others will read this book, improve the ideas and help build a better future for all Americans.

Chapter 1 Building a Strong Country

<u>Background</u>

The first European settlers to the United States were escaping religious persecution. Much of this emigration was the result of the Protestant Reformation, which split Europe into Catholic and Protestant countries. If you were not of the same religion as the monarchy, then you were persecuted. As a result, many Protestant sects left their home country and settled in America. Subsequently, other groups arrived, fleeing persecution (Jews) and escaping famines (Irish, Italians). Many others were searching for a new start in a place with unlimited opportunity in a new country where everyone was equal under the law; there were no restrictions on land ownership; and everyone could rise based on their own merit.

It was the strong religious grounding of early Americans that created the Judeo-Christian foundation for American beliefs. The founding documents reflect these beliefs and the justice system as well. This is the core of the value system of America.

Because the country was originally inhabited by Dutch and English in the Northeast and spread out from there, the core beliefs were inculcated into the original

13 colonies and spread as new territories were added. English institutions and rights (*Magna Carta*) were also implanted into the culture of the colonies.

As more settlers arrived from a variety of countries, communities reflected their ethnicity. Mexicans, Germans, Swedes, Norwegians, French, Greeks, Italians, Russians, Hungarians, Swiss and Chinese until the present. America now has immigrants from more than 100 countries with numerous religions. For those fixated on diversity, it is probably the most diverse country in the world. Our shared values are those rights enshrined in the Constitution. The American people embrace the rights the constitution guarantees, and they have fought for more than 200 years to protect and maintain them.

The present American culture is a blending all these cultures. It is mixed up like a giant stew and changes over time. Politicians, entertainers and local restaurants all reflect the various ethnic groups that inhabit America. These hundreds of ethnicities and numerous religions are the real diversity, not the politically motivated Diversity, Equity, Inclusion (DEI) movement currently under way, which is a façade to provide more privileges to Democratic grievance groups.

America has done a better job than other countries (e.g., England, France, Germany) to integrate various cultures together. This is probably true because America was always a melting pot while the countries mentioned were homogeneous, adding immigrant groups usually from their colonies. In many of these countries, the immigrants still live, work and are educated almost completely separated from the major ethnic group.

Initially, immigrant groups came to America and settled in ethnic ghettos consisting mostly of people from the same home country. They settled together due to a common language, proximity to family and friends, religion, employment, access to ethnic food stores and security. As their children grew, many left the neighborhood due to military service, college, marriage or employment. They were integrated into new neighborhoods. Their ties to the old ethnic neighborhood continued to fray as parents died, friends left, and they moved further away.

All these immigrants integrated into America. They left their old country for good. They were not in America for a few years for a job and planning to return when they saved enough money. They embraced their new country and its culture, learning to speak English, adopting the customs, (e.g., Thanksgiving dinner), and celebrating American holidays (e.g., July 4th). They enjoyed the freedoms guaranteed to all American citizens. When their country was at war, they volunteered to serve. In some cases (German, Italian, Japanese), they were fighting their mother country.

While there are still some groups that live apart from

the mainstream (e.g., tribes, Amish), most Americans live in integrated communities, work together and attend school together. Another group that separates itself from the mainstream of Americans is the inner-city black population. This is not due to their desire to be separated but, in fact, due to government policies that continue to promote welfare over work and public housing that is built in the inner-city creating black ghettos.

America underwent massive immigration in the late 19th and early 20th century. Congress enacted the Immigration Act of 1924 to curtail immigration and allow time for the immigrants to integrate into American society and absorb the American culture and value system. They were concerned, rightly so, that the country would become a group of neighborhoods reflecting the old-world values.

In 1995, immigration was extended, and the United States began allowing millions more people a year into the country based on several immigration programs.

In 2009, waves of illegal immigrants began crossing the southern border. Democratic administrations under President Obama and President Biden especially touted policies that resulted in virtually open borders for anyone who came. Immigrants from around the world travelled to Mexico so they could cross the U.S. border. Thousands of others crossed without registering with the border patrol. The continued onslaught of these mostly Hispanic immigrants has changed the texture of the country. Hispanics are now one of the largest immigrant groups in America. Voting cards are now printed in English and Spanish, the first time any other language has been used. This breaks more than 200 years of precedent that immigrants who wish to become American citizens should first learn to read and write English.

The practice of printing voting ballots in Spanish is part of a trend by politicians to pander to various groups to win their support. It sets these groups up as being privileged, which is the opposite of American values and our Constitution. We strive for everyone to be equal under the law. We keep saying the words, "All men are equal," but talk is cheap. It is the practice of making it so that is important. Pandering to specific groups with legislation that provides them preference over others is not what the founding fathers envisioned. The effect is to alienate the other non-preferential groups, such as those coming from Asia.

What does a country produce? Of course, the answer is products and services. This is the response every economist will provide. However, there is a much more important product the country must produce if it expects to survive. That is citizens who are trained and educated to be self-sufficient and productive members of society. This is one of the major reasons the country has enacted laws to require that children attend k-12 school to provide a level of education required to join the workforce and to participate in governance by voting.

The country has been very successful at producing citizens able to take care of themselves for more than 200 years until FDR decided to implement a massive number of governmental programs to overcome the effects of the Great Depression. This was a fortuitous decision and in hindsight, a bad decision for the country. Instead of choosing a path to create a huge government welfare state, he should have mobilized the private sector to overcome the depression. His programs, higher taxes on business and high tariffs on imports led the rest of the developed world to follow and, as a result, they transitioned a recession into a worldwide depression that lasted until wartime spending revived the economy. It was this depression that helped set the stage for totalitarian regimes in Italy, Germany and Japan. Unfortunately, his large government continued to grow until now the federal government accounts for 24 percent of the U. S. economy.

It was at this point the country began its transformation from a place of opportunity to a place of entitlement. These socialist policies produce an ever-growing segment of society who are unable or unwilling to take care of themselves. This has resulted in a weaker country. A people who are no longer willing or able to make the tough decisions necessary to maintain competitive industries, to educate the population and to feed, clothe and house themselves. In our new society, the federal government has added layers of new welfare programs that provide cradle to grave federal assistance. The effect of these socialist programs is to provide increased incentives for people to not work at all and just live off the government. These non-workers are living off the taxes of the people who are working. For some, it is difficult to reject the easy lifestyle that government assistance offers. Once captured by the system, it is almost impossible to escape. Unfortunately, politicians love to expand the programs and capture ever more people in the web of poverty and perpetual dependence. These are lifelong democratic voters and the key to achieving a one-party communist society, the goal of the Democrats. As this group of non-workers increases, their political power also increases making it ever more impossible to curtail the entitlement programs.

In his article, "The Decline of Work," by Andy Kessler (1) he states, "work has become a dirty word, ... no not coal mining jobs but the inhumanity of digital monitoring of coders, cashiers and others." People are looking for the "perfect job" to find fulfillment and "the correct work and life balance", searching for nirvana but not willing to work hard at the job at hand.

The American people have watched in horror as news feeds broadcast protests throughout the country, burning flags, cars, buildings and whatever is available to the chants of Death to America. Most of these protesters are college-educated students who have been brainwashed by Marxist and Communist ideology in American Colleges. "The left's long march through the institutions is all but completed. Extreme intolerance has now replaced the liberal notion of negotiated compromise that is the sine qua non of democracy. The ignorance of history is the hallmark of the current crisis. Few seem to be able to grasp the complex, often painful, but on balance grand story of America, one that is an example of what a people committed to individual freedom can achieve. The American ideal offered something no other culture could, namely the chance to reinvent and renew one's life, advance one's position, and create a better future for one's children. It is a tragedy that the young seem to have jettisoned this foundational American ideal, or more likely were never exposed to it in the first place. The traditional view that political victory and loss are both part of the democratic process and the gist of a self-constituting polity has been replaced with a Leninist drive to nullify one's opponent. The principle of the radical politics now consuming the country seems to be "I win, you disappear." (2)

While Americas leading families and industrialists of the past were always tethered to a philosophy that they are Americans first, the newly anointed plutocrats define themselves as citizens of the world, and no longer have allegiance to the United States. To many, their business interests in China are more important than those in the United States. We have witnessed several tech companies that refuse to work for the Defense Department while at the same time are more than happy to provide China the means to improve their technology, undermine U. S. security, and help to monitor and control the Chinese people.

<u>Wokeness</u>

"Wokeness is a force that undermines the middle class. You could not have wokeness without an elite contempt for the values of the middle class," said Fred Siegel, a professor emeritus at New York's Cooper Union. Political correctness also undermines these middle-class values he stated. The American middle class sees political correctness as a threat to peoples' ability to speak their mind, a direct violation of their first amendment right. Seigel traced wokeness back to Herbert Croly, co-founder of the New Republic. Croly's idea was that "the college-educated should become the elite, new aristocracy. While liberals were always open to debate, wokeism is a new religion that asserts the important truths are already known. Therefore, the American aristocracy must impose those truths on the country." "These are given positions, irrefutable and sacrosanct. It says, "We don't need debate. We don't need free speech. We don't need freedom of religion or any other freedoms. We need to obey." (3)

Wokeness certainly sounds like a form of Nazi authoritarianism with the elites taking the place of the Aryan race as superior to the working class, whom they deplore, thus the moniker deplorables, coined by non-other than Hillary Clinton, for the gun carrying, Bible toting, smelly Walmart shoppers.

Hyper Intolerance is rising in America, promulgated by the ruling class, academics and legacy media and enforced by their acolytes including, Hollywood celebrities, Google, Facebook and Twitter. Under the guise of blocking racist, false or misleading information, these companies have censored all speech they dislike. As history has shown us, efforts to censor the opposition do not end well. In 1959, Cuba had its share of journalists who believed a Communist government would benefit the country. They conspired with the new Castro government to attack the free press, and eventually, it was killed off by the government. The full story is documented in the book *Harnessing the Intellectuals*, by Carlos Ripoll. Leftist journalists helped take over the newspaper *La Prensa* in Peru, shutting down a major voice against the military dictatorship. Intellectuals also helped Hugo Chavez shut off free speech in Venezuela through a combination of license cancellations for broadcast companies, denial of newsprint and the cancellation of advertising. (4)

America is becoming a weaker country because its value system is rotting from within. While the economy may be growing; wealth is increasing; and other measures of success still are showing prosperity, the work ethic is corroding. Marxism is the prevalent curriculum in colleges. Law and order have disappeared from cities across the country. As a nation, we have been preoccupied with defending ourselves from other countries who are enemies. We have been blind to the rise of communism and lawlessness within our borders instituted by the Democratic Party and their acolytes. Like empires before us, we are a nation in decline due to internal corrosion of our values.

The good news is that American citizens seem to be waking up to the threats to their children's education and the lawless cities. Hopefully it is not too late.

"For the past four years, potted histories have warned about the rise of fascism in the United States. But the real danger is the transformation of 'tolerance' into an ideology with its own courts, informers and punishments, all of them reminiscent of the Soviet Union. "(5)

"One of the pillars of the Soviet Union was a controlled press in which all coverage was organized to conform to a mendacious ideology". In the Soviet Union, this task was given to TASS, the government-owned and controlled news organization. One example of this type of news reengineering was a report that Fuji prisons were so comfortable that people preferred to stay there rather than to be at liberty. TASS rewrote this story stating life was so unbearable in FUJI that people preferred prison. (5)

"These practices would have been unthinkable in the United States at one time, but in August 2016, Jim Rutenberg, media columnist for the *New York Times*, wrote that if journalists believed that President Trump was a demagogue playing to the nation's worst racist and nationalist tendencies, it was necessary to throw out the textbook of American journalism. *The Times* started to characterize President Trump's statements as lies in news stories and suppress news that worked to his advantage, such as the Hunter Biden laptop story." The New York Times' decision ended honest news and replaced it with Soviet/Nazi style propaganda. The other legacy news outlets quickly followed. Freedom of the press was used to suppress truth.   (5)

This propaganda program was expanded to all types of speech as any individuals who are not ideologically "pure" are summarily cancelled for inane reasons at almost every college in the country. Only the voices of the communist/fascist WOKE Progressives are allowed. One party, one message. America has become a communist country. (5)

America is following the example of our European socialist/communist friends in becoming an increasingly secular society focused on accumulating wealth, power and self-aggrandizement. We both continue to turn away from the God of Abraham to the god of government. "The family -- man, woman and child -- is not one lifestyle choice among many. It is the best means we have yet discovered for nurturing future generations and enabling children to grow in a matrix of stability and love." "When husband and wife turn in faithfulness to one another, we come as close as we will ever get to God Himself, bringing new life into being, turning the prose of biology into the poetry of the human spirit, redeeming the darkness of the world by the radiance of love." "Europe's embrace of secularism has resulted in its refusal to have children. The result is that "Europe is dying." America is following it. (6)

<u>Government Economic Policy</u>

Congress continues its ever-increasing intrusion into the American economy to transform it in some way to gain political support. Both parties share the guilt here, but the Democrats continue to be acknowledged as the spend-and-tax leaders. More spending to reach nirvana, the place where the climate reverts to its ancestral cleanliness (prior to Columbus) and everyone is equal economically (except for Democrat leaders like Nancy Pelosi, the Clintons and Bidens) and the oligarchs in Silicon Valley and Wall Street who support the Democratic Party financially. They get to keep their limousines, private jets, numerous homes and yachts.

These new schemes include buy American, hire American, make it in the United States, a federal directorate for technology and of course, the Green New Deal. Our illustrious leaders believe that their programs can re-industrialize and re-engineer the American economy to solve the inequity and climate change challenges that they dream about every night. Unfortunately, history has a few lessons that show planned economies do not work including the Russian failure that resulted in mass starvation in the 1930s, and the Japanese and European failures to support special industries.

The federal government can help the economy grow by establishing good sound policies, such as low taxes, a cost-effective regulatory environment, modern updated infrastructure and outstanding schools that prepare students for the workplace. Unfortunately, ideology and political payback are continually prioritized. The economy would be stronger if the federal government would just get the hell out of the way. (7)

Identity Politics

The identity politics of today have their roots in the riots that occurred between 1965-1970 in the urban ghettos. Policy makers never understood the underlying causes of the riots and were intimidated by aggressive activists into policy decisions that have created more division and extended the poverty and crime still present in the urban ghettos. Policy makers in the federal government, including McGeorge Bundy, adviser to President Kennedy, proceeded to create ethnic and racial categories and racial preferences to government hiring, government contracts, employment and college admissions. Once formalized these new groups became the basis of new centers of political power and for the institutionalization of victimhood by these preferential groups. The Census Bureau followed by replacing its historic categorization by national origin with the new system of preferred racial and ethnic groups. Everyone else was summarily cancelled out. They no longer mattered. They lost any political power they had. It was transferred to these new groups. The vision of Dr. Martin Luther King Jr. and the leaders of the Civil Rights movement was dead. No more color blindness. "I have a dream where every man is judged by his character" was discarded. In its place was the opposite, every man is prejudged by the color of his skin and little else. In the Supreme Court case, Regents of University of California vs. Bakke, the court established race as a basis for college admission. What followed was a piling on by academics, business and state governments to embrace racism as a basis for everything. Merit was out, racism was in. Welcome to identity politics. (8)

Fast forward 50 years and the country's policies continue to be racist, but the problems of blacks continue. How can that be? This new race-based preference society was supposed to solve the blacks' problems of crime and poverty. Blacks have taken control of many major cities, especially on the East Coast. They had claimed back in the 1960s that if they could run the cities, the problems would be solved. What in fact has happened in every case is that the problems became worse, much worse. Of course, these black politicians, continue to blame everyone else for these problems except themselves.

Black politicians and the rest of the Democratic Party establishment continue to fail black Americans. Their policies do not fix problems, they perpetuate them. The fix needs to center around two issues: 1) building strong black families and 2) excellent educational outcomes in k-12 grades.

Black ghetto families are fatherless. About 70 percent of black children are born out of wedlock, a figure that has risen for 50 years. The welfare system prevents women from marrying as they cannot obtain benefits unless they are living without a husband. Fathers are an absolute necessity in the development of children. School dropouts, crime and even suicide rates are significantly higher for children living in a fatherless home. Prior to welfare, black families had higher marriage rates and problems with children did not exist. **Welfare is the problem.**

For more than 50 years, the difference between black educational attainment and whites was substantial. Politicians and experts all had opinions about this difference. Blacks could not learn; systemic racism gave black kids an inferiority complex; they need better qualified teachers and of course they had to be paid more. They had to attend integrated schools. As the debates raged on policies were enacted to bus children all over town to reach racially "balanced" levels. Nothing worked for 50 years. Suddenly, along comes a New York City teacher, Eva Moskowitz, who starts Select Academy Charter schools in New York and the results for these same impoverished children are astounding. Many are scoring better than any other public-school children in the state.

Black leaders, white Democrat politicians and the teachers' unions all united to shut down these schools. WHY? The only answer to this can be that they want black kids to remain poor, uneducated and dependent upon the largess of the Democratic Party. Moskowitz should have been accorded the very highest national recognition, but instead she is persecuted by the Democrats.

Political Polarization

The political chasm between the left and the right has grown exponentially in the past 50 years. The major reason is the divergence of priorities.

"The left prioritizes social justice over truth, free speech or the facts of a situation." This is why regardless of the facts of any situation; the narrative takes control and becomes the conclusion of the event in question. One version is allowed and continually repeated until it becomes the "truth." Thus, the repression results in speech codes, microaggressions (a term that is not in Websters Dictionary), safe places, conservative censorship and whatever other form of control required to eliminate any other viewpoint. If this sounds like Nazi Germany, it is. (9)

"The left does not see people as individuals who are unique with different opinions, skills and aspirations. They are just a member of a variety of groups defined by race, class, and sexual orientation." Therefore, the group that the individual is part of determines the destiny of the person. Every instance of a disparate outcome is further proof of this philosophy. John declared bankruptcy. It was Not due to his gambling, excessive spending, mortgaging his house to take expensive vacations and buying luxury cars. "They" forced him to declare bankruptcy because he was gay. The left demands all individuals within these groups to adhere to their ideology. When they resist, they are labelled. Asian Americans who reject liberal views are denounced as "twinkies" and blacks who disagree are "Oreos." (9)

The left celebrates victimhood and rejects merit, resilience and self-sufficiency. At the same time, their children attend private schools and elite universities.

Following the teaching of Karl Marx, the left embraces

redistribution as one of its core beliefs. If wealth were redistributed the ills of the world would be cured, overnight. Of course, any history student could recount the failures of many dictators who have started out with this philosophy. Their countries became impoverished. The smart ones changed to a capitalist economic philosophy. China is the poster child for this epiphany. (9)

The left, like their communist teachers, worships secularism, which is a euphemism for atheism. They are increasingly hostile to all religions, agreeing with Lenin's infamous statement that "religion is the opiate of the masses." Many of the practices supported by the left are in violation of most major religions, including abortion, same sex marriage, transgenderism and homosexuality. Therefore, they must stamp out religion. Thus, the persecution of Christian churches in America. (9)

The left has achieved its power from its crusade against racial oppression that began in the 1960s combined with the Democrats War on Poverty, which created a multitude of federal programs to right the evils of slavery and racism in America. These programs have transferred trillions of dollars into the hands of Democrat-run cities to convert them into one party fortresses controlling the lives of poor blacks. Fast forward 60 years, the American people see for themselves the failure of welfare, public housing, school busing, affirmative action and the diversity programs. Giving black people privileges not enjoyed by whites and money for not working has not lifted them from poverty. If anything, it has entrapped them forever while destroying their families, children and culture. However, the crusade is running out of steam as Americans see the hypocrisy of millionaire black athletes bending a knee for racial justice. (10)

The 1619 Project, taught in schools across America, is, in fact, racist propaganda. Its goal is to divide Americans based on the theory of unequal opportunities due to race. Race has become the pretext for a fight to reduce and subsequently eliminate personal freedoms enjoyed by ALL Americans regardless of their race. "These are to be replaced by mind control, a surveillance state and manipulation of information to mold public opinion through traditional media and social media outlets. All of these working together to transform America into a totalitarian state run by the Democrat Party. Wokeness is a methodology used to achieve this goal." On the surface, it is pleasant and almost enticing, but beneath the surface, a vicious Marxist ideology allows no alternative viewpoint. (11)

<u>Income Inequality</u>

For the past 30 years, much of the support for the ever-expanding increase in government programs to help the poor has been justified by the Census Bureau's continual reporting of the widening income gap and growing income inequality between the rich and poor. Many economists have added their voice and of course, the Democratic Party has used this as a clarion call for more government spending to help the poor. However, in an article co-authored by Phil Gramm and John Early, they enlightened us with a review of the methodology of the Census Department and observed errors that completely changed the conclusions. Gramm and Early discovered that the Census Department failed to deduct the taxes paid by the wealthy groups and failed to include many transfer payments (earned income tax credits and food stamps among others) to the low- income group. The corrections show income inequality increased by 2.3 percent, not the 21.4 percent reported by the Census Bureau previously. These are rather significant errors, and any skeptical citizen must wonder if they were made purposefully to arrive at a conclusion favoring Democratic policies.

In any event, there are two important conclusions for the reader. First, be skeptical of information coming from the government and any other organization with a political point of view. Second, the important conclusion of the report was that the explosion in transfer payments to the poor over the past 50 years (an increase of 300 percent) has resulted in a corresponding implosion of people in the bottom income quintile who work. More than 90 percent of their income is from the government. The wage equivalent of poverty programs in Milwaukee is to provide a standard of living equivalent to $112,000. Everyone must agree. It is a tremendous incentive Not to Work. (12)

<u>War on Poverty</u>

Lyndon Johnson stated in 1964 that the purpose of the War on Poverty was for all the poor to develop their capabilities. However, by 2015, 37.1 percent of families in the lowest earning fifth of the country had at least one person of prime working age but no one in the family working. Transfer payments for a myriad of federal programs have reduced the actual American poverty rate from 14.7 percent in 1966 to 3 percent in 2015. The result is clear. The War on Poverty has increased dependency and failed to bring the poor into the mainstream of American economic life. President Roosevelt predicted this in 1935 when he said, "The lessons of history show conclusively that continued dependency upon relief induces a spiritual and moral disintegration fundamentally destructive to the national fiber." A wise observation but then why did he initiate it? (13)

<u>The TRUMP Factor</u>

"The left is sustained day and night by one thing only -- their hatred for President Donald Trump. They hate his vulgarity, his unwillingness to walk away from a fight, his bluntness, his willingness to call everything honestly, to answer all questions in a press conference, his distrust of the elite and his love of simple ideas that work." He is a throwback to an earlier era in American history. Alex Tocqueville, commented in his observations of Americans that he admired their ability to see a problem and then get together, find a solution and fix it. That is the essence of the American spirit. That is what makes Trump successful. Regular Americans see this trait in him. They admire it because it works. He will not retreat or be intimidated by the usual power brokers in the press or Congress. Some consider him a bully, but he is the peoples' bully. Fighting the ruling class, who view regular citizens with utter contempt.

His wealth makes him immune to the normal politicians' unwillingness to take a position that may offend anyone and their inability to get anything done. While they wallow in indecisiveness, he has the job completed. Trump is a blue-collar guy with a billion-dollar real estate portfolio. (14)

Regardless of whether you like Trump or not, his power is about the results of his policies:

- government support for large and small business

- lower tax rates for individuals and corporations

- reduced regulation

These policies accounted for the strongest economy in history.

"Between 2017-2019 median household incomes grew by 15.4 percent among blacks and 11.5 percent among whites. A Goldman Sachs report showed pay for those at the lower end of the wage spectrum rose at double the rate of those at the high end. This was the first time since 2009 that the bottom half of wage earners were benefiting more than the top half." (15)

Finally, the proof was irrefutable that low taxes and less regulation would grow the economy and benefit the poor and middle class more than the democrat's belief in more government rules, regulations and handouts. The fact that these policies were proven to work was the ultimate threat to the left, which preached government management of the economy. Threats must be eliminated. The result is the persecution of anything Trump.

Footnotes:

1-"The Decline of Work," Andy Kessler, *WSJ*, 11/14/2022

2-"The American Experiment is on Life Support," Andrew A. Michta, *WSJ*, 10/27/2020

3-"An-Ex Liberal Reluctantly Supports Trump," The Weekend Interview with Fred Siegel by Tunku Veradarajan, *WSJ*, 10/17/2020

4-"How Free Speech Dies," Mary Anastasia O'Grady, *WSJ*, 10/26/2020

5-"Soviet Politics, American Style," David Satter, *WSJ*, 12/23/2020

6-"What Gentiles Can Learn from Lord Sacks," Meir Soloveichik, *WSJ*, 11/13/2020

7-"AmericaDoesn't Need an Industrial Policy," Thomas J. Duesterberg, *WSJ*, 6/23/2020

8-"We Might Get Fooled Again," Mike Gonzalez, *WSJ*, 7/10/2020

9-"The Roots of Political Polarization," Bobby Jindal, *WSJ*, 11/2/2018

10-"Why the Left is Consumed with Hate," Shelby Steele, *WSJ*, 9/24/2018

11-"Can Freedom Survive the Narratives," Lance Morrow, *WSJ*, 5/17/2021

12-"Incredible Shrinking Income Inequality," Phil Gramm and John Early, *WSJ*, 3/24/2021

13-"Government Can't Rescue the Poor," Phil Gramm and John Early, *WSJ*, 10/11/2018

14-"The Real Reason They Hate Trump," David Gelernter, *WSJ*, 10/22/2018

15-"The Trump Boom Lifted Black Americans," Jason L. Riley, *WSJ*, 1/29/2022

Chapter 2 Is Inner City Poverty Fixable?

Inner cities throughout America are plagued by high crime, poverty, few jobs, single-parent households and structural decay. Alcohol and drug abuse are rampant. Most of these residents are black. According to many people, the cause of this poverty is racism. This picture is played out over and over by Democratic politicians and is the rallying cry for support of an endless number of programs and initiatives to eliminate poverty, including Lyndon Johnson's famous War on Poverty and Great Society legislation. However, for the interested citizen, the question is what is true and what is hyperbole about this depiction?

In the 1920s to 1950s, black inner-city neighborhoods were very different than today. Most blacks worked. Crime was relatively low. Drug and alcohol use were low. Unwed birth rates were low. Blacks had cohesive neighborhoods held together by churches, social clubs, black nightclubs and entertainment, and most of all, strong families with fathers almost always present.

What happened? Liberal Democrats assumed control of the narrative of poverty in black communities. Columbia University social scientists Francis Fox Piven and Richard Cloward believed blacks should join the welfare rolls. In 1966, the Mobilization for Youth movement in New York City encouraged poor blacks to apply for welfare. These activists believed poor blacks would be better off not working at low-paying jobs but instead having the state support them.

The National Welfare Rights Organization encouraged blacks nationwide to apply for Aid for Dependent Children (AFDC), a program that previously was reserved for widows and their children and was designed to provide a food supplement. The result was that, in a few years, the welfare rolls in major cities across the country ballooned from a few thousand to millions. Cities were forced to increase existing taxes and add new taxes. Sales taxes, payroll taxes, property taxes, occupancy taxes, hotel taxes and income taxes rose rapidly.

At the same time, cities began giant urban renewal programs to transfer the welfare recipients from sub-standard housing into large, new, government housing projects. Tenements, slums and older buildings in "undesirable" neighborhoods were torn down and replaced by large housing complexes containing thousands of families. Federal, state and local politicians basked in the glory of transporting the poor from the "ghetto" to these new homes. Unfortunately, this urban renewal destroyed established neighborhoods and the cohesiveness that held the black community together in many cities.

To enter these new welfare programs, a woman had to be unmarried with children. This requirement was the opioid of the black community although it was not apparent at the time. Welfare changed the structure of the black family in these inner cities. Woman received the benefits, and they became the heads of the family. The community changed almost overnight from a traditional patriarchal system to a matriarchal system. Men were no longer needed, except to impregnate woman. They were no longer visible as many of the projects did not allow anyone to reside who was not a registered family member. Black men had lost their role in society. They were no longer an essential piece of a family unit, no longer a legitimate partner in raising a family and no longer needed as the primary breadwinner. The results for the men were catastrophic as they drifted in and out of jobs, trouble, addiction and prison. Large numbers of single, untethered men roamed the streets with no sense of purpose. With no need to have a regular paycheck many drifted into crime. The illegal drug industry was an opportunity to make "real money" fast. The result was a dramatic increase in crime in the black community that continues to this day.

	Welfare By Race 2019 (Includes SSI, TANF, SNAP)	
Race	Millions	% of Race
White	25	12.6
Hispanic	14	22.8
Black	13	32.5
Asian	2	10.7
Other	5	40.6
Totals	59	

Source: Census

(Other category consists of Native Americans and other ethnic groups)

"A new way of thinking infected blacks and liberal whites that discouraged blacks from doing their best in school or work and taught concerned whites that providing hand-outs, exemptions and lower standards for blacks was a sign of moral sophistication." (1)

Liberal authors and social scientists postulated that years of racism had created a "psychological barrier" that prevented blacks from achievement. This became the foundation of the argument that the system was rigged against blacks, and therefore, it was useless to attempt to be successful. The corollary to this is that blacks should then reject everything white people do, and welfare is the method to get even because white people will pay the bill. Welfare then became more entrenched to fight back against white racism. Unfortunately, the "hate what white people do" mantra sealed the continual poverty for blacks. White people had built a social system based on thousands of years of experience that concluded that the road to success was education, work and marriage. Blacks rejected each of these things.

During the 1960s, America experienced the assassinations of President Kennedy in 1963, Robert Kennedy in 1968 and Martin Luther King Jr. in 1968. While these tragedies were felt throughout the entire nation, they were felt much more intensely in the black community. The civil rights movement was in full swing during this decade and these murders were believed to be part of the historical attempt by some whites to subjugate blacks. The ensuing riots in black inner cities only made the situation worse as burned-out store fronts, buildings, homes, cars and looted property signified the bankruptcy of thousands of small inner-city businesses and the further deterioration of the neighborhoods. Most of these small businesses were owned by minorities including Asians, blacks and Hispanics. Most would never be willing or able to rebuild again. Riots scare away insurance companies and without property and liability insurance it is difficult to operate. The destruction of these businesses further reduced the job opportunities in these cities. Many of these neighborhoods have still not recovered and the riots of 2020 set them back further. Ironically, the inaction of Democratic mayors and governors to protect the property of these minority businesses only leads one to believe they want the minority business community destroyed.

It is important to note that, in the 1920-1950 era, there were numerous prosperous black communities. John McWhorter, in his book *Winning the Race*, uses the example of Bronzeville, Chicago, which included:

- several newspapers, including the *Defender*

- $100 million in black-owned real estate in 1929

- Brookmont-finest colored hotel in the world

- 192 churches

- 731 black-owned businesses

- Provident hospital

- numerous jazz clubs

- extensive literary community

In 1950, everyone in the black community worked. By 1990, only four in 10 worked. (1)

It is also important to remind readers that ethnic communities were prevalent in many cities and included black, Italian, Irish, German, Hispanic, Greek, Polish, Chinese and Jewish Americans among others. People congregated in neighborhoods where their friends and family lived, where they had access to ethnic restaurants, food stores and shops that catered to the ethnic group, specialized religious institutions (Catholic masses in Italian), social clubs and where there were many who spoke their native language. Whether you called these neighborhoods ethnic or ghettos, they were primarily composed of one ethnicity and met the needs of these groups.

Liberal authors have attempted to explain the continuation of inner-city black poverty. The reasons they give are as follows:

1-The black underclass developed because factories moved out of inner cities and took away the low-skilled jobs. This is not substantiated by the facts. (1) The facts indicate that millions of blacks moved to the suburbs during this period. Also, while suburbanites commuted to the cities the buses/trains ran both ways, so inner city people could commute to suburban areas for jobs.

2-White people enforced housing covenants to prevent blacks from moving to the suburbs. Like any law it could have been challenged by reporting it to the federal authorities. The facts are somewhat different. In 1970, 3.6 million blacks lived in the suburbs. In 1995,

10.6 million blacks lived in the suburbs.

3-White people built sterile towers to house the blacks that discouraged residents from developing a sense of community and the dark staircases provided a cover for criminal activity. The Democratic politicians who cleared the sub-standard rodent infested housing with walk-up access, leaking roofs, inadequate electricity, poor plumbing, etc. believed that moving poor people to new buildings with elevators, new electrical wiring, new plumbing and air conditioning was a way to improve their lives. Unfortunately, these massive housing complexes did create other unforeseen problems, primarily the destruction of the cohesive black community.

4-White people pumped crack into poor black neighborhoods. Here, we are to believe two things: First, all the dealers in crack and other opioids were white, and no blacks were ever involved and second, the dealers of crack only attempted to sell to blacks, 13 percent of the population. What about the other 87 percent?

5-Middle-class blacks moved to the suburbs. The poor blacks no longer had role models. Here we are expected to believe that only poor blacks, not poor Jews, Italians, Irish, Puerto Ricans or Chinese fell apart when their middle-class neighbors moved to the suburbs.

6-Housing projects made social chaos inevitable for poor blacks. Their underclass behavior is a result of the shock of moving them from their neighborhoods into the tall buildings. Substance abuse, crime, unwed births and fatherless families are all the result of moving these people to new apartments in tall buildings. What about the shock of moving from rural farm communities in the southern states to big cities? Or for the millions of people who moved from countries around the world? These events did not cause social chaos.

7-Highway construction broke down poor blacks' sense of community as new roads were built in black neighborhoods. This is difficult to understand. Do blacks want housing restrictions lifted so that they can move into white neighborhoods with better schools, less crime and more job opportunities or do they want to stay in the "old" black neighborhoods with the rat infested and poor-quality housing in inner city black neighborhoods? Hard to have it both ways.

8-Drugs came into black neighborhoods. Somehow, we are to believe that drugs were "imposed" on blacks without their acquiescence. Poor blacks were unable to resist abusing drugs? What about the other ghetto neighborhoods of Jews, Italians, Puerto Ricans, Irish or Chinese. They were somehow able to resist when blacks could not. Drugs were available in the 1940s and 1950s. Why weren't they a problem then?

White flight to the suburbs was a product of changes

in society. A portion of the suburban flight was due to the Democratic strategy of increasing the number of welfare recipients. Paying for welfare and other social programs caused taxes to increase for businesses and residents of the city and they responded by moving to lower tax venues. Inner cities began to record ever higher levels of crime against businesses and individuals. The increased levels of crime also contributed to the move to suburbia. Businesses in high crime neighborhoods were having trouble attracting good employees who did not want to commute into these neighborhoods. Retail establishments experienced high levels of shrinkage due to shoplifting, vandalism, robberies and the effects of occasional riots. The national highway program built new expressways to the suburbs and people wanted their own home with a yard. In addition, as the middle-class shoppers left downtown, sales revenues declined. These factors also led to rising insurance rates. Collectively, these factors forced retailers to close downtown stores and move to the suburbs.

Unfortunately, this negative cycle of increased flight from the inner cities led to fewer businesses and fewer inner-city jobs. As business and working people fled the inner city for the suburbs, the tax base shrank, and this caused the city managers to raise taxes even more on the remaining taxpayers. This resulted in more flight and a continuing reduction in the tax base. The cycle was almost never ending, and the result has been catastrophic for many cities across the country. Detroit became the poster child for this process when it finally was forced to file for bankruptcy in 2013. Its inner city is filled with burned out buildings and empty lots where homes once stood. The population declined from 1.8 million in 1950 to 600,000 in 2020, a decline of 66 percent in 70 years.

Cities lost their middle classes as the working-class jobs fled the inner-city problems.

What changed? A new way of thinking evolved in the 1960s by liberal whites and blacks. It discouraged blacks from emulating the white culture. It was now cool for blacks to reject everything the white man did to pursue the American dream, work hard to get good grades in school and graduate, learn a trade, get a job and when you are financially able, get married and then have children.

Liberals substituted government handouts, exemptions and lower standards. "Cannot make the grade to graduate? No problem. We will pass you anyway. Cannot gain admission to college? We will make an exception and lower the scores required for blacks and blame their sub-standard performance on racism. Not qualified for a job? No problem. We will enact affirmative action laws that force business to employ a percentage of blacks even if they are not qualified."

Blacks were making economic progress until American

liberalism came in under Lyndon Johnson (die-hard racist) and said in effect, to black people: "We don't have any faith in you. We don't believe you can make it on your own. We hurt you. So now, we'll make it better. A downward spiral ensued in much of black America. (2)

"Today, by contrast, blacks enter the American mainstream as a matter of course where they're far more likely to run into racial preferences, be celebrated for their race and be promoted above their skill level than held back. Steele said that he doesn't know anywhere where blacks are held back. They're not just pushed forward, but they're dragged forward into American life." (2)

One of the major changes was the rise in the number of violent young men. The Democrats continue to blame the violence on the availability of guns, and they continue to erase the rights given to Americans by the Second Amendment. "Guns have always been plentiful in the United States. Young men killing strangers in large numbers for sport have not. The overwhelming problem is that the socialization of young males is failing. This has been true of African Americans since the 1960s when black on black violence began to soar to small-army levels. But young black men, perhaps because they are a deeply rooted minority, have not seen this killer instinct escalate to indiscriminate mass slaughter. Historically, the only thing that stops such young men is older and stronger men who compel emulation through example, love and coercion.

"And so, the cycle is clear, welfare eliminated the men from the family. The absence of those older men has allowed the younger men to grow up without their control and guidance and the result is uncontrollable violence. (3)

<u>Race and Policing</u>

On Sunday, May 31, 2020, 18 people were killed in Chicago. None by the police. Over the entire weekend, 25 people were killed and 85 wounded. Sounds like a battlefield report from Afghanistan. No, this is everyday life in Chicago. According to the *Sun-Times*, there were 492 homicides in Chicago in 2019. Only three involved the police. These are the facts, not the media hype. Black men are responsible for more than 50 percent of the crime while black men and women comprise only 13 percent of the population. That means blacks are committing crimes at six and half times the rate of whites. If we do the math using only black men comprising 6 percent of the population, you arrive at a crime rate 12 times (1200 percent) the rate of whites. Black men, who comprise 3 percent of the population commit 50 percent of the crime. This is why inner-city police departments have a higher level of policing in the black neighborhoods. They are trying to prevent crimes and save lives, BLACK lives. These are real facts, not Democrat propaganda. It is also why the residents of the inner cities do not want the police defunded or reduced (although we never hear from them). They want MORE policing. They want protection from criminals. They do not want their children killed. (4)

The media are in business to sell more advertising and high-profile crime, especially police vs. black perpetrators, sell. Add Jessie Jackson and Al Sharpton to the story and the money just rolls into their coffers. Thus, their coverage of these incidents is at best biased but mostly purposefully inflammatory accusing the police of racism and excessive force to incite hate and division. On the other hand, no stories about the 25 blacks killed over the weekend in Chicago and no Jessie Jackson or Al Sharpton presence either. They can't extort any money from these black-on-black deaths from their rich liberal donors. They don't care about dead black people. Only the mothers and family of these mostly young men are at the funerals crying as we have all seen so many times on TV. (4)

<u>The Job Conundrum</u>

One of the major issues for inner city poor is the insufficient number of good-paying jobs. This is a valid issue. We have heard politicians; community leaders and residents complain vigorously about the problem. Let us discuss the problem from the business owners' perspective.

Consider the issues for locating three different types

of businesses in an inner-city location; manufacturing facility, retail store and a corporate headquarters.

A manufacturing facility would seem to be an obvious fit in an inner-city location, especially if the company was able to obtain some type of government aid such as a tax holiday or training funds. The obstacles however are still significant for the company. Manufacturing site selection is complex with numerous considerations for finding or possibly constructing a one level facility that can receive raw materials, produce the product, ship orders, maintain inventories of raw materials and finished goods. A site is difficult to find in a built-out city center. Freight in and out is a serious issue in a congested city center, and it would cost more than at a suburban location.

Hiring a motivated, trainable or experienced workforce is always the foundation of a good production facility. In an inner-city location this is a challenge as the neighborhood is a repository of under-educated and low skilled labor. Employers may see this population as not experienced in some of the basics usually taken for granted in other locations, such as good attendance, ability to follow complex directions and ability to operate machinery.

Asking the management team to commute into an inner-city neighborhood either by car or public transportation would not be something many would welcome and recruiting this group would be a major obstacle.

Security would also be a major concern and the plant may need armed security guards 24 hours a day in addition to a robust system of security cameras. The concern and the cost would be significantly higher than at a suburban location. Customers, vendors and other visitors may also be reluctant to commute to an inner-city plant if it were in a crime area.

When a company decides they need a new facility, a team is formed, and the team considers the major requirements for the facility, such as a rail line, water shipping, output and overall size of the facility, expansion capability and labor availability. Based on a cursory set of requirements, several locations are considered. The next step is a side-by-side evaluation of all factors for each location. They weigh them and select the preferred site.

Logistics usually favors the suburban sites almost from the start because of the availability of large tracts of land that can be built to the company's exact specifications to maximize efficiencies, reduce freight costs, and lessen security requirements. Also, the belief that the suburban workforce will be easier to train and be more reliable over time.

Next, we will consider a retail business. Retail site selections are based on traffic patterns, local area demographics, especially age and income, although these will be different depending upon the type of business. If they have a fried chicken franchise that is searching for a location in the inner city, then they would be identifying where other fast food, especially fried chicken, restaurants were in the area. If the area is dominated by high-rise apartments and condominiums, then a store front may be suitable for foot traffic. If the area is mixed with homes and high rises and some customers will expect to drive to the restaurant, then a drive-through option and some parking will be a consideration.

If we are considering a site for a clothing store, department store or some other retail operation that will sell a variety of items laid out on shelves, this presents other issues for consideration. The major issue is theft. Pilferage is a serious problem in these neighborhoods. Although stealing is rising in other neighborhoods, inner city shrinkage can be too expensive for even major chains to overcome. The retailer cannot afford to staff the store with enough people to watch every customer and especially customers who come in groups and then split up. Security costs become prohibitive. With Democratic laws that reduce penalties for theft and district attorneys who do not prosecute "minor crimes," shrinkage has become the cause of even major retail stores to close. Giant retailers Walmart, Walgreens, CVS and Nordstrom are closing stores due to excess shrinkage.

As a result of the pilferage issue, the retail outlets most likely to prosper in the inner-city environment are those with counters where the customer orders and the merchandise is given in exchange for payment, such as banks, dry cleaners, fast food and convenience stores with merchandise arrayed BEHIND the counter. In some locations, the crime is so blatant that only bulletproof stores are viable. Sheets of two-inch reinforced plastic are set up over the counter to separate and protect the employees from customers/criminals.

For chains, the obstacles are daunting but for the small independent owner, who is usually black, Hispanic or Asian, the challenge is enormous. While chains can get insurance because they can spread the risk over numerous locations, the independent retailer may find property and liability insurance difficult to obtain or so expensive that it is unaffordable. This places the entire financial risk on the owner. Shrinkage, robbery, fire, riot or whatever the risk is exclusively his or hers. The summer riots across black communities tell the tale, most of the burned-out businesses were owned by minority businesspeople. Many had no insurance and were financially wiped out. NO one helped them rebuild. The city, the state and the federal governments were all AWOL (absent without leave) for these victims of crime and casualties of war.

For retailers to thrive, they need traffic from customers who have the income to buy their goods and they need to be in a secure location where pilferage and robbery are not significant problems to obtain insurance and attract good employees willing to work in their store.

Now, consider a corporate headquarters. This is an office environment dominated by college-trained professionals with degrees in business, engineering and the sciences, depending on the type of company. A site selection for corporate headquarters, small or large, would include an assessment of the local workforce. Does the area have enough of the experienced, trained staff that the company would need to hire? Is the location conducive to attracting these people to commute? Is it safe? Are there restaurants and other amenities in the neighborhood for employees, vendors, customers and other visitors?

Yes, there are companies headquartered in inner-city and other high crime neighborhoods across the United States. In almost every instance, they have stayed because they were there for many years and the neighborhood surrounding their facility changed. However, looking at the challenges, it would be safe to say that no company would consciously move into these neighborhoods as they contain nothing that attracts a company, and the problems and risks are too great. No amount of tax incentives by the government can overcome the inherent problems of inner-city neighborhoods.

The difficulties to be overcome in these inner-city neighborhoods are daunting, but unlike many, we believe ALL problems can be overcome. So, what can be done to improve the lives of the inner-city poor?

First, we need to understand why people are poor. In modern society, so much poverty is a result of not having job skills that result in wages to support themselves or a family. The rush by social scientists and the Democratic Party to enlist poor black women to apply for welfare (AFDC) is a direct consequence of not being able to find a good-paying job. When the movement to AFDC began, black inner-city women still had low out of wedlock birthrates and the AFDC application was a choice. Work at low-paying job or don't work. It always sounds good to get something for free. As the Democrat Party always starts their recruitment into another program, it begins with something for nothing. Of course, there was a catch (there always is), a woman had to be unmarried to receive the benefits. Yes, unmarried. The entire tradition of black Americans before this time was to be married. Black parents exercised a strong hold over their children, especially their daughters, to do the right thing and get married before having children. But the lure of free money was too great to ignore, and official marriages gave way to common law relationships to "qualify" for the benefits.

We will stop here and give the politicians, bureaucrats and social scientists the benefit of the doubt as to their good intentions at the start of the welfare state. Unfortunately, as with so many of the ideas of the intelligentsia, their science is poor, and the unintended consequences are never considered and eventually disastrous for the individuals involved. As the smartest people in the world, they can never admit their mistakes. As Rahm Emanuel said, "never let a good crisis go to waste." The creation of the welfare state is a gift that has solidified Democratic power in major cities and states. They will never give it up, and that means millions of blacks and Hispanics must live in the urban plantations forever.

The truth is that tearing down old buildings and slums does destroy the vitality of a community. The crucial question is: Does the benefits of replacing the dilapidated buildings outweigh the disadvantages of the social upheaval created by destroying the ethnic community? These are tight-knit communities with a sense of belonging and attendant political participation, ethnic character and the economic mobility that springs from property ownership. History now tells us NO. Unfortunately, the armies of public housing "experts;" university housing policy staffs; and the federal, state and local housing bureaucracies are all for build it back better. That is how they get paid. That is what they did, and now black Americans are living with the results. In retrospect, the plan should have been to renovate the old buildings and maintain the community spirit. (5)

Back to our point of finding a solution to the inner-city poverty problem. In truth it will not be just "take-a-capsule-three-times-a-day-for-30 days" type of solution. It will require a series of solutions, each specific to the parts of the system that create the enduring problem. In short, the welfare system caused the problems and now to fix the problems, the welfare state must be disassembled. The incentives against work must be eliminated and the area must be reconstituted as a thriving economic neighborhood with high levels of employment. Economic recovery will reduce the level of crime.

Step one is to diagnose the population in the inner city and break it down into smaller groups with specific problems. For example:

- young women with children without a high school diploma and no job skills.

- young men and women with criminal records without a high school diploma and no job skills.

- women with no children without a high school diploma and no job skills.

- men with no children without a high school diploma and no job skills.

- male and female alcoholics.

- male and female drug addicts.

- older males and females who are partially disabled or have limited work opportunities due to a disability.

- older males and females who have physical issues and are unable to work.

Step two requires government to test and determine their education level, ability to follow directions and work with others toward a common objective. What type of job do they prefer? Do they like to work in an office setting or outside as an individual or in a team?

The government has to change the rules of its welfare state to encourage the behavior of a citizen who is responsible. Programs are needed that can be customized for individuals. They should depend on private sector training programs that do lead to well-paying jobs, and not the politicians' training programs that provide training for low-paying jobs that do not exist (hairdressers) because no company is involved. They also do not pay enough to live on in any event.

The program should include an educational phase and social skills training to prepare people who have always lived in the ghetto to work with the people whom they will encounter in the non-ghetto environment.

Programs like the Federation for Advanced Manufacturing Education described in the chapter on Education under community colleges, are exactly what is needed for inner-city residents seeking to start a good paying career.

(It is important to remember that many of these people have lived in a ghetto their entire lives. They have absorbed the ghetto culture and attitudes toward outsiders and may have a difficult time adjusting to living outside the ghetto without significant assistance.)

The government will also need to accept the risk created by each individual. For example, many insurance companies will not cover individuals who have a criminal record for driving or as part of a liability policy. Other firms like banks, insurance companies, credit card companies, armored car services will need the government to provide insurance coverage (bonding for theft) for these specific individuals as they are deemed a high risk. As we have learned, the biggest hurdle for an ex-con is to find a job because the system punishes them forever. To help these people carve out a successful life, they need a job! Remember the old adage: "how do you get a job? You get experience. How do you get experience? You get a job." How you get the job to get the experience is somehow never explained. However, it exists and must be addressed.

The next step is critical. The question of whether a person is willing to move must be broached. If they are

NOT willing to move, then the chances are great they will not find a job with the pay they need to support themselves (and their families). High-paying jobs, as discussed above, are not coming to inner city neighborhoods any time soon. However, there are opportunities in cities. Electricians, air conditioning technicians, carpenters, welders, transit operators, heavy equipment operators, computer repair technicians, real estate agents, property managers and insurance adjusters. These jobs and thousands of others do not require a college education and pay well. A training program sponsored by the company and supported by the federal and state government is the goal. Success will depend on making good matches between the candidate, the job and the employer.

Next, the job applicants must be matched with the company who will make the decision to offer a training program and a moving package to help them get settled in a new location. Here again, the government can assist. Moving may be to the suburbs of the city or to a new state, which is miles away. While moving can be traumatic, it may be of great benefit to get away from the local gangs, troublemakers and temptations that were a large part of the problems.

By separating individuals into smaller groups with similar situations and issues to be resolved, the counselors will learn more about the job seekers' concerns about the program. Women with small children who might have had relatives help care for the children will want assurances that good childcare will be available when they leave for work every morning. This will be a learning process for the facilitators.

Success breeds more success. One way to help these transitions is for the agency to seek out and hire individuals who were successful in transitioning to new careers to return and provide testimonials to the next class of people aspiring to build a new and better life.

<u>Disassemble the Inner-City Ghetto</u>

As stated earlier, Democrats built the inner-city ghetto and now it is time to disassemble it. There are several key elements to this initiative.

1. **Make Drugs Legal** -- This is completely necessary to destroying the inner-city gangs and thus the crime that prevents the normal regentrification of old neighborhoods. Dealing drugs is one of the primary job opportunities for young black and Hispanic men. They are recruited, and many times this recruitment is forced or at least coerced, when they are young teenagers. From then, their indoctrination continues to develop them into hardcore believers in the gang ethos. Unfortunately, following this path results in death or imprisonment for many of these young

men before they reach 25.

The government oversight of the manufacture, distribution and sale of all previously illegal drugs sold by the cartels and drug dealers across America essentially puts them out of business. Any addict should be able to go to a drug store, present an ID showing they are over 18 and buy a dose of the drug. (*Refer to the section on Drugs)*

2. **End Perpetual Welfare** -- Anyone with common sense can now admit that welfare has been a failure for the very group of people it was intended to assist. Women with dependent children did not receive aid from welfare and then move on to a better life. Help for them was not a temporary crutch to be removed when their economic condition improved. It became an urban plantation, a form of incarceration without walls. Yes, they could move, walk or take a trip to anywhere, but they would return because they could not escape economically from the plantation.

    The focus of welfare must change to re-employment of people. All individuals receiving welfare must work 40 hours a week to receive benefits. The benefit should be an income-support mechanism depending upon monthly income. This formula should encourage work and increased income. It also must encourage women to marry by not providing greater benefits to single women. The core problem with welfare that destroyed black families was its requirement that women be single. Government assistance should be completely redesigned to encourage people to BE MARRIED.

It is essential to keep these people working for a variety of reasons. Getting up each morning and going to work keeps them connected to outside society. They maintain the basic work skills of attendance, punctuality and their ability to interact and socialize with fellow employees and customers. They are available for training and promotion opportunities with higher wages. They build a resume for opportunities outside of their current work setting. Working also acts as a deterrent from participating in destructive behavior as they must be up and ready for work in the morning.

The philosophy of welfare should be changed from life-long dependency to a transitional stage working toward the goal of perpetual self-sufficiency as the individual acquires skills that provide higher wages.

3. **Tear Down the Tenements** -- While well-inten-

tioned to provide homes that replaced older, rat infested and dilapidated structures with faulty plumbing and electrical infrastructure, these buildings have become worse than the tenements they replaced. Most of these building are themselves now old with faulty plumbing and electrical infrastructure, but worse, they are controlled by gangs and centers of violence and drugs. In New York City, public housing advocate Jumaane Williams has included the city's housing authority on his *Worse Landlords Watchlist* with nearly half a million open work orders that would cost $45 billion to complete. (6)

4. **Treat the Addicts** -- Individuals with drug or alcohol addictions must be referred to treatments centers that help them overcome their addiction. For the individuals who cannot fully live without drugs, they need help to learn how to live with the addiction and still have a normal life. Presently, many of these treatment centers must turn away people after 30-60 days as Medicaid funding stops. The addict finally gets in but cannot stay long enough for an effective treatment regimen and goes right back to doing drugs when released.

5. **End Racial Preferences** -- Although the Amer-

ican left has continually used racism as the primary reason for income disparities between whites and blacks, this simplistic rationale completely discounts the fact that racial and other income disparities exist and have existed around the world forever. For example, "the income gap is greater between eastern and western Europeans than between black and white Americans." Is this caused by racism? Both groups are white. "Black poverty fell by 40 percentage points since 1960. It continued to fall after the Great Society initiative but at a slower rate." The greatest success of the civil rights movement was not a new government program but getting government off the backs of blacks by eliminating Jim Crow." (7)

"Liberals also insist that more black political representation will increase black upward mobility, but the record says otherwise. Poor blacks in Marion Barry's D. C. and Sharpe James' Newark saw their economic plight worsen." Even under the country's first black president, the economic condition of blacks regressed. It was under President Trump that records were set for the lowest rates of unemployment, highest new business formation and lowest unemployment for black Americans. (7)

"If history is to be our guide, what will help black

Americans the most is for government to just get out of the way." Stop interfering with the black people and let them figure out how to improve their economic condition. (7)

Racial Justice

Racial Justice consists of two beliefs. "First, adherence to the doctrine that racial equity requires more, and greater expansions of the welfare state and civil rights law is needed. The constant expansion of state and federal welfare bureaucracies and programs, such as Medicaid, food stamps, unemployment insurance, head start, public housing and rent assistance has done more harm than good. Government at all levels has a duty to monitor the business and social practices of citizens through an array of civil-rights divisions and commissions empowered to prevent any form of actual or perceived discrimination. You must believe that more money for public schools is always in the best interest of minority children." (8)

Second, if you express any sentiment at all that can be construed as "racist" in any way, you can expect a variety of social punishments." This political correctness doctrine has now morphed into cancel culture as the progressives control social media.

In 1965, Daniel Patrick Moynihan, then an assistant

secretary of labor, issued a detailed report concluding that generational poverty among black Americans was the result not of an insufficiently generous welfare system but of the black family's dissolution. He was denounced as a racist. He was correct.

<u>Anarchy</u>

The summer of 2020 was scandalous featuring politicians who not only let criminals out of prison with their no-bail-get-out-of-jail-free cards, but also then encouraged them to riot, loot, mug and murder others by failing to prosecute them and calling out to defund the police. All the laws that have held civilized societies together were turned upside down by Democratic mayors and their acolytes and the result was a summer of fear if you were unlucky enough to live in one of the urban jungles, we call major American cities.

This hate fest was encouraged by the usual crowd, Hollywood celebrities, progressive Democrats and the media with help from the leftist billionaires, like George Soros. They of course watch the chaos on their big screen television from the comfort of their homes in the Hamptons, Malibu or Palm Beach. The poor urban dwellers suffered the most. Some of them had their businesses looted or burned to the ground. They are now financially ruined but maybe thankful they are still alive.

The violence was orchestrated by the Black Lives Matter, Antifa and other anarchists controlled by the Democratic left, just like Hitlers brown shirts and Mussolini's black shirts to incite riots and create a climate of fear.

While many cities suffered riots, the main culprits were Portland, New York, Chicago and Minneapolis, all of whom have been completely controlled by the monolithic Democratic machine for more than 50 years.

This summer has only added fuel to the exodus of business and people from these and other large American cities. While city leaders are recreating the conditions that caused the massive exodus in the 1960s and 1970s: accelerated violent crime, urban blight, crumbling infrastructure, schools teaching radical social ideologies and the mobs running the streets as the police withdraw afraid of lawsuits for doing their job. All of this encouraged by major American corporate heads to establish their credentials with the left. (9)

<u>The Victims</u>

Both the national media and the politicians have moved on from the summer of love in Minneapolis. The victims have not. "Much of the Twin Cities are still in ruins. Boarded-up store fronts still display makeshift notices that read "black owned" or "minority owned" to ward off further destruction. Many locals are reluctant to speak on record, but some are eager to do so. (10)

"It has been agony," said Mohamad Ali, a native of Somalia. "I respect the public anger," but I think we carried it too far to burn our city." At the height of the chaos, rioters set a large fire in front of his <u>apart-ment</u>, which sits atop several streetside shops. He spray-painted several desperate appeals onto plywood affixed to the storefront windows: 'Don't burn please, kids live upstairs.' This was a thriving area. Now, a lot of minority businesses are burned." (10)

"They never told us what they was gonna do," Ms. Westbrooks said. "What are you going to do for us? We have no job. We have no income. What are you going to do for us?" She had no insurance. (10)

Minneapolis abandoned these people, the police never came to file a report, the customers are afraid to come. Truly these people are the forgotten victims of the BLM and Antifa riots, sponsored and supported by the Democratic Party and their acolytes.

"Mass-produced, 'Black Lives Matter' signs dot the yards of countless leafy homes across the area." Hopefully, these people will remember and vote for law-and-order candidates the next time they vote, such as Republicans. Don't bet your lunch money. These riots will occur again in a few years."

Black Americans living in high-crime neighborhoods understand that it is the neighborhood that is the problem. That is why they lined up in Chicago to participate in a lottery to relocate to housing projects in suburban locations close to functioning schools and better job prospects. They are not alone in their belief. Baltimore's Abell Foundation long ago called for policies to "allow poor families to leave violent neighborhoods in the short run instead of being trapped in the low-performing schools and poor-quality housing that exist while their communities await larger redevelopment investments."

"While residents overwhelmingly want out, the thrust of public policy in recent decades has been to keep them in place, partly because doing so maintains some of the safest seats in American politics. Among the unhelpful gestures: elite opposition to charter schools, high marginal tax rates on people moving from welfare to work and housing subsidies tied to downtrodden and jobless neighborhoods." (11)

Under the banner of Justice for George Floyd, mobs have been able to burn hundreds of businesses and cause damages in the hundreds of millions to mostly poor inner city retail store owners who were black, brown and Asian store owners. Is this violence the remedy for the crime? Or is violence the objective and crime the excuse? It seems more likely the latter scenario. Mayhem shuts down debate and any opposing view is immediately attacked by the same characters in the media, social media and Hollywood. Bullying is common.

"There are people hell-bent on destroying this republic" says Robert Woodson, "And we cannot allow them to win. We must resist." (12)

"Low-income black neighborhoods throughout the United States are becoming more isolated and more dangerous in part due to the efforts of social justice warriors, including members of Black Lives Matter. These activists demonize law enforcement, resulting in a reduced level of trust by the citizenry of police and the increase in police reluctance to investigate and prosecute criminals in these neighborhoods. This results in more crime in the very neighborhoods the social justice warriors claim to be helping." (13)

"Adding to this devastation, many black social critics, pundits, professors and politicians articulate a message of despair, victimhood and conflict. They tell people trapped in these inner-city killing fields that regardless of what blacks are doing to each other, it isn't their fault. For them, blame lies only with the legacy of slavery and Jim Crow." (13)

"To avoid having to explain why these problems persist after 40 years of black political rule in many of these cities, the same critics go to their all-purpose villain -- systemic and institutional racism. Police and

prosecutors are merely enforcers of a white suprema-
cist culture that pervades society. The most dangerous
thing about this message is that it exempts inner city
blacks from personal responsibility and suggests they
are helpless to improve their circumstances." (13)

The elite evangelists of these lies never have to suffer
the consequences as they do not live in the inner-city
Zip codes where the crimes are committed. After they
make their hate filled speech, they drive to their suburban home in a place where crime is almost non-existent because the police and prosecutors do their job.

<u>Stopping the Violence</u>

Fortunately, there are some social scientists in America who care about finding solutions to the inner-city
crime epidemic that is killing thousands of mostly
young black men in the inner cities along with other
victims. Christopher Winship and Thomas Abt analyzed over a thousand anti-violence programs worldwide. They discovered that urban crime was concentrated in tiny pockets of these communities. They
labelled it "sticky" to account for the fact that there
were few people really involved and a very small geog-
raphy. (14)

One city was Oakland where the analysis identified 400
individuals, 0.1 percent of Oakland's population were
at the highest risk for violence. Once this was determined, "a group of community leaders, social service

providers and law-enforcement officials began meeting in small groups with these individuals. Their message was that their community wanted them to stay out of prison and stay alive. These interventions were aided by social service support in the form of job training, educational assistance and other services to steer those toward better outcomes. They made it clear that help was available, and the community was ready and anxious to provide it, but the shooting had to stop." (14)

This initiative, called Oakland Ceasefire, resulted in a 50 percent reduction in the city's homicide rate from 2012, when the program began, until 2019. This program was modeled after Boston Ceasefire, a police initiative in Boston in the 1990s where it reduced homicides by 60 percent in the first two years. Similar programs were initiated in a total of 12 cities and produced positive results in each. (14)

Failure

"Since the 1960s, essentially little has changed in the neighborhoods at the center of those long-ago urban riots. By current telling, they are about as poor, as crime ridden, as under-educated and in poor health as they were when LBJ said he would change them. That means five decades of stasis and stagnation in America's most marginalized places, virtually all of it under Democratic-no Progressive-political control". American taxpayers wonder what has happened to the trillions of tax dollars spent on Medicaid, food stamps, welfare, public housing, rent subsidies and federal aid to public schools. They were told 50 years ago if blacks would run the cities everything would change for the better. Now most American cities are run by black mayors, police chiefs, district attorneys and what? Cities are the same or worse. The players have changed but the system is the same. The Democratic system of government results in poverty, crime, white flight, business flight, poor schools, illiteracy, alcohol and drug addiction and hopelessness. Now the narrative has shifted away to "systemic racism" as the most recent explanation. (15)

The election of a black mayor in New York City was greeted with the usual hoopla as the usual Democratic supporters used the election as a reason to present it as a new beginning for the poor black residents. Instead of a new approach to the problems of crime, poverty and unemployment, the new mayor has doubled down on the policies of Bill DeBlasio, the former failure. The only difference is that Mayor Adams continues to talk about fixing the problems. Maybe he is dumb and does not understand how to fix the problems or maybe he is just so wedded to the Democratic Party playbook for managing a city that he cannot change. For everyone who was hopeful of improvements in city life in New York, sorry, same old, same old. The Democrats never change.

"Moreover, there are limits to what government can do to address inequality, because what drives group disparities today is mostly rooted in cultural differences -- attitudes, habits and behaviors -- that don't easily lend themselves to political solutions." (16)

Following the deaths of two children in Chicago, McDonalds CEO Chris Kempczinski sent a message <u>to the mayor, Lori Lightfoot. It said, "with both, the parents</u> failed those kids, which I know is something you can't say and even harder to fix." She released it to the media and immediately the calls started for Kempczinki's resignation. He then went on a prolonged apology tour. This is one of the major problems, that you cannot discuss the problem itself. There is a narrative in place blaming all inner-city crime on "white supremacy." No one, especially white men, can deviate from the narrative. Unfortunately, the narrative is a lie. It also prevents all the residents of the inner city from any responsibility. In this specific instance, the parents, who were gangbangers, took the kids with them when they knew they were targets of another gang. The kids became the victims. (17)

<u>The 1619 Project</u>

Public schools are teaching the 1619 project to students. This false history argues that the United States is a corrupt country fundamentally built on slavery. Latasha Fields argues "that individual choice and personal responsibility is why she opposes programs that create dependence on the government. Ultimately the success or failures of the black community come from the choices we make." "More than 100 years ago, Booker T. Washington wrote, 'There is a class of colored people who make a business of keeping the troubles, the wrongs and the hardships of the Negro race before the public. Having learned that they can make a living out of their troubles, they have grown into the settled habit of advertising their wrongs-partly because they want sympathy and partly because it pays. Some of these people do not want the Negro to lose his grievances because they do not want to lose their jobs." (18)

Unfortunately, nothing will change. Check back in another 50 years and you will find the same poverty, crime and urban decay. Why? Inner city poverty is the power base of the Democratic Party. All the federal funding comes back through the city administration and is used to ensure enough of the poor are paid off to continue to vote Democratic. The white Democratic power brokers and black city overseers do not want to lose their jobs. The municipal unions do not want to lose their sweetheart contracts. The National Democratic Party elites understand that these inner cities are necessary to offset the Republican rural balance of the state in elections for federal and state offices to maintain their power in Washington.

Footnotes:

1-*Winning the Race*, John McWhorter

2-"How Equality Lost to Equity," interview with Shelby Steele, Tanku Varadarajan, *WSJ* Opinion, 2/13/21

3-"Violent Young Men, Here and Abroad," Reuel Marc Gerecht, *WSJ*, 8/14/2019

4-"The Full Truth About Race and Policing," Jason L. Riley, *WSJ*, 6/10/2020

5-"The Poor Side of Town and Why We Need It," Howard Husock /The Tragedy of the Progressive City, Barton Swaim, *WSJ*, 10/30/2021

6-"New York, I Love You, but We Can't Go on Like This," Mark E. Kingdon, *WSJ*, 2/16/2021

7-"Progressives Put the Racial Equity Squeeze on Biden," Jason Riley, *WSJ*, 2/3/2021

8-"Radicals Have a Point About Racial Liberalism," Barton Swaim, *WSJ*, 8/10/2020

9-"The Elites Fiddle While America Burns," Gerard Baker, *WSJ*, 8/2/2020

10-"Riot Torn Cities Are Already Forgotten," Michael Tracey, *WSJ*, 7/8/2020

11-"Race Problem or Crime Problem," Holman W. Jenkins, *WSJ*, 6/1/2020

12-"The Mayhem is the Message," William McGurn, *WSJ*, 6/9/2020

13-"America's Inner-City Cartels," Robert L. Woodson, *WSJ*, 11/19/2019

14-"To Cut Urban Bloodshed, Focus on Violent Hotspots," Thomas Abt, *WSJ*, 7/6/2019

15-"America's New Nihilism, Daniel Henninger," *WSJ*, 6/4/2020

16-"Eric Adams Should Remember David Dinkin's Legacy," Jason L. Riley, *WSJ*, 1/5/2022

17- "McDonald's CEO Apologizes for Telling a Simple Truth," Jason L. Riley, *WSJ*, 11/10/2021

18-"God, Parents and 1619 Project," Latasha Fields, *WSJ*, 9/22/2020

Chapter 3 The Need for Better Education

<u>Overview</u>

For years, newspaper and TV stories have documented the continual erosion of the American education system. Lower test scores in schools throughout the country and especially in inner city schools is bad, but even more alarming is the fall in ranking of American children compared to other countries.

PEW Research conducts the Program for International Student Assessment (PISA) evaluating the test scores of 15-year-olds around the world. The U.S. students ranked 38th in math, 24th in science and 24th in reading. Students consistently at the top live in Singapore, Hong Kong, Japan, South Korea and Finland.

For a country to stay at the forefront of technological innovation and continue to make gains in productivity, which is the foundation of rising living standards, it needs a well-educated population. But by far, the most important reason for having a well-educated population is that the populace is responsible for the continuation of the republic. It is their collective judgment and ability to discern the best policies that makes democracy work.

Elementary Education

Improving elementary education is an issue that has spawned a huge American industry. Many groups participate in the education conversation and their output is a litany of opinions about the causes of the education problem and the proposal of a variety of solutions. However, when the disinterested observer wades through the hyperbole and posturing, it becomes apparent that the students' needs are somewhere down the list of priorities in "solving the education crisis." Teachers, parents, politicians, school administrators and other vested interests determine what action is taken. Teachers' unions are politically powerful because they are the largest donor group in every state and federal election to Democratic politicians. As a result, their voice is heard above all others. Politicians extoll their magic programs to improve education, then package them up like an ad campaign with slick names such as "No child left behind." However, what we see is a rerun of an old movie. Someone gets elected. More money is spent. Funds are reallocated and after a few years, the results are the same, and the problem is worse. Schools have continued to fail the children.

One of the greatest scams of the past 30 years was the introduction of state lotteries to benefit education. Politicians promised a large percentage of the profits would go to education and of course, this money would "improve education." This was the selling point to overcome the objections of the people, many of whom did not want to introduce legal gambling. Initially, there was some money added to the education budget, but in many states, these funds were gradually removed or reallocated. No one was ever held accountable. (1)

So let us go back and become more focused on the needs of the students. Let's treat students as customers instead of pawns to be manipulated by the adults.

The place to begin improving elementary education results is by ensuring that each child who enters the local school system is physically able to do the work expected of them. This means a comprehensive test of their vision; hearing; ability to follow simple directions; read materials off an instruction sheet, blackboard, chart or a computer screen; and a thorough evaluation of the child's learning style. Approximately 20 percent of children entering 1st grade have some physical disability preventing them from doing their best in the classroom. Special education professionals are more aware of the variety of learning disabilities than can be both identified and treated successfully. The good news is that most of these disabilities are, in fact, physical problems, such as inadequate hearing or vision. Hearing aids, glasses, eye strengthening exercises and moving children up to the front of the classroom have yielded exceptional results for many children. However, the most important point is that early diagnosing is essential to ensure that the child will not face physical and emotional obstacles and begin to believe they cannot learn. Minor physical impairment undiagnosed often leads to the child, teacher and parent all believing the student cannot succeed. A young child who struggles can quickly reach the conclusion that they are stupid and tune out all schoolwork. Parents and teachers unwittingly contribute to this false impression if they cannot help the child progress.

Educators have also become more aware of different learning "styles" of children which are cultural or cognitive in their origin. For example, some people are visual learners and retain information better if they read it. For others auditory learning provides an easier way of comprehending information. As a result of this improvement in understanding more about learning methods, we now refer to them as learning differences. The bad news is that most children in public and private schools are NOT diagnosed and treated until the problems with their schoolwork and/or behavior force the school or the parents to search for answers outside the classroom. Even then, the problem is usually misdiagnosed as behavioral and then referred to a psychologist or psychiatrist for medical treatment with Ritalin or some other drug. Ask yourself the question, the child has a problem learning the information presented in school, so they act out in the classroom their frustration. Now, we give them a drug to "calm them down." Really? In fact, the treatment compounds the child's frustration and hatred for anything associated with education. Shame on the system. The United States is the only country that treats children in this manner. No other country uses drugs to treat children's behavioral problems in school. Something is seriously wrong with the educational and medical practices that are supposed to be caring for American children. Is it Big Pharma, bad doctors or unqualified teachers? Or is this part of a larger mission to destroy K-12 education and consign these children to a life of underachievement and poverty?

Children with dyslexia, severe attention deficit disorder (ADD) or other medical ailments, such as diabetes that require special assistance must be enrolled in programs that can actually meet their needs and help them maintain grade level performance. Often, the remedy is a smaller class or specific tutoring. (Not medication) Few public school systems provide this level of support. The parents are on their own and many cannot afford the tuition for the private school their child needs.

<u>Teacher-Centric Instruction</u>

The core of classroom education should remain teacher-centered, wherein the focus of the class is on the teachers' instruction, not child-centered where the education is delegated to the child in the form of individual learning. According to E. D. Hirsch "If you want equity in education, as well as excellence, you have to have whole class instruction" in which a teacher directly communicates information using a prescribed sequential curriculum. He cites history in explaining how education went wrong. The decline began in the 1940s, when schools unbolted the desks and kids were no longer facing the teacher. Instead, children were divided into small groups and instructed to complete worksheets independently with occasional input from teachers. That was also when our verbal test scores went down, and the relative ranking of our elementary schools declined on a national level. On the International Adult Literacy Survey, Americans went from being No. 1 for children who were educated in the 1950s to No. 5 for those in the 1970s and 14th in the 1990s. And things have only gotten worse. Between 2002 and 2015, American school children went from a ranking of 15th to 24th in reading on the Program for International Student Assessment (PISA). (2)

<u>The Importance of Play Time</u>

While learning inside schools is vitally important. It is also necessary for children to learn in an environment that is low stress, filled with fun, happiness and a joy in learning. School should be the place children are excited to get to every morning, not the place they dread.

American educators, pressured to improve children's test scores nationally, have rearranged the school day to increase childhood stress and eliminate the arts, physical education and almost all play time. No wonder children hate school. American parents suffer from two preoccupations: First, they fear that something will happen to their children and thus, they limit the child's freedom. They become helicopter parents accompanying their children everywhere and never allowing the child to explore his immediate neighborhood on his/her own terms. Second, they push to get the very best grades so the child can go to an Ivy league college and be a success. Happiness is nowhere to be found. (3)

Finland has the best school system in the world year after year and American school systems should study and learn their methods to improve the educational and emotional health of children. One reason is the extremely high academic requirements to enter teachers' colleges. (3)

In the Finnish system, parents and educators agree that the work of children is to play. The benefits are better grades, social growth, emotional development and happiness. The American Academy of Pediatrics agrees, "the importance of playful learning for children cannot be overemphasized." (3)

<u>School Choice</u>

For years, we have all witnessed and participated in the debates over school choice. The argument for choice is that parents can choose to send their children to a school that they believe will provide a better education for their child. The argument against is that the best children will leave the public school system. The argument against choice is interesting, in that the opposite, namely free choice, is fought for vehemently in every other sphere of American society but bitterly **fought against** for school children. As Americans, we value the right of free association to choose our friends, our doctors, lawyers, accountants, religion, cars and neighborhoods. Why is the idea of choosing a child's school the focus of so much opposition? The answer is MONEY. "Democrats and the teachers unions officially wed in 1979 when President Carter signed legislation to establish the Department of Education. Three years earlier President Carter had cut a deal with the National Education Association, the nation's largest teachers union, to create a new federal department in exchange for the union's support in the election. The Democratic Party has been doing what teachers' unions demand ever since." (4)

Public school education mandates are a form of coercion and a denial of the freedom of speech of parents over their children. In effect, the state has inserted themselves between the child and parent to insist that the state's education is superior to that of the parent. Honestly, most parents cannot afford private school tuition and so they are forced to go along with this system of coercion. The state should provide a voucher to each student and allow the parents to regain their "right" to direct the child's education. After all, the voucher is really a refund of the taxes the state collects from the parent to fund the public school. (5)

Unfortunately, when trying to solve a problem one must confront the facts, as unpleasant as they sometimes are. In this case an analysis of the data proves public education in the United States is a complete and total failure.

Therefore, alternatives must be available for the parents and students. This is their right. In the past private school was available only to higher-income families because they could afford to pay for the education twice -- first in their local school taxes and second with private school tuition. This reality excludes the middle class and certainly those living in poverty from choosing their own school and receiving a high-quality education. The exception has been religious schools which derive a large amount of their financial support from congregation members and other sources, such as Catholic school bazaars or the diocese.

When each child is provided an education voucher, suddenly, the playing field for educational possibilities becomes level, for poor, middle class and wealthy students. Parents should be not only able, but encouraged, to take their business to an organization who can educate their children -- public, private or religious. Now, the middle class and poor children can look to enter private schools by having a voucher for a major portion, if not all, of the tuition and pay the difference with a scholarship, a grant or cash. Just like in every arena of a capitalist society, the businesses that provide better products and services will thrive and the ones with inferior products or services will close from lack of support. This model works around the world and certainly is the cornerstone of American life. Why is it so revolting a concept for education?

"An analysis of 40 educational choice programs has shown the programs save taxpayers approximately $7,500 per student." While opponents continue to claim that choice programs drain the public schools of funds that support public school education and degrade their effectiveness, no data are available to support these claims. More and more evidence supports the fact that private school programs educate children at 50 percent of the cost of public schools and do a SUPERIOR JOB. (6)

Diversity, Equity and Inclusion

One of the fastest growing obstacles to quality education is the new orthodoxy being taught in schools under the banner of diversity. Children are continually being separated by race with white children taught they are the oppressors of people of color and colored children being taught that they cannot get ahead because of white racism. Children are segregated in the school into "affinity" groups, groups of children with the same skin color. "This promotes radical concepts, such as 'spirit murder' (what public schools supposedly do to black children) and 'abolishing whiteness' (a purported precondition for social justice). In the classroom, critical race theory inspired lessons have often devolved into race-based struggle sessions with public schools forcing children to rank themselves according to a racial hierarchy, subjecting white teachers to 'anti-racist theories therapy' and encouraging parents to become "white traitors." (7)

Unfortunately, while parents have been asleep believing that when they send their kids off to school they are learning how to read, write and do math, they are being brainwashed into activist racists. "The lightbulb has gone on for many families who weren't aware of the things going on in their children's schools." (4)

Schools in Albemarle County, Va., (Charlottesville) had a reputation for excellence with a strong core of the basics, like reading, writing and math. When the county decided to change its direction and adopt a new curriculum, "Courageous Conversations About Race," parents began to get organized to fight back for a reinstatement of the three Rs. The new curriculum is based on the works of Ibram X. Kendi, who wrote

How to be an Antiracist and discusses topics such as cisgender, white privilege and non-Christian folx. This curriculum encourages children to view their lives through the prism of race, gender, sexuality and class. These parents were part of the group that organized support for the eventual election of Glenn Youngkin as governor. Parents want to stop the divisive teaching in Virginia schools and get back to the basics of a quality education. (8)

Charter Schools

"One reason for their success is that charter and private schools enforce stricter discipline than public schools." If the students don't behave, they are expelled. Period end of story. Public schools have been politicized over the past 50 years and have unfortunately lost their focus on education and have become nurseries for wayward students who are not disciplined at home and cannot be disciplined or expelled by the public school. "The Cato Institute's Corey DeAngelis and Western Carolina University economist Angela Dills analyzed the correlation between adolescent suicide rates and the enactment of private school voucher programs over the last several decades. They found that states that enacted charter school laws witnessed a 10 percent decrease in suicides among 15-year-old to 19-year-old students." They postulated that the effect would be greater if more students received vouchers. This study is a small window to view the level of stress students are under from other students in public schools and the complete lack of help they receive from the teachers and school administrators.

"One criticism of charter schools is that while a few energetic principles show success, it is impossible to replicate. A recent study in Boston disproved this false narrative. Sixteen charters seeded an additional 16 charter schools, mostly with rookie teachers with an average of 1.4 years teaching experience. Their results matched the success of the original 16 charter schools. These charters succeeded by using "a highly standardized model that limits variation in practices across schools and classrooms." Given the success of this program, parents were flooding them with applications. A referendum in Massachusetts, which was opposed by Sen. Elizabeth Warren, to expand the number of charter schools was voted down. Democrats and the teacher's union are not in favor of high-quality education for inner city children. Their power and money are more important." (9)

The attacks on charter schools are increasing as the teachers' unions see parents voting with their feet as they remove children from public schools to enroll them in charter schools, private schools and home schooling. California public school enrollment is down by 155,000 children; New York City has decreased by 43,000; and about 25 percent of public schools have lost 10 percent of their students. (10) Fewer students in public schools means less funding, fewer teachers and less union dues to contribute to the Democratic Party. So, the charges of racism, resegregation, Jim Crow, White Supremacy surround charter schools. However, the facts continue to support charter schools over public schools. In almost all instances, charter school children outperform the public-school students. Charters are filled with minority children, so the race charges are completely unfounded. "We succeed where others fail because we do things differently. Our classical curriculum, direct instruction methods, additional instruction hours and focus on orderliness are a proven formula for successful learning." (11)

While the charter school students excel, the public-school children continue to fall behind. "A new report by *Wirepoints*, using Illinois data shows children unable to perform at the most basic level. Statewide, in 2019, 36 percent of all third-grade students could read at grade level. The number drops to 27 percent for Hispanic students and 22 percent for black students. In the Decatur system, 2 percent of black third graders were reading at grade level and 1 percent are doing math at grade level. Third grade is the year that children need to achieve reading fluency that will prepare them to tackle more complex tasks in upper elementary grades. A child who can't read in third grade can't do word problems in the fourth or science experiments in the fifth. By 11th grade, 5 percent of Decatur's students are reading at grade level and 4 percent are on par in math." (12)

While protection of the teachers' unions is the primary reason Democrats fight so hard to preserve the failed public school system, the secondary reason is the indoctrination of the children into the WOKE ideology. Indoctrination of children is the most successful method of societal transformation. Using Critical Race Theory as their rationale, teachers' unions and their co-conspirators have redesigned schools as places where they prohibit any speech that is counter to theirs. Black and brown children are brainwashed into believing they have been harmed by intergenerational racism. White children are then made to feel responsible as they are the oppressors. The goal is to achieve "collective liberation", where society is transformed into a collective state, stripped of individualism and replete with reparations.

In the fall of 2020 as it became clear that children were the least vulnerable to the virus, 92 percent of Catholic schools across the country reopened, compared with 43 percent of public schools across the country. The 2022 National Assessment of Educational Progress (NAEP) report showed conclusively how important reopening was for learning. The average score for 4th grade Catholic school students was 17 points higher than their public-school counterparts. In eighth grade reading, the average score was 20 points higher than for public school students. Superior performance for about $5,300 per year, or one-third of what the average state spends on public schools per pupil. (13)

High School

When American children enter 9th grade, very few realize the enormous affect the following four years will have on the rest of their life. Schools (and most parents) do an extremely poor job of impressing on these young adults the consequences of poor grades on their prospects for an enriched life, a rewarding career and the opportunity to earn a good income. In fact, there is little discussion of careers in high school and no sustained effort by schools to provide information about the vast number of possible occupations available in the United States The strident involvement of some parents is probably responsible for the success of their children in later life. Unfortunately, the lack of comprehension of this truth and lack of involvement of parents is a major cause of their children's inability to reach their potential.

Part of this is due to the teachers themselves who live in their own bubble of education that understand little about the outside world. In fairness, if the teaching community was asked why more time is not devoted to career planning, the answer would probably be that we hardly have enough time to teach the required course curriculum. We certainly do not have time or money for career counseling. But let's ponder this for a moment. Here is a child who is constantly told to do well in school, study, read and learn but for what goal? Is there a connection for a child who wants to be a baseball player? For most high school students, their knowledge of the various possible occupations is not much further developed at the start of high school then when they read the golden books describing doctors, nurses, police and firefighters in early elementary school. Of course, during their brief lives, they have encountered the dentist, the various teachers and relatives who had other careers. Outside of these encounters, the world is a big unknown.

The children who already know what their career goal is exhibit more focus, more determination and more effort to excel academically because they understand the relationship between academic performance and the achievement of their dream. If the majority of children were better connected to a dream, it would inspire them and increase their effort and academic performance.

The answer is to connect each child with a dream and then focus them on achieving that dream. This is not as simple as it might seem. Many children do not have any idea what they will do once they leave the protected confines of school and their parents' home and are thrust out into the real world. Their options are limitless. The problem is to identify one thing, just one, to pursue.

In the past half century, the military provided part of the solution for men as much of this time young men either joined or were drafted into the military. It provided them with a bridge to adulthood while getting paid, growing up, learning discipline, respect and maybe a trade. They travelled and gained some perspective of the cultural differences within and outside of the United States and had time to decide what occupation was of interest to them.

For many others, they followed in the footsteps of family members to work in a local factory, farm, family business or occupation, such as police or firefighter. Unfortunately, as factories have closed, the opportunities in these occupations have gone. While factories of old required more brawn for jobs, modern factories contain more complex equipment requiring strong reading and math skills to operate proficiently.

A good place for parents and educators to begin with children is to highlight the effects of not having a skill or profession achieved by additional education or training.

This is the toughest time for young men or women because they need to find their way into a place that is willing to pay them a livable wage and offer career advancement with experience and education to increase their standard of living.

This is where states can help by adding to the high school curriculum four years of career education. No, not by school counselors who also know little about the world outside of education but by a combination of movies, books, pamphlets and career fairs that provide information to students beginning in the 9th grade about the millions of occupations in the world. The tasks that comprise the occupation, the skills required, the education required and most importantly a path to get from where they are to one of the entry level positions. An essential part of this is bringing people to schools who are actively working these jobs currently or are retired who can describe what the job entails and answers questions posed by students. For those who believe that this type of outreach is beyond the scope of the school system, we should ask them what the goal of education is, if it is not to provide the skills to manage your life. The sum product of a person's education is to be able to support yourself and your family. With the media technology available, this should not be difficult. However, too often, high schools push students toward college even if they are not the type who could do well or who do not want to attend college.

<u>The Trades</u>

Much more coordination is required among local unions, businesses and community colleges to provide a path for high school students into the skilled trades, such as electricians, carpenters, welders, air conditioning technicians and plumbers.

In the United States, unions do this, but their efforts are separated from the school system. Business does most of the training for the trades. Small contractors hire and train people usually only requiring a high school education. One problem is the low status of blue-collar workers in the United States. In Germany and other European countries, blue collar workers are highly trained, well-paid and an integral part of the factory team that designs and manufactures high quality products. In other industries such as power generation, oil, gas, construction and transportation, blue collar workers are important members of the work force and are paid good wages. Highly educated parents have no problem seeing a son become a factory worker or electrical contractor in Germany. This is NOT the case in the United States and should be changed. It is not cost-effective to convince children to attend college, major in one of the soft sciences, rack up thousands of dollars in debt and then work in a factory or retail store in an unskilled job because the degree program they selected does not lead to a real job. Accounting, computer science, engineering, medicine, law and finance are where the good paying jobs are. They all require strong math skills.

Apprenticeship programs are a great method for training inexperienced people for jobs in the trades. This is an area for federal and state programs to help businesses train people without incurring all of the risk and cost of unproductive employees. These programs are measurably more effective in providing real job training because the employees are connected to employers who have real jobs. Apprenticeship programs have a 90 percent success ratio for individuals accepted into a program. The United States has millions of open blue collar job opportunities and millions of unemployed. The challenge is getting the unemployed into these jobs.

One of the stumbling blocks is the tension between unions and private employers for control. Construction unions who train 68 percent of the nonmilitary apprentices do not want private employers to begin training. They worry that wages will decline, and training will be poor. Employers on the other hand see union-controlled apprenticeships as stalking horses for unionization of their facilities. Unfortunately, the problem persists as the country is suffering from a shortage of skilled workers in all the trades and in many areas of manufacturing. "While the number of active apprentices has grown by 25 percent in the three years through fiscal 2019 to 633,522, enrollment remains small relative to the 17 million Americans in college." In fact, if we use 30 percent as the percent of high school students who attend college then 70 percent do not, the remaining figure is 56 million. A percentage of this figure should be the goal for apprenticeships. Nearly 640,000 is barely a drop in the bucket. This is a problem that must be fixed by the government, but it probably will not because politicians cater to the demands of the two constituencies. Without a solution, the country will not bring manufacturing back to the United States to provide better paying jobs for those high school graduates and inner-city minorities. (14)

Perpetual Education

Our world is changing at an ever-increasing rate and that means many of the jobs that once existed will either change radically or be replaced. As a result of these changes and the continued advance in life expectancy, many more people will change careers over their lifetime requiring additional training and education. One of the ways educators can help is by modularizing the degree programs to reduce the amount of time required for an individual to transition between careers. For example, if you are an accountant and after 20 years want to become a high school English teacher, you need a core course that provides a degree in English. If the core curriculum for a major in any specific field is 24 credits, use that as the requirement to obtain an add-on major and qualify as an English teacher. With more standardization of degree requirements and course curricula and cooperation among colleges, students can take the classes in many different places and transfer them back to the original college for the add-on major. This would allow someone who attended college in New York City to obtain an add-on degree later in their career from a college in Texas. Because colleges are resistant to awarding transfer credits toward a degree without taking a large percentage of the hours at their institution, this initiative will require a substantial level of coordination from states and maybe the federal government. Online colleges may be a significant part of the solution in this case. The national college accreditation groups could also be helpful.

This type of retraining is necessary, to keep the individuals' retraining cost affordable to them both in money and time. Most people seeking to be retrained cannot take off two to four years to complete a degree program and the government cannot afford to pay people for this time away from work. The focus must be fast, cost-efficient retraining of the individual to get them back to being a productive member of the workforce as soon as possible. This training also would help people who are released from prison to give them skills to start their lives again without them getting caught in the cycle of prison life.

<u>The Inner-City School Dilemma</u>

Inner-city parents and black leaders continually state that "we need better schools" to provide the children a better education. Sometimes "better schools" sounds like a product we can search for on the Internet, compare prices and just order it with overnight service from FedEx. Nothing could be further from the truth.

There are many theories as to why inner-city schools are failing. None of them explain the present and historical divergence in outcomes. This author believes inner-city schools fail because the community is not invested in education as the remedy for their poverty. Notice that community groups in Jewish neighborhoods do not cry out for better schools because wherever Jews live, the schools are already very good. That is because the community itself believes in and supports education. Each child in a Jewish community receives continual reinforcement from parents, relatives and other adults about the importance of education. Educated people are REVERED and are community leaders. Educational achievement is highly sought. The same is true in Asian communities.

Investing in education requires taking a long view of life. It requires the student to have a long-time horizon for the investment that is required before education begins to pay off in terms of personal gratification, recognition and financial security. The inner-city kid doesn't have a long time. They may not live that long. Community values reflect this as well. Most people live from welfare check to welfare check. They live in an urban prison and long for immediate escape. This is why sales of lottery tickets per capita are the highest in every state in poor inner-city neighborhoods. They want out NOW!

Kids in these neighborhoods look around and see the people who are glorified by their friends, family and neighbors -- sport stars, movies stars, musicians and drug kingpins. They have the money, the big homes, nice cars and women. Nobody is famous in the inner city for getting 100 percent on the citywide algebra exam.

The real question is how can these poor people be convinced to get on the education express? The government has NO solution other than throwing more money into the local school system. They have tried many things to improve school performance including incentive pay for teachers, increasing education qualifications for teachers (master's degrees), smaller class sizes, computers and the elimination of everything (art, music, gym) except the core curriculum -- all with limited success. Of course, in many schools, the core curriculum has been changed over the years from math, science, English and history to gender and black studies. Are these supposed to make students more qualified to be hired by business? If you don't know the answer, it is NO.

"Boston and New York City each spend $25,000 per year per student. Philadelphia spends $24,000 but only 17 percent of eighth graders are proficient in reading. Nationwide, black mothers can expect their children to learn 30 percent of what they are supposed to learn to be successful in life. Even if the black children go on to attain a college degree, they will earn 23 percent less than whites." A $15,000 school voucher would allow an inner-city child to attend a religious, private or charter school. Any remaining funds would accrue in the child's education account and could be used for college or trade school. (16)

"In 2012, the Education Department released a study showing that black students were more likely to be suspended than white students." Instead of trying to determine the cause of the disparity and work to fix it, Democrats in Washington in the Obama administration jumped on the racist train. They asserted that white teachers are prejudice against black students. They need to be investigated and prosecuted. Because most black students attend school with other black students and are taught in schools run by black principles and black teachers, there was no white on black racism. But a good racist narrative should never be corrected by adding the facts. Schools were pressured; suspensions decreased. The disrupters were allowed to stay in the classes. Bullying and school violence increased. It is regrettable that the government would not even consider non-racial reasons for the difference in suspension rates. If you wonder why so many black children do not get a quality education, this is but one more reason. Racial politics is more important to Democrats than the education of black children. (17)

Worst Inner-City School System

There is always one of something that stands out as the example of the best or the worst. It appears that the worst inner-city school system is not in one of the major cities but in Providence, R.I. It should not be surprising. This city has a reputation for being run by corrupt Democratic politicians whose only goal is to enrich municipal unions.

The Johns Hopkins Institute for Education review of the city's school system chronicled their observations in a 93-page report released in May of 2019. "Peeling lead paint, brown water, leaking sewage pipes, broken asbestos tiles, rodents, frigid and chaotic classrooms, and student failure were all documented. "(18)

"Very little visible student learning was going on in the majority of classrooms and schools we visited, most especially in the middle and high schools." Not surprisingly, only 5 percent of eighth graders were proficient in math during the 2015-2017 period. One cause is the policies that discourage student discipline. Based on claims that school suspensions target mi-norities, the legislature passed a law limiting teachers' ability to suspend students. Instead of learning, class-rooms are full of students talking to peers, checking phones, staring into space, talking on their phone or watching YouTube videos. (18) The bad teachers cannot be fired because the union is so powerful. The good teachers get no support to discipline the students and are afraid of some students. In inner cities, many are gang members.

In contrast, the Providence charter schools are doing very well, but the city cannot decide whether to expand charter schools or limit their growth. Really? The city cannot decide to increase funding to schools to provide more black students with a high-quality education? Of course, the culprit is the same as always, insufficient funding. Providence spends $18,000 per student per year, 50 percent more than the average nationally. However, moving a child from a public to charter school entails no additional cost. Another falsehood to keep black kids in poor schools. (18)

<u>What Is a Good School?</u>

In New York City, there are several high schools rated outstanding, The Bronx High School of Science and Stuyvesant High School are among them. They are great high schools because the students are highly motivated, intelligent and work hard to achieve. Acceptance is determined by a competitive exam open to all New York City residents. A great school is a function of the student body that attends it. If we took the lowest scoring high school in New York City and switched the location of the students to the Bronx High School of Science campus, they would perform as poorly at the Bronx High School of Science campus as they did in their original school. The teaching staff MAY make some difference but not much. Teachers can identify shy students and children with a troubled home life and encourage them to take more difficult classes and enter science fairs but in the end, they cannot take their tests nor do their studying. Even outstanding teachers cannot motivate students who are not interested in learning, nor can they get parents to make education the priority required for the children to apply themselves to learning and graduate from high school.

The lesson here is that the only improvement possible in school is improving the motivation of the students to learn and most of this is derived by the immediate family and local community. Yes, inner cities have poor schools, and this will never change until the community embraces education as the solution to their poverty. Obviously, there are many thousands of parents in these communities who understand this and that is why the waiting lists for charter schools In New York City are so long. Charter schools have proven that poor blacks can learn and perform as well or better than the white kids in middle class schools.

"According to the most recent data from School Digger, a website that aggregates test score results, 23 of the top 30 schools in New York State were charters. In a *U. S. News and World Report* ranking released the same year, three of the top 10 public high schools in the country were charters, 23 of the top 100 were also, even though charters made up only 10 percent of the nation's 24,000 public high schools." (19).

"The average charter school SAT scores were 654 on math and 611 on verbal compared with 475 and 485 for a similar national demographic." This is more impressive because 80 percent of the charters' student body consists of black and Hispanic students. (20)

<u>Success Academy</u>

For many years, we have engaged in a discussion of the difference in educational achievement between black and white students. The basic question was whether the gap in test score performance could ever be closed. Now, it is organized by the Success Academy charter school network in New York City. "Their predominantly black and Hispanic students already pass tests in mathematics and English at a higher rate than any school district in the entire state. These results undermine long held theories of genetic determinism, claims of cultural bias in the tests and assertions that "racial integration" is necessary for blacks to reach educational parity with whites." WOW. Stop here and think about all the hate-filled rhetoric and trillions of dollars wasted on public school programs, such as busing that have been spent by STUPID politicians, judges and "expert educators." Obviously, real high-quality education as practiced by this charter school demonstrates what is possible when the effort changes from political activism to education of children. (21)

One secret to Success Academy's success may be the selection criteria used by the school to not select the best students but the most motivated parents who will provide the "at home" portion of the education. "The parents are reminded in a series of pre-approval meetings of the school's expectations which include strict behavior codes, school uniform compliance, supervising homework, reading with children every night and recording what's read in a log." Much of this is reminiscent of traditional Catholic schools, and they produced many years of well-educated children from working class families. (22)

In Boston, the charter schools' story is the same. Charter schools are among the best in the state with a graduation rate of 90 percent. However, the Democratic political machine has managed to defeat a referendum to expand charter schools. In the meantime, the Boston Public School system is continuing to spend more and more taxpayer money. The district is losing students but adding teachers. 220 teachers were added in the past five years as the student population declined by 5,000 students. They also added 150 administrators. The current cost per pupil is $27,000 ($17,000 in Atlanta; $22,000 in D.C.; $28,000 in NYC) and it is easy to see where the money goes, excessive staffing of teachers and administrators. (23)

Gov. Phil Murphy of New Jersey has followed the same Democratic Party policy to clamp down on the expansion of charter schools in his state. The two largest charter school systems, NorthStar Academy and Phillips Academy operate in the inner-city neighborhoods of Newark and Camden. The governor has refused to increase their enrollment, leaving over 800 parents on waiting lists. Yes, parents of black and Hispanic children while the Democrats continue to whine about equity. These schools continually outperform the other schools in the state, but the teachers' union does not want to be shown up for their poor teaching performance. (24)

The real issue is why Democratic politicians across the county continue to erect every obstacle possible to deprive these poor black kids of a great education. Perhaps they should begin by explaining their reasoning to black parents.

Ben Chavis became the principal of the American Indian Public Charter School (AIPCS) located in Oakland, Calif., in 2000. At that time, it was among the worst schools in the state and scheduled to be closed. He asked the board of Education for a reprieve to try to turn around the school. The schools' founders focused on "bead making, drumming and self-esteem." The school day began with a discussion of students' feelings. Chavis fired the staff and replaced them with competent teachers focused on structured learning. The 2004 statewide test results showed AIPCS ranked highest in Oakland. By 2008, it ranked 5th of 1,300 schools in California. In 2011, he decided to expand the number of charter schools. Shortly afterwards, the police began an investigation into alleged mail fraud and money laundering. He resigned from AICPS in 2013 to defend himself from the false allegations. In 2017, he was formally charged. In May of 2019, the U. S. attorney's office dropped the charges, and he was given a suspended sentence for a technical violation. He filled out a form incorrectly. (25) Another instance of using the Department of Justice to persecute enemies of the Democratic Party.

What we learned from this experience is that the Democratic Party and their acolyte, the teachers' unions, will resort to any method to stop charter schools from expanding in cities across the country. Any method to attack and discredit the founders and staff of charters is acceptable. However, once again, it is the students who suffer. Democrats and teachers care nothing about the students. (25)

Nationwide "exam schools," those schools that determine admission by a competitive exam, are under fire by Democratic politicians like Bill DeBlasio and Virginia Attorney General Mark Herring. Their charge is that the results of these entrance exams have a "disparate impact" on the Democrats' favorite minority, urban blacks. Bluntly stated, there are few black and Hispanic students who excel so they do not gain admission to these select high schools. These politicians, spouting racial equity as a justification, insist on destroying the merit system of admissions and replacing it with a system based on the racial makeup of the area. This would destroy these institutions as superior learning environments. Of course, if someone suggested that all the high school sports teams, which are dominated by black athletes be subject to the same type of racial equity and contain more Chinese, Philippine, Japanese, Jewish, Mexican and Brazilian American students to balance them out racially, the outcry would be enormous. Where blacks outperform others, it's OK for them to dominate. However, where they underperform other groups, it's always due to racism. (26)

<u>Obstacles to Better Education</u>

Unions

The teachers' unions in the United States have long been the target of the wrath of parents and education reformers who point out that the unions' policies continually favor the interests of teachers over students. No place is this more visible than in the debate for inner-city school choice. The debate is not new but perhaps it is more heated now that parents have become more aware of 1) the real curriculum taught in public schools and 2) the success of charter schools in providing a superior education to the most disadvantaged children. The COVID-19 lockdowns shined a light on the divisive and hateful critical race and gender studies curriculum and the support of this trash by the teachers' unions.

The people of the United States have decided that they want to provide a fully paid primary education (grades K-12) for every child. Unfortunately, with this clear goal, the execution becomes bogged down in politics by the adults.

Should a student who prefers to attend a religious school, military or trade school be denied this right? Most people would say of course not. A student should go to the school of their choice. Now what about the cost? Why shouldn't the student be able to get a voucher for the cost of his/her education at the local school and take it to the school he/she prefers to attend as payment for the tuition. After all, if the student is not attending the local school the expense of his/her education is saved. Correct?

The teachers' unions' point of view is that the cost of the local school remains the same if a student leaves for a private school, and the tuition voucher removes funding for the public school system that then causes the quality of education for the remaining students to decline. If students leave for another school, then fewer classrooms are needed; fewer teachers are needed; and fewer principles are needed. While the fixed expenses may remain, the variable expenses are reduced. The building is a fixed expense, but the people working in it are variable expenses. (The unused space in the school is then rented to the charter school.) Therefore, there will be fewer teachers', union teachers. Of course, unions are against vouchers.

The question to be asked here is whether a student should be denied choice because the local school administration will be forced to change. This is an interesting argument. Of course, it would be immediately struck down if it were used as a reason to deny the busing of inner-city students to suburban schools. Once again, the rationale used to defend one policy cannot be carried over to another policy. When the rationale for a policy is only good for that specific situation, it is usually a flawed principle.

The primary advocates for students are their parents, but they are subjected to so much propaganda about education that many cannot make a good decision even if they had the power to make changes. However, parents pay the taxes, and they are the best advocates for their children. They should have the right to choose.

The teachers' union's job is to fight for the union membership and because of that, they are not advocates of children. The union wants higher pay, better benefits, life-time employment, non-termination agreements and non-performance metrics for teachers. In other words, high pay without accountability for results is the norm. The students do NOT belong to the union. They do not pay union dues and therefore, the union does NOT represent them in any of their dealings. This fact seems to be overlooked by everyone in this debate.

Self-Interest

We all have experienced the self Interest of one group prevailing over the interest of another. This is human nature around the world. In American schools' superintendents obtain their positions by selling new solutions to school boards and the public to improve or fix the performance of the school. New teaching techniques, computers and a new curriculum are the diet pills of education. When the present school superintendent is fired because the performance is bad, new people are interviewed and sell the board a story about how they can turn things around. The present learning system is abandoned and a new one is installed. The new superintendent comes with glowing credentials and gets a huge salary, but five years later when his or her contract is up for renewal the performance has not changed. The answer is to find a new messiah who will also sell you a new program and after five years or whenever their contract has ended, the performance still will not improve.

In any bureaucracy, people position themselves for recognition and promotion. Schools operate the same way. They have friends and they do not want to make their friends look bad or become subject to criticism and certainly not termination. This breeds a style of management where the blame is always on something other than the people teaching or running the school.

Public schools are government bureaucracies and are run in similar fashion to government agencies. Mediocracy is the standard. No one is to blame. No one gets fired. Merit and accountability are two concepts that are not allowed to exist. The students change; the parents change; and new ones come into the school system. The same poor education is provided to them. The message is that children are less important than adults.

Sports

Some readers may be surprised to see sports listed as an obstacle to the development of high attainment schools. In the top three rated school systems in the world, Finland, South Korea and Poland, there are NO organized sports programs. Yes, read it again. There are NO organized sports programs, and NO the children are NOT obese.

All team sports are strictly organized privately and after school hours. In South Korea, the regular school hours are 8 a.m. to 10 p.m., including the *hagwon*, (after school tutoring), so in effect there are no sports on school days. Sports are NOT important to these people.

In American schools, sports are very important. Sports stars are school heroes from middle school to college. Many children, especially boys, would prefer to be a sports star than an honor student. The glory and status of being a sports hero and the potential financial reward of a major league contract as a player or a coach are the dreams of many. It is easy to understand the lure of fame and money for a young person. They cannot see the benefit from calculus or history classes. A lifetime as a certified public accountant, computer programmer, doctor or dentist is not very exciting or rewarding compared to becoming a sports star.

School systems encourage this behavior from elementary school and the role of sports increases as the students move on to high school and then college. One wonders if many universities should change their names to better state the school's mission, such as Ohio State College of Football and Basketball or Notre Dame Football College. Of course, the immediate denial from the administration is that the sports programs bring in large amounts of money that "fund" other sports and activities. This may be true for some, but is it true for all of them? There is a movement within the country to pay college athletes. This may be the catalyst for the AAU to require a separation of colleges into learning institutions and semi-professional athletic institutions. This would be better for students.

Of course, what we never see as parents is the "real cost" of sports in terms of its deleterious effect on learning. In high school, the teams spend thousands of hours practicing and are allowed to miss classes to travel, practice and participate in games. In college, it is more of the same. Some students thrive on this pressure-packed schedule, but many do not and are mediocre students at best who are allowed to take watered-down courses to generate passing grades to help the teams win to provide for the glory of the institution.

Unfortunately, for the students who are not great athletes, sports are another obstacle to a better education. School resources are provided to team members and the staff who support and manage the team. Coaches are paid millions and ordinary professors dramatically lower salaries. The message is there for all to see, education is less important. It affects the mindset of the youngest children. Sports stars make more money than honor students. Don't study hard. There is little gold at the end of that rainbow.

In the end, when a student who is not an athlete completes 12 grades and four or more years of college, what is the takeaway from organized elementary school and college required (if required) gym classes? They do some running, play touch football, play some soccer and basketball. Maybe the school has a pool, and they swim. Most of the exercise is calisthenics, but they all miss what the goal of school sports should be for them -- namely to develop life sports, activities for non-athletes that adults can participate in for their entire life. These would include basketball, soccer, running, yoga, tennis and swimming. Instead of encouraging everyone to participate in sports in school, the others are excluded because they are not good enough to make a team and thus do not acquire the basic skills to participate in sports for life. Stupid, Stupid. The focus on teams should be changed to a focus on intramural sports where life sports are stressed, and everyone participates. We say we want a healthy society. This is a good way to achieve that goal.

Wealth

Another factor that deprives American children from obtaining a superior education is the country's wealth. Of course, you are thinking how can this be? You have always learned that it is the poor countries that cannot afford great schools. We are rich.

In America, being rich is the sole reason that politicians have not recognized a sense of urgency to improve education in the United States. They continue with the same old excuses and alibis, stupid and worthless schemes that will fix the problems of American education, and the taxpayers keep buying the bad dog food.

When the Russians launched Sputnik in 1957, it was a moment that galvanized the people to force changes and accountability in American schools. School systems across the country reorganized their curriculum to emphasize science and math. Teachers who taught these subjects were highly sought after, paid higher salaries, and the results were noticeable because more students became engineers and scientists.

Being rich means that there is no sense of urgency to make the necessary changes and force accountability into the American education system. There are many ways to be successful in America and many do not require a strong education, so we continue the cement mixer strategy, forever churning but making no visible progress. Technology is rapidly changing the world. Those who were ahead for many years (America, United Kingdom, EU countries) now find they are behind China, Taiwan, Japan, Singapore and South Korea. Wake up America.

Status Quo

A person can make the case that most Americans are indeed satisfied with the status quo. Let's look at the stakeholders in American education: the teachers' unions; the education service providers; the companies and experts who make a living selling products and services to the school systems; the politicians in cities and states that are closer to and thus more visibly accountable for performance; and college administrators who are enlarging their staffs, increasing their salaries, enrolling more students who cannot graduate or cannot find a job when they graduate. All these groups are happy to keep the American education system as it is.

Local Jobs

Another obstacle is that schools represent jobs for the community. In many American counties, school systems are one of the largest employers. Control over these funds is important to local politicians as they can use jobs as patronage for friends, relatives and supporters. When 75 percent of a school budget goes to pay salaries of administrators and teachers, the impact on the local economy is obvious and fodder for politicians' campaign speeches. However, very little money is left over for actual education. Once again, the children's educational needs are trumped by the needs of the adults.

As shown, the problems with the American education system cannot be readily fixed without much change in attitudes. These are problems in kindergarten to high school, but colleges have their own problems described in the next chapter.

Chapter 4 Four- or Five-Year College Indoctrination

The Greek philosopher Plato supported the value of free thinking at his Academy, a "community of thinkers drawn together in the logical quest for truth" and "dedicated to the art of critical debate." Intellectual liberty was the foundation of the Academy. The Roman philosopher Cicero modeled his own academy, Tusculum, after Plato's and embraced the same philosophical principles. Medieval Universities (e.g., Bologna, Oxford), embraced freedom of thought and expanded the concept of academic freedom and protecting teachers' right to debate, write and teach without fear of retribution. This philosophy has created the university system worldwide and successfully expanded human progress in the humanities, technology and science.

If Plato were alive today, he would be extremely disappointed that his philosophy of free speech and thought had died in American universities and was replaced by a "one thought fits all" mentality mated to the rabid persecution of those who do not submit.

Colleges have historically been havens for socialists and communists around the world and the United States is no different. This recent move to the left by college faculty is a result of the Marxist radicals of the 1960s, Students for a Democratic Society, they decided that controlling academia was the way to transform America. Brainwash students and then each succeeding generation of students will take these beliefs into society. Over time they reduced the number of conservative faculty at many universities and forced their views on faculty and students.

"The passage of time finds the faculty ever more wildly radical in its teachings, indulging in increasingly preposterous flights of absurdity. This zealotry upsets not only conservatives; prospective students also realize the limited utility of a degree in lesbian, gay, bisexual and transgender studies." (27)

Why is there a fixation of sexual perversion in college? The answer is because that group is totally loyal to the Democratic Party. The reward for that loyalty is preferential treatment. Heterosexuals must be made to submit to the LBGTQ community wishes.

In recent years, the left leaning academics have become even less tolerant of any views on campus except for theirs. Their communist propaganda machine cannot tolerate conservative views. Conservative professors are not hired, those who are in colleges do not receive grants or promotions, may be disciplined or forced out. Conservative faculty and students are a "minority without minority rights, including the right of free speech." This is not only acceptable in colleges in the United States and Great Britian. It is the policy of the universities. (28)

This communist theory is taught by faculty who do not brook any contrary point of view. This is the real problem for students and for American democracy. It is the professors' way, or you are labeled a *&^%phobe of some type and dismissed. Students are forced to learn and regurgitate this theory, much of which is completely contrary to American Democratic beliefs and has no foundation in fact.

At prestigious colleges across the country, student activists act as a mob to intimidate the silent majority while they protest "antiblackness" and the "erasure of Marginalized voices." As a result of this continual bombardment, many students are forced to keep their heads down to stay out of the lines of fire. This creates a tier of second-class students. "The term used by sociologists to describe this is 'dhimmitude,' a class of people who have internalized their second-class status." After years of enduring this treatment, "it can become a permanent condition, a form of moral and spiritual surrender." People who have been chastened into submission are more apt to continue this behavior after college and will not develop into strong independent thought leaders in whatever area they pursue. In fact, the behavior is likely to continue once they arrive in the workplace and encounter a new group of Diversity, Equity and Inclusion (DEI) zealots. Perhaps, this is the problem at Disney, Target, Anheuser-Bush and many Silicon Valley companies. (29)

"University of Chicago geophysicist Dorian Abbot argued in a *Newsweek* article that universities obsession with "diversity, equity and inclusion" (DEI) threaten to derail the primary mission: the production and dissemination of knowledge." He should know, as his lecture at MIT on climate was cancelled due to his article. The DEI police have taken over most college campuses. They control who is hired, what is taught and what is said throughout the college. They force the hiring of black, LBGTQ and women applicants and place barriers to the hiring of white men. They demand an ideological commitment and a level of activism in all new hires, transforming the college into a radical army. This is the Chinese cultural revolution on steroids, and it is here in the United States of America whose constitution guarantees each person the right of freedom of speech, except on college campuses. (30)

Harvard Business School has vowed to eliminate racial bias in their admissions, stated the dean, Nitin Nohria. After apologizing for not fighting racism as "effectively" as we could have, he stated that recruitment efforts at black colleges will be increased. Although the school has a large population of international students with varied ethnic backgrounds this isn't good enough for the Diversity, Equity and Inclusion police. They want more black students. Other ethnics, including African blacks, do not count. Therefore, more African American black students with lower grades will take the places of white, Asian, European and Middle Eastern students who deserve these positions much more. (31)

Unfortunately, the progressive left running colleges continually distort the meaning of words to cloud their true agenda. Equity is a perfect example. The dictionary meaning is; the equal treatment of everyone. The progressive use is to allow their grievance groups, namely blacks, gays and women (unless transvestites are competing) to get in the front of the line for admission to selective high schools, colleges and private industry and government job opportunities. Equity to a progressive has the opposite meaning as the dictionary. It is a purely racist concept, developed and spread throughout the country under the false guise of being a social justice "solution." (32)

One example of the misuse of diversity to discriminate is the Brown University policy prohibiting "caste discrimination." This is described as a "subtle, often misunderstood form of structural inequality." The university has never experienced a complaint based on this discrimination and probably never will because as they state that it is "subtle and often misunderstood," it is another weapon in the arsenal of discrimination against students and faculty of "South Asian Descent." This is illegal under the U. S. Constitution but the Diversity, Equity and Inclusion police at Brown don't care about the constitution or the rights it provides. Anyone charged will be persecuted and forced to leave. (33)

Asian Americans suffer racism across the board in education because of their high achievement status. The left cannot allow them to succeed because they ruin the narrative that systemic white privilege denies people of color the opportunity to succeed in America. Therefore, they are discriminated against in merit-based admissions to selective high schools and elite colleges. Their places are given to black students with lower qualifications.

"You have almost certainly heard some of the following terms: cisgender, fat shaming, heteronormativity, intersectionality, patriarchy, rape culture and whiteness." These concepts have been developed in colleges for many years and are now being introduced into the mainstream culture. These are nothing more than fake academic concepts that have been transformed into accepted realities, without any factual basis whatsoever. Biologist Bret Weinstein calls the process 'idea laundering.'"

The steps are as follows:

1. A group of academics find a topic they can agree to have strong moral feelings about.
2. These academics start a peer-reviewed periodical. They organize the studies of this topic to be submitted to a journal, the journal has a board of directors, a codified submission process, guest editors and of course a pool of "credentialed experts."

3. Ideas go in, garbage comes out, but it is labeled as "knowledge."
4. University libraries are petitioned to carry these publications, increasing the circulation and funding.
5. Eventually, there is a large canon of academic work, ideas, prejudice, opinion and moral impulse that have been laundered into "knowledge."
6. With all this published material, the subject then becomes recognized as a new field of study.
7. The final step is the affirmation by the college that this is an acceptable field of study with department status, tenured professorships, higher salaries and academic standing for worthless garbage, unproven baseless theories espoused by racists. Welcome to the communist propaganda industry.

Thus, the rise of the grievance industry in today's colleges and the decline in academic rigor. (34)

America is experiencing a social regression wherein disagreements are now being resolved by violence against individuals who do not conform to the orthodoxy of the left. Not surprising, "the regression has begun on college campuses. Many colleges are one-party campuses and do not brook any divergent viewpoint. Campuses are in a constant state of hysteria about systemic racism with small armies of diversity adminis-

trators always eager to jump at the slightest infraction
and the communist mob ready to punish the offender.
No faculty, administrator or student is allowed to hold
a view contrary to the Marxist ideologues. This left-
wing orthodoxy is also replacing traditional civics in
colleges. Recent graduates know much less about U.
S. government than older Americans do. In 2018, the
Woodrow Wilson National Fellowship Foundation gave
a sample of Americans a test based on the exam for U.
S. citizenship. Only 19 percent of the people under 45
passed, while 74 percent of those over 65 did, meaning elderly people who learned the material 40 years
prior can summon it from memory better than recent
grads." (35)

American universities used to lead the world in cul-
tivating an environment open to all ideas, opinions
and thought and encouraging a serious and rigorous
debate of the merits of each, exactly as Plato had envisioned. Currently American universities act in the
same manner as universities in totalitarian countries
and banana republics, espousing one propaganda message for all. Conform or be punished.

The American Association of University Professors
standard for behavior states that professors "should
not take unfair advantage of the students' immatu-
rity by indoctrinating them with the teachers' own
opinions before the student has had an opportunity
to fairly examine other opinions upon the matters in

question." California's constitution states that the University of California "shall be entirely independent of all political or sectarian influence and kept free therefrom." Despite this, "the UC Santa Barbara campus now offers a minor in Poverty, Inequality and Social Justice. The Berkley campus has a school of social welfare that is committed to developing leaders for social justice."

Yale University's mission statement for many years was "to create, preserve and disseminate knowledge." It changed in 2016 to "committed to improving the world," which is code for social justice. This is being accomplished by marginalizing professors and substituting administrative staff to make most of the policy decisions for the university. Equity and diversity demand total adherence to the gospel of that church and no other voices are allowed. Thus, the transition from free speech and inquiry into only ideas acceptable to the equity police has happened. (36)

The result of this shift left by American universities has been a serious decline in real education. "In their 2011 book, *Academically Adrift: Limited Learning on College Campuses*, Richard Arum and Josip Roska found that over 45 percent of students surveyed are progressing through college without any measurable gains in critical thinking, complex reasoning and writing," precisely the skills that a student is expected to learn in a university. (37)

"The sad fact that behind the glorified status of a handful of supposedly elite colleges and universities resides a rather shabby reality. Apart from the great scientific schools, Caltech, MIT and a few others, most contemporary universities are increasingly given over to political rodomontade: race, class, gender and all that. Outside science and engineering, students are unlikely to get much of an education under the current dispensation at any of these joints." (38)

Perhaps this focus on activism at colleges instead of a strong educational commitment is finally catching the attention of parents. The University of Missouri is suffering from a reduction in new student applications. Freshman enrollment dropped 35 percent between 2015 and 2017. The university has been forced to lay off 185 people in addition to the 308 staff they terminated the prior year. They have declined to renew expiring faculty contracts, and not fill positions of retiring staff. This is a result of the public pushback over free speech limits. The University has since adopted the Chicago Principles, which guarantees "the broadest possible latitude to speak, write, listen, challenge and learn." Unfortunately, some people are not convinced the university is truly supportive of this ideal. (39)

Even the prestigious Rhodes Scholarship trust has devolved into an organization that no longer searches for "the best men for the world's fight," now the emphasis has switched to "radical inclusion" meaning the scholarship should be awarded to black men, gays and women. In fact, in 2021, 21 of the 32 winners are people of color and one is non-binary. "Diversity is often their preferred academic specialty, along with sexual harassment, racism and the status of prisoners." The Rhodes Trust, who administers the scholarship, has become another WOKE organization, catering to the educational illuminati. (40)

One of the major causes for the breakdown in education standards throughout the American education community is the increasing influence of the social sciences. Unfortunately, "many social scientists have difficulty separating **Facts** from **Faith,** reality from the way they would like things to be." Unlike real science, social science theories are never subjected to rigorous analysis and proof before being forced on students by acolytes in teaching positions. Professor stardom is particularly perplexed by the idea of "implicit bias," which holds that unconsciously held beliefs about social groups perpetuate racism." This is a preposterous concept, which, if accepted, could be applied to any crime. Social scientists have become more like modern day snake oil salesman, travelling from town to town selling the elixir to cure all human ills. Instead, they seed new ways to increase anger and hatred. (41)

<u>Some Colleges Are Still Committed to Open Thought</u>

Bard College continues to pursue knowledge and believes that a variety of opinions is necessary for that pursuit. Although many believe that listening to views you don't agree with means you agree with it, at Bard, they listen respectfully and disagree where they feel it is necessary. All teaching must then accept the questions and criticism from an involved audience. In the end, one must persuade others, not force them to believe in what you are saying. "Gathering evidence and formulating arguments is the fundamental enterprise in the pursuit of knowledge. A scholar must accept the fallacy of their own point of view and the ability of everyone to change their mind." "The doctrine Bard subscribes to, is the power of reason, the power of argument, the power of language, the power of critical thinking and the willingness to try stuff out, and to revise one's point of view." (42)

<u>Community Colleges</u>

In the previous chapter, we discussed how high school students are not given any career options or training other than a push toward college classes. This could be changed with the help of community colleges.

The major roles of community colleges at this time are to 1) accept students who could not meet the higher standards of four-year colleges but want to pursue a college education 2) to provide a less-expensive college alternative for many students for the first two years of college 3) separate the competent students who will continue on with higher education from those who have decided that college is not for them.

Another important role for community colleges is to become an advocate and training resource for jobs with the trades, both independent trades, such as general contractors, air conditioning technicians, plumbers and factory/industry focused trades such as welders. Working with local industry, the Community Colleges can develop short-term certificate and degree programs, such as apprenticeship programs that combine the educational theory and practical experience working for a local company. They can also help these students to prepare for the state licensing exams to become certified in the trade (where necessary).

Community colleges can also assist individuals who wish to run a small business with programs that combine basic business skills such as accounting, finance, sales and marketing with the trade skills and experience. These courses should provide a real-world road map for individuals who want to start a business but do not understand how to get the required training, business education, experience and licensing. Obtaining an associate degree in business administration is not enough to enable an individual to operate a small business. Community colleges are ideally suited to help bridge this gap by partnering with counselors at the Small Business Administration and other local experts to provide support for start-ups.

However, their most important contribution should be rapid retraining of individuals who have lost their jobs. One such program, "the Federation for Advanced Manufacturing Education (FAME), began in 2010 as an experiment among several companies, including Toyota Motor Co.'s, Georgetown, Ky., factory, which was having trouble finding "middle skill" workers to operate new technology. The program pairs employers with community colleges. Today, nearly 400 companies participate in 13 states. Students at FAME, a mix of new high school grads and older factory workers well into their careers typically spend two days a week in class and three days working on the factory floor, earning a part-time salary. They learn to maintain and repair machinery, English, math, philosophy, work ethics and teamwork. After earning an associate degree, most work full time for the factory that sponsored them." (15)

When automation replaces workers, the machines then need to be maintained and repaired. They require a higher level of skills, and these are the people who do that work. Because their skills are greater than a factory worker's, their salaries are higher. In the decade before the pandemic hit, the United States added 1.3 million manufacturing jobs. FAME graduates help to support this increase as the need for people to repair robots and other sophisticated machinery continues to increase.

<u>College Admissions and Ratings</u>

What is a college or university? According to the Merriam-Webster online dictionary, "a school that offers courses leading to a degree and where research is done." They are also places involved in training basketball and football athletes for professional careers. While this definition would not necessarily apply to other countries, it does encapsulate the focus of U. S. institutions of higher learning.

In the United States, we have a tiered system of colleges. On top is the Ivy League, consisting of mostly the oldest colleges founded in the country. Some date to the 18th century. Due to their longevity and the fact that mostly wealthy families could afford to send their children to college up until the past 50 years, these institutions have history, tradition, wealth and a notable list of alumni that enhances their prestige. For many years, these institutions were affectionately known as the "old boys' network" as relationships built while in college were responsible for successful careers in business and government. As such, the saying, "it's not what you know, but who you know" that counts fits this group more than any other.

The next group is non-ivy but high academic, such as Northwestern, UC Berkley and Duke.

The third group is the technical schools including MIT and CalTech.

The final group is all other colleges that may have various rankings, specialties and other advantages.

Everyone knows that admission to one of the Ivy League colleges is the ticket to success in every field. Alumni of these institutions are given the social and professional status equivalent of British peerage. Americans almost genuflect when a person is introduced to them, and their college credentials include an Ivy League diploma. All colleges vie to have them on their teaching staff. Corporations entice them with promises of rapid promotions and early access to the executive suite and of course, Wall Street and the major consulting firms hire them almost exclusively. This group represents American nobility.

We have been led to believe for many years that entrance to this austere group was limited to those of superior intellect, the brightest people in the country and around the world. However, court documents from the college admission scandal and the Asian student lawsuit against Harvard have revealed some startling facts regarding the "real entrance" requirements _and_ composition of the student body at our "elite" universities. In fact, they are NOT that elite after all. A large percentage of the class is composed of 1) children of alumni 2) children of wealthy donors 3) children of politically or socially well-connected individuals (Obama, Bush and Schumer) 4) children of faculty and 5) athletes or those with other special but non-academic abilities. More spaces are then filled with the Democratic Party's super minorities (Blacks, Gays, etc.) and finally, the academically gifted obtain the remaining spaces. Hardly, the mix required to be revered as the finest universities in the world, but the mix required to pay the exorbitant tuition and obtain legacy gifts from the wealthy. This assemblage of student pales in comparison with a country like South Korea whose students compete in national exams for admission to the top universities. Maybe, the fact that Americans purchase an increasing array of complex electronics, appliances and cars from South Korea proves their students and universities are in fact far superior to the Americans? (43)

Of course, rating organizations disregard the facts and instead adhere to the myth. Ratings are not based on the SAT scores and high school rankings of those accepted. They use criteria like the size of the library and the number of applications denied. It seems that the low acceptance rate of these schools has been driven by a scheme in which the schools purchase names from the College Board, the nonprofit that is responsible for SAT testing. Once they purchase the names, they send brochures to the children who then apply. Most of them are rejected and then ask the question, why did you solicit me if you were not going to accept me? The answer is that extra applications are used to inflate their rejection rate. This increases the selectivity rating for the college. It is a sick game that uses the applicants as pawns to artificially increase the reputation of the college. As such, it should be deemed illegal by state lawmakers. The College Board should also be censured for its part in selling this information. (44)

The Harvard Delusion

Harvard University continually tops the rating agencies as America's best university. It is considered by many as the modern-day Delphi, the ancient Greek site of the Oracle. Whenever an ancient king wanted the answer to a serious question, he sent someone to visit the Oracle at Delphi for the true answer. Thus, Harvard students and professors are sought out for their opinion on every subject facing the world. But what is Harvard? Is this a college that, like select charter schools in New York City, takes the poor and disadvantaged off the streets and molds them into exceptional students who can compete for places in the city's select high schools via a placement exam? NO. Select has a system of education that produces a superior product to almost all other K-12 schools in the country. Select is the epitome of what every educational institution should strive to be. They educate students. Harvard and other Ivy League colleges do not have a system of education that produces the best graduates. It is the opposite. It selectively accepts only the cream of the crop, the wealthy, well-connected students, the most academically superior then throws in some ethnic and other equity applicants, to virtue signal that it has a "diversified" student body. Of course, the students will be successful because Harvard does not graduate students. It anoints them into the ruling class. Other elite universities do the same but to a lesser extent because they are not "the Oracle." These institutions are living proof that the axiom "it's not what you know but who you know that is the key to success in life" is correct. The Ivy League universities who advertise their exclusivity are the purveyors of privilege, not merit. (45)

<u>SATs</u>

Numerous Ivy League and other "highly competitive" universities have announced their decision to eliminate SAT scores for consideration of college admissions. This was done under the usual quest for "diversity and equity." This means that the university will accept applications from individuals with black skin and reject applications for individuals with white or brown skin. Maybe to cut through all the lies, applicants should just write their name on the application and affix a color photo of their skin, no grades and no letters of recommendation. Black-skinned applicants will be accepted and others, well maybe, if there is room. (46)

The story continues from the left as they are re-engineering society to account for the unfairness. Rich children have the advantage of being able to take college prep courses and increase their scores. That is why they have better scores. If this were true, what about the poor Asian kids who score among the highest applicants? Why doesn't the university offer FREE prep courses to alleviate the advantage? The SATs have proven to be great predictors of college performance. They do not cause black and Hispanic students to score poorly. They just provide unbiased evidence of their inability to do the work. The accusation that the SATs are racist is absurd. The children from inner-city schools are poorly educated and thus poorly prepared to attend college, any college. Instead of fixing the problem, it is easier to attack the test as biased. (46) Our great jurist, Antonin Scalia, summed up the matter in a 2003 Supreme Court case about affirmative action at the University of Michigan Law School. He said the state chose to have an elite law school and that requires it to select only the very best students. Unfortunately, the best students are often NOT black or Hispanic. The state has a choice. If racial diversity is the most important criterion, it can elect to have a less elite law school. Otherwise, it must follow the constitution and select students based on merit.

Harvard has decided to ditch the requirement for an SAT score in its admissions process. Its goal is to create a diverse and equity driven campus by eliminating the objective measurements of student proficiency and replace them with subjective measurements, such as "kindness, courage, integrity and likeability." It uses these soft measurements to accept students it wants to fill its equity and diversity goal and to discriminate against others, such as Asians and Jews who score high on standardized tests. This is a replay of how it discriminated against Jews in the early 20th century. Unfortunately, these types of changes hurt minority students because employers are never sure they are getting a Harvard graduate or an affirmative-action graduate. The black students who are admitted and do the work are forever tainted by tokenism. If Harvard believes black students don't score well because they do not get a good enough K-12 education, then it should support charter schools across the country that have demonstrated their ability to produce high school graduates from inner-city neighborhoods who are able to compete with private school students for admission. Of course, as a co-conspirator of the Democratic Party, Harvard must keep black kids in poor schools, poor and dependent on Democratic Party welfare programs while supporting the teachers' unions continual drive for higher salaries and no accountability. Harvard would not get any social justice credit if the black kids were proficient. It gets the credit by accepting people who are not qualified. (47)

Harvard's new "holistic" approach to assess the qualifications of applicants includes academic, extracurricular, athletic and personal. It is in the personal category where racial bias is practiced. Asians in the top 10 percent academically have a 12.7 percent chance of admission. This compares to 15.3 percent for whites, 31.3 percent for Hispanics and 56.1 percent for blacks.

<u>Racism is still racism; however, it is practiced, and</u> <u>Harvard has a lot of experience after denying Jews</u> <u>admission for many years under a similar pretext.</u> The <u>truth is that a Harvard graduate is now not much bet-</u> <u>ter than the graduate of any state college. The ques-</u> <u>tion is when </u>will the premier hiring groups consisting of consulting firms, Wall Street investment banks and Big Tech realize this?

It seems that MIT agrees with this writer. After years of abandoning the SATs under pressure from other colleges, MIT has decided to reinstate the requirement for an SAT score from all applicants. MIT explained it as follows: "Our research shows standardized tests help us better assess the academic preparedness of all applicants and also help us identify socioeconomically disadvantaged students who lack access to advanced coursework or other enrichment opportunities that otherwise demonstrate their readiness for MIT." As stated previously, these disadvantaged students could be prepared for MIT if they attended charter schools, but the Democrats want them to stay disadvantaged. There is no social justice credit to Democrats if blacks start scoring well on standardized tests. (48)

The fact is that inner-city schools will NOT improve in the near term because the Democrats want to control blacks and Hispanics by keeping them poor, under-educated, dependent and residents of the inner city to continue to support Democratic candidates. This is precisely why Democrats fight so hard against charter schools and vouchers for children to escape their terrible schools. The highest correlating factor in predicting college success for students is whether they live with their biological parents. The source of most problems in the inner city is the lack of these family units.

The Impact of the Education System

Having a strong education system is certainly a goal shared by many countries. But how exactly does an improved education system impact the country and its citizens? One way to measure the impact is to rate the countries by the number of patent applications. The stronger the education system, the more scientists, engineers and entrepreneurs are produced. Below is a table that ranks the top 20 countries. The absolute figures are adjusted for the size of the population. Not surprisingly, the No. 1 country is South Korea, which also is the country with one of the three best school systems. They perform at almost four times the United States' level.

PATENT APPLICATIONS

PER MILLION POPULATION 2019

Country	Number
South Korea	3319
Japan	1943
Switzerland	1122
China	890
Germany	884
United States	869
Denmark	645
Sweden	601
Finland	548
Netherlands	530
Austria	496
France	363
Singapore	303
Norway	297
Belgium	288
United Kingdom	272
Italy	227
Russia	165
Israel	151
Iran	140

SOURCE: World Intellectual Property Indicators, Wikipedia

Over Credentialization

One of the real issues in education is the constant desire to add educational credentials to the requirements for job qualification. Americans have been brainwashed to believe that the more time a person spends reading books, the better they will be at a specific job.

In the medical field, pharmacists were required for many years to complete a five-year degree program. Then, it was expanded to a master's degree and more recently a doctorate is required to become a pharmacist. WHY? Certainly, there are more drugs available now than before, but can anyone ever learn all of the drugs and the possible interactions? NO. This is a job for computers that can store up-to-the-minute information for easy access by a pharmacist or better a doctor who prescribes the medication.

The requirements for a nurse practitioner were also increased from a master's degree to a doctorate. If the non-doctor specialties in the medical industry are all required to have a doctorate-level education, then wouldn't it be easier to just have them all complete the requirements to become a medical doctor?

Not singling out the medical profession alone, this over credentialization is also true in business where four-year business degrees are required where high school was sufficient or master's degrees where a bachelor's degree was sufficient for many years.

Another example of the overpriced education is the three-year law school. Why isn't law a major in an undergraduate setting instead of requiring a student to complete a four-year bachelors' degree in some worthless subject like political science and then attend law school? "Graduates of these programs could expand the availability of low-cost civil legal services." (49)

American society is appalled at the huge debt incurred by students seeking college degrees, but they are to blame by continually increasing the credentials required. Another degree does not always confer additional skills, motivation or success in a position. In fact, when you ask individuals when they finally land jobs, what would be more beneficial, they invariably say on-the-job training and real-world experience.

It appears that colleges and professional organizations conspire to add educational requirements that are unnecessary to provide colleges with additional students and money to expand. Increasing the educational requirements means more professors, more facilities, larger budgets, more administrative staff and more time to indoctrinate children into the Marxist ideology. The professional organizations also use their power to continually increase the requirements as a barrier to entry and to justify higher salaries. Unfortunately, job salaries have not increased as fast as the requirements and costs to obtain these additional degrees. Many students graduate, fulfilling all the educational requirements for a job and then discover they cannot live on the salary nor pay back their student loans.

Another reason for the expansion of graduate degrees is the continual watering down of education at every level. America has traded a rigorous learning mentality in education that weeds out students who cannot perform into a mediocre nursery school environment, just like T-ball, where everyone gets a trophy. The tradeoff has been the lack of real educational achievement. Therefore, students need more and more education or they turn to other areas of financial compensation, such as illegal activity or theft.

Footnotes for Chapters 3 and 4:

1-"U.S. Students Fail to Gain Ground in International Test," Tawnell D. Hobbs, WSJ, 12/4/2019

2-"Bad Teaching Is Tearing America Apart," The Weekley Interview with E. D. Hirsch by Naomi Schafer Riley, WSJ, 9/12/2020

3-"To Really Learn, Our Children Need to Play," Pasi Sahlberg and William Doyle, WSJ, 8/10/2019

4-"Betsy DeVoss is on a Mission to Rescue Teachers Union "Hostages," Jason L. Riley, WSJ, 6/22/2022

5-"Is the Public School System Constitutional? Philip Hamburger," WSJ, 10/23/2021

6-"School Choice Saves Money and Helps Kids," Martin F. Leuken, WSJ, 2/13/2021

7-"Battle Over Critical Race Theory," Christopher F. Rufo, WSJ, 6/28/2021

8-"Youngkin Makes the GOP the Parent's Party," Brad Wilcox and Max Eden, WSJ, 11/4/2021

9-"Do Charter Schools Replicate?" Review and Outlook," WSJ, 5/13/2019

10-"The Tragedy of the Schools," Daniel Henninger, WSJ, 2/3/2021

11-"The Smear Campaign Against Charters," Baker A. Mitchell, WSJ, 8/14/2019

12-"Illinois Shocking Report Card," Review and Outlook, WSJ, 10/5/2022

13-"Amid the Pandemic, Progress in Catholic Schools," Katherine Porter-Magee, WSJ, 10/28/2022

14-"Trump Risks Unions' Wrath on Training," Eric Morath, WSJ, 11/29/2019

15-"Apprenticeships Offer Path into Middle Class," WSJ, 10/20/2020

16-"Money for Children Not Schools," Jeff Yasss, WSJ, 6/23/2022

17-"Classroom Chaos in the Name of Racial Equity is a Bad Lesson Plan," Jason L. Riley, WSJ, 5/12/2021

18-"An Education Horror Story," WSJ, 7/8/2019

19-"Have Teachers' Unions Finally Overplayed Their Hands?", Jason Riley, WSJ, 2/10/2021

20-"Charter Schools vs. Eco-Tours: It's No Contest," Steven Galbraith, WSJ, 12/24/2020

21-"Charter Schools Enemies Block Black Success," Thomas Sowell, WSJ, 6/19/2020

22-"The Secret of a Charter Schools Success? Parents," Robert Pondiscio, WSJ, 9/7/2019

23-"Massachusetts May Take Control of Boston's Public Schools," Roger Lowenstein, WSJ, 4/23/2022

24-"Phil Murphy Stifles New Jersey's Charter Schools," Jason L. Riley, WSJ 3/16/2022

25-"A Charter School Principal Won't Go to Prison," Jason L. Riley, WSJ 5/1/2019

26-"A Progressive Assault on Selective High Schools," Chester E. Finn, Jr., WSJ, 11/27/2020

27-"The Future of Higher Education: A Few Stars, Many Satellites," Daniel Pipes, WSJ, 3/22/2021

28-"Academic Freedom is Withering," Eric Kaufman, 3/1/2021

29-"Why I Stopped Hiring Ivy League Graduates," R. R. Reno, WSJ, 6/5/2021

30- "How Diversity Turned Tyrannical," Lawrence Krauss, WSJ, 10/21/2021

31-"Harvard Business Vows to Tackle Race Bias," Patrick Thomas, WSJ, 9/24/2020

32- "The Secret Meaning of Equity," William McGurn, WSJ, 11/1/2022

33-"Brown University Discriminates Against South Asians," Suhag A. Shukla, WSJ, 12/22/2022

34-"Idea Laundering in Academia," Peter Boghossian, WSJ, 11/25/2019

35-"Woke Universities Lead America to Primitive State," John M. Ellis, WSJ, 11/3/2020

36-"Higher Education's Enemy Within," Jose A. Cabranes, WSJ, 11/9/2019

37-"Campus Culture Seizes the Streets," John M. Ellis, WSJ, 7/6/2020

38-"The College Admissions Game Brings Out the Snob in Everyone," Joseph Epstein, WSJ, 3/20/2019

39-"More Misery in Missouri," Review and Outlook, WSJ, 6/16/2018

40- "The Rhodes Scholarship Turns Against Its Legacy of Excellence," David Satter, WSJ, 5/8/2021

41-"Science Needs Criticism, Not Cheerleading," J. Peter Zana, Opinion, WSJ, 2/20/2021

42-"The Reopening of the Liberal Mind," Daniel Akst, WSJ, 5/25/2019

43-"Colleges Rethink Legacy Preference," Douglas Belkin, WSJ, 2/24/2020

44-"Universities Buy SAT-Takers Names and Boost Exclusivity," Douglas Belkin, WSJ, 11/6/2019

45-"Who Deserves to Go to Harvard?", Heather MacDonald, WSJ, 6/14/2019

46-"Is the SAT Really the Problem?", William McGurn, WSJ, 5/26/2020

47-"By Ditching the SAT, Harvard Hurts Minority Students," Jason L. Riley, WSJ, 12/22/2021

48-"MIT Leads the Way in Reinstating the SAT," Jason L. Riley, WSJ, 4/6/2022

49-"Eliminate the Bar Exam for Lawyers," WSJ, 3/16/2021

Chapter 5 Illegal or Legal? Drugs

<u>Overview</u>

There are more than 30 million illegal drug users in the United States today, a number that continually grows notwithstanding the massive and ever increasing federal, state and local interdiction efforts. Americans are in love with illegal drugs.

Yes, drugs are everywhere in America. They span the economic ladder from the very poor to the super wealthy. We read about the impact of drugs on the inner-city minorities and the rich super stars who die of overdoses.

According to the Rand Corp., U. S. illegal drug sales equal $150 billion a year. Frontline estimates the total to be $65 billion. Using the smaller number, it is the equivalent of 20 Mary Kay cosmetic companies.

Criminals enter the illegal drug business because of the insanely high profits. Cocaine sells for $1,500 a kilo in Columbia. In contrast, the price is $66,000 a kilo on the streets of New York. That is a profit margin of more than 98 percent and a markup greater than 4,400 percent. There is no legal business with this type of profit structure anywhere in the world.

Drugs are involved in all types of crimes but particularly gang wars over sales territories. If this reminds you of the Al Capone gangster era, you are correct because the elements of both are the same. Organized gangs controlling an illegal business selling products that Americans want but the government has banned.

History

To understand how America has devolved to the present state of crime from illegal drugs, it is necessary to travel back in time to the beginning of the war on drugs.

The seeds of the drug war were planted in the United States with the birth of the Temperance Movement In the late 19th century. For many people, liquor was the bane of society. Public drunkenness was prevalent in almost every city and was blamed for poverty, crime, poor health, abandoned children, failed marriages and low worker productivity. The Temperance movement reflected a belief by many that if alcohol could be banned, the country would see an immediate increase in all things good, such as happier, stronger families, more productive workers, less crime and poverty and more prosperity for the nation. Women were the force behind the Temperance Movement that was an umbrella for the abolition of alcohol and illegal drugs in addition to supporting racial and gender equality. In 1873, Frances Willard founded the Women's Christian Temperance Union (WCTU). From then, the movement continued to grow with support from many Protestant churches and other organizations who believed in the various causes.

Prohibition

Apparently, the support for banning illegal drugs was stronger, or it was easier to convince the legislature that the downside was smaller, because Congress passed the Harrison Act in 1914, which made cocaine and opiates illegal to manufacture or sell. It was a clear victory for the Temperance Movement and helped galvanize support for the passing of the 18th Amendment to the Constitution on Jan. 19, 1919, which made the manufacture and sale of alcoholic beverages illegal. In any event, an Amendment to the Constitution is a significantly stronger form of legislation than a federal law. It requires the ratification of 75 percent of the state legislatures. Once passed, it was inconceivable to anyone that it would ever be rescinded.

One of the basic laws of physics postulates that for every action there is an equal and opposite reaction. This was certainly the case for the laws that barred Americans from liquor and drugs. Liquor was an especially divisive topic for Americans. Shay's rebellion, an armed rebellion to protest Washington's administration after the imposition of a federal tax on corn whiskey was the first protest by American citizens. The fact that many of the protesters were also Revolutionary War vets demonstrates how important whiskey was to the economic prosperity of the protesters. Corn whiskey was the value-added product of farmers corn crop. It was easy to store, transport and convert into cash and thus extremely popular in Colonial America.

The major impact of these laws was the organized resistance to each of them by groups of people. The term "organized crime" was first used to describe the activities of criminals, particularly in the business of manufacturing, selling and distributing some beer but mostly hard liquor. The second aspect of these laws was the public's belief that they should never have passed. Thus, America had two laws that banned the sale of products the public did not believe should be banned. The result was the development of local and regional organizations to bypass the law and deliver to Americans the booze and drugs they wanted.

Profits from the illegal liquor business were very high and that allowed the gangs to bribe everyone from the corner cop to judges, city councilmen, mayors and members of Congress. Since the major cost was detection and the loss of a shipment, liquor was sold in higher proof (more concentrated alcoholic versions) to maximize the value of each shipment. Richard Cowan developed the "Iron Law of Prohibition," which stated that the more intense the law enforcement, the more potent the prohibited substance becomes and the more adulterated and dangerous the final product becomes. Formerly 80 to 90 proof (40 percent to 50 percent alcohol) liquor was now sold at 150 to 160 proof (75 percent to 80 percent alcohol).

The high profits of the liquor trade resulted in many more Speak-Easies being opened in a city than the number of saloons that were closed due to Prohibition. Gangsters were selling a product people wanted and there were many entrepreneurs willing to invest money to accommodate the retail sale of the product.

Prohibition set the template for the present illegal drug trade. Once again, a highly profitable product that many people want to consume, has been made illegal by government fiat. The high demand also has created a large army of people willing to sell it; thus, transportation and sales opportunities are endless to satisfy the consumer demand. Just like the endless number of speak-easies selling liquor, there are a huge number of gangs and individual sellers of various types of drugs in every neighborhood across the country.

Prohibition was sold to the American people as a way to reduce crime, poverty, disease, broken homes and numerous other social ills. However, according to the CATO institute, the homicide rate in large cities rose from 5.6 per 100,000 inhabitants during the 1900-1910 period to 8.4 homicides per 100,000 inhabitants in the decade following the enactment of the alcohol and narcotics prohibitions.

The final judgment on Prohibition was that it was a failure:

- higher proof and adulterated alcohol were more dangerous to consume

- crime increased and became more organized and systematic.

- police departments, courts and prisons were overtaxed with the increased violent criminal activity

- many public officials became corrupted due to bribes

- eliminated a major source of revenue for the federal and state governments

- increased government spending on interdiction, prosecution and incarceration of gangsters

- liquor drinkers unable to satisfy their need switched to opium, marijuana and other drugs

Federal Interdiction

Fast forward to 2021. We see another monolithic federal agency trying to prevent people from buying a product they wish to consume. The federal government has never learned its lesson about trying to prohibit people from engaging in certain activities. It lost the war against alcohol and during its epiphany realized it could regulate and tax alcohol. The government lost the war against gambling and once again, jumped into legal gambling with state lotteries. Why it does not see that it cannot win the war on drugs is just plain dumb. Certainly, the country cannot in the 21st century, blame its Puritan ethos for the lack of common sense in dealing with human vices. Yes, we all admit drug addiction is harmful to any person who is afflicted with this disease. Maybe, in the United States, that is the crux of the problem. Just as we could not admit alcoholism was a disease for many years, we still cannot admit drug addiction is a disease. It is, and the better way to deal with it is to help the addicts by making the sale of these restricted drugs legal and removing the stigmas attached to being an addict. After all, there are millions of functioning alcoholics in the country. Accepting the research that 30 million people use illegal drugs, then there are millions of functioning drug users as well.

Americans seem to need to label and hide certain behaviors of humans and force the participants underground and therefore into the arms of criminals. The behavior does not stop, and the organized crime expands and extends into places that a legalized system would never tread, such as the sale of drugs to children. Legal or illegal, drugs have the same effect on people. Legalizing drugs eliminates the criminal part of the industry. Have you read about any gang wars over the illegal sale of liquor recently?

In 1970, Congress passed the Comprehensive Drug Abuse Prevention and Control Act. The following year, the federal government created the Drug Enforcement Agency (DEA) with a charter to enforce all federal drug laws. Its 2019 budget was more than $3 billion to cover a total staff of 10,000 agents. This is a very large agency and very large commitment by the federal government to eradicate illegal drugs in the United States. Unfortunately, the DEA is fighting a war it is continually losing and can never and will never win. The present cost of fighting the war is estimated at $51 billion per year according to the CATO institute. Unfortunately, this huge and ongoing drain on the taxpayers is only effective at interdicting 10 percent of the illegal drugs crossing the border. About 90 percent still arrive on our city streets.

<u>Drug Use</u>

The perception of the typical drug user is a poor urban dweller who is completely addicted to a drug, unable to hold a job, manage his or her own life and his or her personal responsibilities. Drugs transform people into savage criminals that the police have difficulty controlling, resulting in violent confrontations or they become homeless and transform city streets into sewers.

However, this picture is a distortion of the truth according to Dr. Carl Hart, a Columbia University professor and an expert on illegal drugs. He argues in his book *Drug Use for Grown-Ups*, that there is a polar difference between the picture painted by the media and politicians and the actual research. He discusses each of the major drugs and presents the conclusions of his actual research on the people who are users. To wit, they are well-adjusted people, many of whom are professionals who are living normal lives and managing their responsibilities without any problem.

Hart's research concludes that the effects of using cannabis, cocaine, heroin and methamphetamine were positive. Over 80 percent of the users were not addicted to any substance.

Hart further stated that it is almost impossible to publish any information that is contrary to the perceived narrative on users and the effects of drugs on them. He offers as evidence his research on users of methamphetamines. His study concluded that they performed equally as well as the control group, yet the *New England Journal of Medicine* refused to publish his study conclusions. Another example shows that "follow the science" only applies to the science and conclusions that are acceptable and conform to the current narrative. He further asserts that many researchers who publish doctor their conclusions to confirm to the accepted drug narrative so that they can continue to receive grants for further research. He specifically accuses them of reporting conclusions not supported by the evidence.

The most surprising revelation in this book was that Hart is a drug user himself. Throughout the book he discusses his use of various drugs, alone and with others, for recreation, relaxation and research. His personal revelation is an extremely powerful testament to his findings regarding drugs.

As a result of highly exaggerated media reports connecting marijuana use to violent crime by blacks, the Marijuana Tax Act was passed in 1937. The effect of this law was to ban the legal sale of marijuana.

After the law was enacted, Fiorello LaGuardia, the highly respected mayor of New York City, commissioned a study of the effects of marijuana. The results were conclusive, "individuals who have been smoking marijuana for a period of years showed no sign of mental or physical deterioration attributable to the drug." Scientific evidence negated the claims made to enact the legislation. Of course, the law was never repealed. Are legislators following science?

According to Hart, there are presently 27 million marijuana users in the United States. Media reports claiming marijuana causes psychosis were not confirmed by his studies of the drug.

In the United States, panic-promoting journalists continue to write stories that increase the public threat from out-of-control drug users, and thus maintain pressure on the politicians to enact ever more stringent drug laws, affecting mostly the users. Recently the public has been forced to endure the opiate threat. This included almost daily counts of the deaths from opioids in the United States. This threat has been replaced by the fentanyl threat with almost daily death counts on the news.

The facts are different. Most opioid deaths are not from the opioid alone but from mixing the opioid with alcohol, antihistamine, anticonvulsant, benzodiazepine or some other sedative for effect or from foreign substances added to the drug. The fact is that illegal drugs are unregulated, and the production and sale are often made by unscrupulous people who add other drugs or other substances to hype the performance of the drug. These additives are both unknown to the user and make the drug usage more difficult to regulate the dose. These are the causes of death for most users. Fentanyl is the additive mostly used now.

<u>Getting Off the Opioids</u>

"Opioids are extremely beneficial to patients' relief of pain from injuries. In fact, they are essential given our current state of medical understanding. However, the patient is faced at some point with the challenge of weaning themselves off the drugs. Too fast and the patient becomes withdrawn, experiences increased sensitivity to pain, flu symptoms, insomnia and crippling depression." Healthcare providers have done a poor job at this very important part of the patient recovery cycle. That has resulted in many patients going back on opioids because the withdrawal process itself was so debilitating. There is no "one-size-fits-all approach, but there are guidelines both for prescribing and withdrawing that need to be taken into consideration for each patient. Together with a trained drug professional who the patient can lean on for support, the process can be improved to cause the least amount of suffering. (1)

The Cannabis Conundrum

Cannabis advocates hoped that the drug would be legalized by the federal government by 2022 because many states had legalized the drug fully, or at least, through a convoluted "for medical use" only loophole. However, recently there has been a substantial increase in public sentiment against legalization. Not from police or physicians, but from parents. They saw first-hand the damage cannabis usage did to their children. Loss of motivation, memory and grades are common among children who use the drug. "In fact, many users prefer semi-synthetic extracts that are between 60 percent and 90 percent THC. Cannabis is more dangerous to teenagers than it has ever been. It contains more THC, the chemical responsible for the drug's high and its psychiatric risks along with less CBD, a non-psychoactive chemical that may reduce some of THC's negative effects. In 1980, cannabis typically contained less than 1.5 percent THC. These days, cannabis often contains between 18 percent and 25 percent THC. The new superhigh-THC-low-CBD products carry serious psychiatric and abuse risks. (2)

More states are acceding to the growing movement to legalize cannabis. New York State legalized the sale of cannabis in 2021. One of the major selling points was the opportunity to generate a huge tax windfall for the state, giving the politicians even more money to waste. New York State has even advertised for people with experience to become licensed drug sellers. This would be a tragic mistake. Individuals convicted of illegal activities are not the best qualified to run an honest business. Marking up the prices to cover the large state taxes would attract a large black market run by the same criminals who run it now. Politicians are so very stupid.

Conclusions

This author is not a drug user, never has been and has no personal interest in the illegal drug trade or the interdiction of drug trafficking. My involvement is purely as a scientist and to observe what works and what does not and report to the reader my conclusions and recommendations.

The first conclusion is that the U.S. government has lost the War on Drugs. Yes, after spending more than a trillion dollars and incarcerating hundreds of thousands of people, the war is lost. There is an old saying that doing the same thing over and over again and expecting a different result is the act of an insane person. The evidence is clear that it has been the strategy of the federal government.

The second conclusion is that 75 percent of deaths from the various illegal drugs are not from the drug but from some contaminated version of the drug sold through an unregulated marketplace. (*Drug Use for Grown-Ups*) This problem is exactly what happened to alcohol during prohibition when illegal contaminates were included in liquor production by the bootleggers. Many people became sick, and some died from these ingredients. These negative effects were eliminated by the repeal of Prohibition as the government regulated the manufacture of alcoholic drinks in the United States. Legalizing drugs and controlling the manufacture and sale in the United States, will eliminate most deaths from impure and contaminated drugs.

<u>Financials of the Drug Industry</u>

As stated earlier, the illegal drug industry has been estimated to be between $65 billion and $110 billion in retail sales per year. That is an enormous industry. For comparison Mary Kay cosmetics, which has a similar retail sale through sales rep structure, annual sales are $3 billion, and it employs 5,000 sales reps.

For this example, we will use the lower estimate of $65 billion in street sales.

Let us assume the average street salesperson sells $200,000 of product each year. Dividing $65 billion by $200,000 is 325,000. This is the estimated number of street salespeople who sell drugs in the United States. Of course, no one knows for certain what the exact figure is, but it is illuminating to start to work with estimates of the size of the industry, sales per street seller and the annual sales. All the numbers are large. (If you don't agree with the estimates above, substitute your own.)

Whatever figures you feel comfortable using, remember these are only the final street salespeople. Every organization has layers of people. Once the drugs are delivered into the United States, they have to be prepared for sale, broken down, remixed and packaged. Then they are distributed out to the next layer of sales and finally to the street sellers. The actual number of people employed is probably between two to three times the number of street sales sellers or 650,000 to 975,000 nationally. Yes almost 1 million people are employed in an all-cash business that pays no federal, state, city or payroll taxes. The tax revenue stream was an important consideration for the repeal of Prohibition. The tax windfall from the legalization of pot in Colorado may eventually be the reason marijuana and other drugs are legalized. It should not be. The focus must stay on the human suffering and death.

As we have learned from Prohibition, massive criminal enterprises have the ability and money to bribe civil servants and politicians for protection against discovery and interruption of their business. The major question never asked is why the war goes on with no victory in sight. Will the bureaucrats and politicians who gained power from this war ever relent and give it up? They say all the right things, but the war continues. In the most recent evolution, the transportation of illegal drugs has been enabled by the Democratic Party's insistence that the southern border remain open to refugees. The cover story from politicians and their acolytes, the communist media, is that America needs to open itself to people fleeing poverty and repression. However, the DEA and Border Control tell a very different story. The refugees are just a cover for the drug runners bringing large amounts of illegal drugs and trafficked women and children across the border. Because they are on site, these are the individuals whose version of events we should believe. Their version of events begs a larger question -- why is the Democratic Party enabling illegal drug traffickers and criminals to cross the border unimpeded? This policy aids the cartels. If the real reason was to help people fleeing poverty and repression, why isn't it done through legal channels and through the numerous airports and ports? Why force the people to undertake the arduous and dangerous illegal journey through jungles and deserts to arrive at the southern border? No, it only makes sense if the Democrats support illegal drug and human trafficking.

History tells us that when trying to understand human behavior, it is always instructive to follow the money. Although this author is unaware of any proof, the public must be left to decide if there is a financial connection among the Democratic Party, drug cartels and traffickers.

How to Get Rid of Illegal Drugs

Make them legal. Yes, it sounds ridiculous at first, but the United States and other democratic countries are already legalizing marijuana. They finally came to the realization that they cannot contain or stop the use of marijuana, so they decided to legalize it. The same is true for the other drugs, opium, heroin and fentanyl. The governments at the federal, state and local levels have been fighting the drug war for more than 100 years. They have lost the war. Illegal drugs are everywhere in the United States with a massive distribution and sales network that is more efficient than those of major corporations. Large profits, in cash, have enabled the drug cartels to expand their network around the world. They bribe whomever they need to bribe. Resist and they will kill you. DEA and other agencies try to fight this type of crime using regular police tactics, but these are ineffective. Instead of doing the same thing over and over again and failing, we need to re-evaluate and learn from previous attempts to restrict people from imbibing in a vice. (3)

America, more than any other country, should have learned the great lesson of how to deal with illegal drug use. The lesson was Prohibition. The federal government passed a stupid law restricting the sale of alcoholic beverages. The problem was that Americans wanted to drink alcoholic beverages. An illegal manufacturing and distribution system was rapidly constructed by gangsters and sold through a network of social clubs (Speak-Easies). Politicians, cops and whomever else, were given the same ultimatum, accept the bribe and look the other way or we will eliminate you. The honest police and politicians fought the war, but in the end, they had to surrender. Why? The people wanted alcohol. The situation for drugs is the same. The people want the drugs.

The American political establishment has continued to reject the legalization of drugs. They reiterate the same old bromides that have been used by the "reformers" in the Temperance Movement. History has shown us that alcohol and drugs are not responsible for all the ills of humanity. Post Prohibition has demonstrated that for the overwhelming majority of people alcohol consumption is not a destructive influence on their life. This template should be used to argue for the decriminalization and subsequent legalization of drugs in the United States.

We know for certain that the cost of criminal interdiction, street violence and incarceration will be eliminated. These savings can be reinvested in programs to help addicts lead a normal life. The estimated cost of fighting the Drug War is $51 billion per year (Cato institute). This massive tax on the American people results in the interdiction of only 10 percent of the drugs across the border.

Consider the following costs:

- Financial grants to producing countries to fight drug cartels in their home country

- Coast Guard and DEA efforts to interdict drug shipments into the United States

- Local policing

- Capture, prosecution and incarceration of drug smugglers

- Gang violence, medical costs and murders

- Destruction of communities

- Loss of tax revenue (sales taxes, income taxes, real estate taxes) in troubled communities

Loss of federal, state and local income and sales taxes and payroll taxes

When the bill for everything is totaled, it must be in the hundreds of billions per year.

Military Intervention

Former Attorney General Bill Barr has recommended in a *Wall Street Journal* article that the United States should send troops into Mexico to attack and destroy the cartel operations. This is not a good idea for many reasons. First, we have witnessed the outrage by regular citizens from the U. S. invasions In Iraq and Afghanistan. Instead of helping us, they help the people we are fighting. Mexican cartels have spent years building good relations with people in their district to turn them into allies who will support them against the federal government.

What Decriminalization Would Look Like

There are two possibilities for improvement of the illegal drug problem in America. The first is legalization. The drugs are removed from Schedule 1 of the Federal Controlled Substance Act. The second, somewhat less effective, but maybe enough to combat the negative effects of having the drugs on the Federal Banned Substance list, is to decriminalize the possession and use of the drugs. This can be done while maintaining the criminal penalties for production, distribution and sale.

Portugal is a case study for the second possibility.

- All illegal drugs decriminalized

- Anonymous drug purity testing services set up throughout the country

- The number of heroin users declined from 100,000 to 25,000 since decriminalization

- Deaths have plummeted to one of the lowest for any democratic country

- Portugal -- six deaths per million population

- America – 312 deaths per million population

There are other countries adopting the same or similar laws:

- Spain -- Drugs decriminalized, drug purity testing for free

- Uruguay in 2013 legalized marijuana

- Canada legalized it in 2018

- Switzerland, Belgium, Netherlands and Denmark have heroin assistance programs. Patients who receive treatment hold jobs, pay taxes and live long healthy lives. Heroin addiction is treated with heroin.

As countries move away from the traditional law enforcement solution for illegal drugs, such as persecution, prosecution and incarceration, to more intelligent and successful programs, it is hoped that the criminal effects will diminish, and the "patients"/addicts will be able to rejoin society.

<u>Recommendation</u>

The illegal drug problem consists of three different problems that are interconnected. They are:

- The gang violence due to the manufacture, distribution and sale of the illegal drugs

- The deaths caused by tainted product sold on the streets

- The addiction of the drugs

The only remedy that solves the gang violence and deaths caused by tainted products is to legalize drugs but in the same manner as the legalization of alcohol. All products would be manufactured and sold through a three-tiered system, under federal oversight.

First, the manufacturers would have to be licensed by the federal government with their production facilities, the dosages and specific formulations proscribed by the Food and Drug Administration (FDA), or the Alcohol, Tobacco and Firearms (ATF) Administration.

Second, manufacturers would then be able to sell the products to a network of state wholesalers, licensed by the individual states that, in turn, would sell the products to state-licensed retailers.

Third, state-licensed retailers will sell to anyone over 18 with no questions asked and no other information requested.

The final prices should be substantially lower than the street prices of the equivalent illegal drug dosages. This is very important as lower prices will eliminate the drug cartels. The goal of the program is to kill off the cartels, not to raise tax revenues. We already see legalization in California enhance sales of illegal marijuana as the illegal product is cheaper than the tax burdened legal marijuana.

The goals of this three-tiered system would be:

1) Provide drug users with safe, unadulterated drugs at reasonable prices

2) Drive the illegal dealers and cartels out of business by selling higher quality product at significantly lower prices

3) Provide the government with legal revenue from the "honest" drug industry

Eliminate the cartel and gang crime from the sale of

illegally manufactured drugs

Provide addicts with better care options for quitting their drug addiction.

This approach would deal both with the problems of supply and demand. Drug users would make the rationale choice of buying the drugs from the legal suppliers where they can be assured of high quality, unadulterated, product.

Unfortunately, it is expected that the cartels and illegal trade will not just go away. They would have to continue to be persuaded. How?

Tougher federal laws will need to be enacted for any "illegal drugs" sold. Individuals participating in the manufacture, transportation and sale must be subject to mandatory life terms in prison. No exceptions. No reduction in sentence for any reason.

Drug users who are caught with illegal drugs would be subject to mandatory 10-year prison sentences. No exceptions. No reduction in sentence.

Can we eradicate illegal drugs? This is probably not a realistic possibility in a democratic country. However, most people believe that illegal drug use has gotten out of hand and must be reduced. The best model for this goal is cigarettes. In the 1940s and 1950s, cigarettes were everywhere. People smoked in the movies, on television, at work and on planes. Legislation was introduced to create no smoking areas, and at the same time, a massive advertising campaign began to present the downside of cigarettes. Testimonials from cancer patients and others with emphysema helped to transition smoking from cool to stupid. That is a better model to follow for illegal drug use.

Society must make using drugs "uncool." Cigarettes were popularized by making smoking the cool thing to do. Movie stars and TV personalities were regularly seen with a cigarette in hand. This promoted smoking. When cigarette smoking was banned due to cancer links, the depiction of smokers was replaced with ads of emaciated smokers suffering from cancer or emphysema. These pictures and testimonials told the true story of smoking and helped reduce smoking in the United States. Using the same strategy will have the same effect of changing the image of drug use and help to reduce the number of people trying and using these dangerous drugs.

Footnotes

1-" The Perilous Blessing of Opioids," Travis Rieder, *WSJ*, 6/15/2019

2-" Marijuana Activists Pass Their High Point,". Alex Berenson, *WSJ*, 6/26/2019

3-" Why the U. K. Isn't Having Problems with Vaping," Matt Ridley, *WSJ*, 10/26/2019

Biography:

An American Disease, David Musto

Dark Paradise, David Courtwright

Addicts Who Survived, David Courtwright

Forces of Habit, David Courtwright

Heroin Addiction Care and Control

The Pursuit of Oblivion, Richard Davenport-Hines

"The Once and Future Drug War," James Marson, Julie Wernau, David Luchnow, *WSJ*, 1/22/2022

Drug Use for Grown Ups, Carl Hart

Chapter 6 What's the Cost of Healthcare?

<u>Introduction</u>

One of the most important and divisive issues facing the United States is the issue of healthcare. The Democrats continually press for a single-payer, government-conceived-and-managed plan covering everyone. They justify this by arguing that the United States is the only industrial country that does not have a single-payer healthcare system covering all citizens. They also argue that healthcare is a human right. Of course, classifying it as a right makes it morally more difficult for anyone to object to their plan to take over the United States healthcare system. However, if the human rights argument is accepted, then other things must then be also classified as human rights, such as food, clothing, shelter, retirement, vacations, entertainment, happiness, a fulfilling career, a cell phone and a car. The list continues. Their goal is always more about control of the program so that they benefit by 1) hiring more workers who can then be unionized and contribute to the democratic party funding drives and 2) changing the rules to aid specific groups who support the Democratic Party. We are already seeing racial preferences in medical care for democratic grievance groups.

The Republicans counter by pointing out that the government cannot be trusted to manage the country's healthcare system. They use the Veterans Administration as their prime example of a government-run healthcare system, which has been fraught with years of complaints regarding the poor level of care and examples of actual deaths from the long wait times for appointments. Care is rationed by this system. That means substandard treatment for patients. Politicians' response to the years of complaints was to continually reorganize and appoint a new head of the Veterans Administration, but the complaints and poor care continued. Obviously, reorganization of a failed organization does not correct the structural and managerial ineptness. The real solution imposed by the Trump administration was to allow veterans to visit private doctors and hospitals. This change has solved the V.A. care problem for veterans.

The first question that must be posed is whether the present healthcare system would be acceptable to most Americans, and the pundits, if everyone could afford health insurance. If so, then the real issue is cost, not structure.

The major healthcare structures will be examined and compared to the U. S. system.

<u>Healthcare Consumers</u>

For purpose of this analysis, consumers are divided into three separate groups:

Group 1 consists of a) the homeless b) the working poor who cannot afford private insurance and do not qualify for government programs (Medicaid) and c) those who can afford insurance but choose, for a variety of reasons, not to purchase it. While none of these groups have a health insurance policy, they do receive medical treatment at hospitals for emergencies and these costs are included in the total U.S. medical costs. The individuals in group 1 pay very little to nothing for healthcare.

Group 2 consists of individuals covered by government-run programs including Medicare and Medicaid. Medicare premiums are set based on an individuals' income while Medicaid is free to those who qualify, but there is an income restriction.

Group 3 consists of individuals who purchase private health insurance. The largest percentage of these are covered by employer-sponsored health plans. The law requires the employer to pay a minimum of 50 percent of the employees' health insurance premiums. Self-employed individuals pay their own insurance premiums. Plans for the self-employed and individuals carry higher premiums than the employer sponsored plans that have many more members and thus qualify for discounts. The larger the pool of employees the better the rates offered by the health insurance company.

<u>Providers</u>

Doctors are the primary providers of healthcare for consumers whether they practice as an individual or are part of a group practice. They have a business wherein they build up a list of clients through referrals from other doctors; patients; or an affiliation with a local hospital, medical center or network. Doctors provide care for Group 2 and Group 3 patients because these two groups have health insurance or pay cash.

Hospitals provide most of the care for Group 1 patients through emergency room visits. They provide care for group 2 and 3 patients.

<u>Types of Healthcare Programs</u>

There are three major healthcare models in use around the world.

The Bismark model, named after the famous German Chancellor, is a social health model. This model requires each citizen to buy health insurance through their employers. Private doctors and hospitals provide the service under contract.

The National Healthcare model or Beveridge Model was developed by Sir William Beveridge in 1948. This is a taxpayer-funded service which operates on an annual budget approved by the legislature. The focus of this model is cost control and it features gate keeping mechanisms for care as well as strict controls on the purchase of pharmaceuticals and equipment. Hospitals are owned by the government and medical staff are government employees. This is a rationed program.

The out-of-pocket model is a private model wherein the consumer pays the cost of their own healthcare either directly or through health insurance or a combination of both. Doctors work for themselves, and hospitals are privately owned. They may be for profit or non-profit. This is the model used by most Americans although the V.A. and Medicare/Medicaid are more like the Bismark and Beveridge models.

<u>Obamacare</u>

Politicians have been urging the adoption of a national health plan to cover everyone for many years. Each election cycle, Democratic candidates for Congress tout the need for universal coverage, downplaying the problems with national health plans. When President Obama was first elected, the Democrats finally held all three branches of government and began the development of a national healthcare plan. President Obama spoke before the nation touting the advantages of this new plan. He promised:

1)everyone could keep their plan

2)everyone could keep their doctor

3)the plan cost would be less than present plans

The 2,000-page plan was written and passed without anyone in Congress being allowed to read it. Nancy Pelosi said, "vote yes and then you can read it." Unbelievable, in a democratic country and an administration continually touting themselves as the "most transparent in history." One question remained. If it was such a great plan, why was Congress provided with a different plan?

As Americans began the process of renewing their coverage, they were told their old plan was "No longer offered" by the insurance company. Rates for a single person rose by 50 percent or more and annual deductibles rose from $1,500 on some plans to $15,000 on the "replacement plan." Single consumers who were paying $400 a month now paid $600, families had similarly large percentage rate increases. Far and away the greatest surprise was the exorbitant increase in the yearly deductible. A single person now had to pay $7,200 a year in premiums ($600 times 12 months), plus $15,000 in medical expenses (the deductible) before the insurance company began to participate in paying medical bills. Who in their right mind would sign up for such a ridiculous proposal, facetiously called an insurance policy? What exactly is insured?

The old health insurance plan based on the 80/20 split between insurer and consumer was now replaced by a catastrophic health policy with a $22,200 premium. WOW, the biggest insurance scam in history. Many also lost their doctor as the doctor was "No longer" in the network. President Obama had lied. You could 1) No longer keep your plan and you could 2) No longer keep your doctor and your 3) New plan was much, much, more expensive. President Obama had in fact converted "health insurance" into "catastrophic health insurance" transferring the premiums paid by consumers in group 3 to pay for the health insurance for those in Group 1 who had no prior health insurance. Of course, neither President Obama, the Democratic Party leadership or the media ever admitted this.

Young people immediately saw this situation for what it was, a scam on them, and they refused to sign up, opting instead to pay the $300 penalty due to the mandate to purchase included in the legislation. They believed their health was good enough to go without a health insurance plan. Older people, especially those with families, had no choice but to pay. Unfortunately for them, they paid their premiums and then still had to cope with health costs the policy did not cover.

It was revealed several years later that the architect of this plan, Jonathan Gruber, an MIT professor, knew in advance that people could not keep their plans or their doctors and that the cost of health insurance would rise significantly for those who chose to sign up. He later admitted to being happy that he could trick the American people by his chicanery, with the help of the Democratic leadership and a compliant Chief Justice Roberts, a man whose name will live in infamy for his decision to place politics above the well-being of the American people.

Along comes President Trump and the healthcare mandate is voted down and Obamacare begins to self-destruct. Instead of one size fits all, new regulations allow insurance companies to customize plans for various groups depending on customer needs (how novel). Insurance companies are also allowed to sell across state lines. Plan rates begin to decline and come back out of the stratosphere. The number of people covered by health insurance rises.

However, the call for a universal health plan continues by the Democrats. In 1950, most people paid for healthcare out of pocket. It has been elevated to a "human right" in 2019. The support for it continues although it is somewhat muted because candidates do not know how to pay for this "human right." But for Democratic politicians, paying the bill is not important. They live in an alternate universe where economic laws that govern the financial behavior of individuals, corporations and governments do not exist. So, stay tuned.

<u>Medicare for All</u>

The most recent form of universal healthcare is now called Medicare for All. It consists of universal coverage for all citizens and non-citizens residing in the United States. Premiums would be on a sliding scale based on income just like Medicare premiums are now. The proponents guarantee that there will be no diminution of service like in countries that have National Health Services. There will not be long waiting times to see a doctor (Great Britain). There will not be long waiting times to see a specialist (Canada). There will not be long waiting times to obtain tests (blood, MRIs and X-Rays), like in those other countries with National Health Services. There will not be long waits in emergency rooms.

In short, they promise the exact same service levels that presently exist in the United States at a significantly lower cost and these services would be available to ALL U. S. citizens and non-citizens who are present in the country. There will not be rationing of service. Of course, No democratic candidate can explain exactly how the costs will be lowered (because they can't.)

Democrats continue to lie to the American people, telling them that Medicare for All would provide "free healthcare" for every person. "It is estimated that California would pay $400 billion for "free healthcare."

Nationwide, the cost would exceed $32 trillion for the first decade ($3.2 trillion per year). (Total U. S. tax collections are $4 Trillion) Doubling corporate and personal income tax rates would not pay for it. Of course, once the "real cost" was acknowledged, then the only realistic option would be to curtail benefits. One of the drawbacks of single-payer systems is the long wait times for treatment. In 2017, the wait time in Canada for a referral from a general practitioner to a specialist was 10.2 weeks. In the United Kingdom, about 362,000 patients waited longer than four months for hospital treatment. In Canada, the wait times for heart disease treatment was three months; neurosurgery wait times are eight months; and hip or knee replacements 10 months. (1)

Democrats promise that Americans can have "free healthcare for all" by taxing the rich. This is another false argument that is supported by a close examination of how the European socialists pay for their welfare states. France, Germany and the United Kingdom all tax the middle class at higher rates than the United States because the rich in their countries are just not rich enough to pay for the never-ending social programs in their respective countries. The same will be true in the United States if we ever adopt the Medicare for All program. Of course, Congress will have a separate program, a much better program. (2)

Bernie Sanders continues to proclaim that Medicare

for All would provide universal coverage, controlled costs, high quality and ready access. He cites Canada as an example of a country that has achieved these objectives. The Frazier Institute published a study that examined 28 universal healthcare systems. Canada was one of the most expensive, and at the same time, its wait times for service were poor for several of the major indices. The study identified the Netherlands and Switzerland as the best overall systems. Both rely on private insurers with the government paying the premiums of those who cannot afford them. These are systems that should be examined in more detail and benchmarked against for improvements that are need-ed in the U. S. system. (3)

Do Americans want to replace their private health insurance with its many choices for care and replace it with a federal government-run behemoth agency where the bureaucrats make all the choices for the patient without consultation with a doctor? Haven't they learned from the bungled management at the V.A.? What about the long wait times? Decline in qual-ity? Decline in innovation? Most of all, do they want rationing of service so that those most vulnerable are left to die? (4)

Bernie Sanders offered up a new version of his Medi-care for All takeover of the American Medical Industry in 2019. He suggested a bailout of all hospitals with a $20 billion package. He asserts that hospital failures are a direct result of corporate greed. The facts, however, tell another story, according to data from the American Hospital Association, Medicare and Medicaid reimburse hospitals at a rate of between 87 percent to 90 percent of its costs for services performed. "I sit on two hospital boards and their finance committee and discuss Medicare with management every month. Our experience is that Medicare generally pays less than 50 percent of the actual cost, not 90 percent." (5)

The hospital in turn charges its private insurance patients' rates that are 140 percent of the cost to cover the shortfall from the government insurance programs. Hospitals get into financial trouble when their patient mix is predominantly Medicare and Medicaid insured. There are insufficient private insurance patients to squeeze money from to cover government-induced losses. "Former Congressman John Delaney, stated during a debate that if you go to U. S. hospitals and ask them one question: "How would it have been for you last year if every one of your patient bills were paid at the Medicare rate? Every single hospital administrator said they would close. Thus, in Bernie's world, we should bankrupt all the healthcare providers and then have the government take over everything. Then, we would have government bureaucrats limiting care to those unworthy (Republicans) or those who will probably die anyway (the elderly or chronically ill). (6)

The COVID-19 Pandemic has been an opportunity to see the various healthcare systems at work. "According to an August study in the *Journal of Critical Care,* the United States has 34.7 ICU beds per 100,000 population compared to 29.2 in Germany, 15.9 in Belgium, 11.6 in France, 9.7 in Spain, 6.6 in the U. K. and 6.4 in the Netherlands. Hospitals in Europe's national health systems operate under global budgets that keep a tight cap on hospital funding. This results in chronic under-investment and rationed care in normal times. Hospitals are lean because they cannot afford to maintain spare beds and staff. During Europe's surge, Covid treatment in many countries was rationed, as it often is, by age. Older and frailer patients were denied admission to Italian ICUs. The *Sunday Times* reported that U. K. patients over age 80, and some over 60 with underlying conditions were left to die. Patients over the age of 80 made up 60 percent of the United Kingdom's deaths, but only 2.5 percent of those in this age group who were hospitalized received intensive care. The American left has long idealized Europe's government-run healthcare because it's less costly, but patients pay a high price." Are you ready to die? (7)

Most of those who are against any form of national healthcare service cite the disadvantages listed above as the actual consequence of any national program. They also cite the decade's long debacle of the Veterans Administration's poor care as the poster child of what will occur in the country. They further argue that once the profit motive is uncoupled from any system the result is poor service. As with Medicare reimbursements now, professional service reimbursements will be reduced. Doctors will retire and students will not be willing to invest 10+ years of education into a profession that does not pay well. Lower reimbursement rates will force hospital closures, unless they can also be placed under the umbrella of the federal government. Thus, not only will the federal government create a single-payer system, but all the providers will also be absorbed eventually by the government because they will not earn enough with the rates of service reimbursements to remain viable as private entities. One can look at the NYC healthcare system to trace the history of hospital closures as the reimbursement rates for municipal employees were reduced and the only alternative for the hospital was to be absorbed by the city system.

"The public option would cause premiums for private insurance to skyrocket because of underpayment by government insurance compared with costs and services. A single-payer option is not a moderate, compromise proposal. Its' inevitable consequence is the death of affordable private insurance." (8)

A two-tiered system will emerge as some doctors will transition to a cash-only system and not accept payment or patients covered by the national healthcare system. This is already the case as some doctors do not accept Medicare or Medicaid patients. The wealthy will have great healthcare and pay cash or have insurance for treatment. Healthcare will resemble public schooling, poor quality for most children while the wealthy children attend private schools. One question to be answered is whether members of Congress will be included in their proposed national healthcare system, or will they continue to benefit from a superior healthcare program exclusively for themselves, paid for by the taxpayers, who receive poor care?

Another example of government incompetence in managing healthcare is their management of both Medicare and Medicaid. The book *Overcharged* by Charles Silver and David Hyman is a 400-page chronicle of the waste and fraud in both government systems. What is unbelievable is that the government never learns from its mismanagement, and the fraud continues. Providers who defraud the government get a slap on the wrist and then start up again under another name and do it again and again without any penalty. This could never occur at United Health Care or other insurance companies because it is a well-managed corporation. Its financial staff oversee the expenditure of every dollar.

The truth is that government must be completely removed from the management of health care. It should set up the programs that the private sector manages.

Comparison of the Different Models

Research shows the Beverage and Bismark systems to be quite similar in terms of outcomes. Overall mortality, infant mortality, life span, cost as a percentage of GDP and cost per capita are the major measurements compared among countries. The Beverage model is somewhat less expensive to operate, and the Bismark model has higher satisfaction levels due to the additional elements of choice and the lack of a gate keeper mechanism. The out-of-pocket system was not viewed as favorably in a comparison for four reasons:

1) costs are higher

2) the infant mortality rates are higher. Infant mortality differences are refuted by the methods used to calculate the numbers. In most of the European countries, infants who do not survive for a specific period are not counted. By comparison the United States includes all infants.

3) life expectancy is less. This difference is attributable to the overall poorer health of Americans due to high levels of obesity, smoking and drug use. (9)

4) everyone is not covered (but they have access to a hospital emergency room for care when necessary.

Many poor countries use the Out-of-Pocket system as they do not have the funds to operate a national healthcare program (Beveridge model) and the citizens do not have the money to pay for a regular health insurance plan (Bismark model).

However, the research studies are somewhat boiler-plate in nature as they all compare the same criteria. This is mostly because these criteria are most easily quantified. Issues that were not analyzed included:

- The time it takes for patients to get their condition diagnosed, a course of treatment created, the treatment implemented and the patient's return to their normal condition or to work

- The quality of doctors, nurses and other technicians who treat patients

- The time required to adopt new more effective and/or more efficient methods of treatment

- The quality of the equipment used for diagnosing patients and its effect on diagnosing, treatment and outcomes

- Differences in use of the latest pharmaceuticals and their effect on outcomes

- Different cultures and their effect on choosing a healthcare system

- The level of service provided to each patient

<u>Private Healthcare System</u>

The advantages of a private healthcare system are:

- Private companies are continually striving to improve their technology to reduce costs and increase service levels

- Private companies are more responsive to patient requirements for plans that fit consumer needs. They do not have a one-size-fits-all mentality

- Private companies value consumer feedback to improve service

- Private companies offer better services than government agencies

- Private companies do not ration care

- Private companies continually invest in research and development to improve treatments and develop new products

- Private companies are nimble and can reorganize and refocus on an objective much faster than a lumbering government agency (e.g., project warp speed)

- Private means more providers to choose from, thus a higher level of consumer choice

Status of the U.S. Healthcare System

An objective look at the U.S. healthcare industry shows that it is one of, if not the best, in the world with well-trained doctors with state-of-the-art hospital care; fast access to specialists and tests, such as MRIs and CT scans for prompt and accurate diagnosis and the worlds' leading pharmaceutical industry developing newer and more efficacious drugs and equipment. In short, if you are sick, U.S. doctors can get you well and back to a normal life faster than almost any other healthcare system. The evidence of this is that sick patients with the means come to the United States for treatment. Another major advantage of the U. S. healthcare system is that it is very nimble. This was evidenced by the significantly better response time of the U.S. drug companies versus European and other countries in dealing with the COVID-19 outbreak. In particular, the speed that the U.S. pharmaceutical industry was able to develop vaccines surpassed others.

Problems With the U.S. Healthcare System

The problems continue however:

11 percent of Americans under 65, or 29 million people, live without health insurance. (10)

2) healthcare insurance is increasing at 12 percent per year.

There are structural problems in the present U.S. healthcare system that contribute to the distortions and problems we have outlined. These include:

1. <u>The federal government's interference in the</u> marketplace in the form of Medicare and Medicaid. More specifically, the reimbursement rates for Medicare patients are below the market costs for those services and significantly below market prices. Service for this group of patients forces the cost of their care to be transferred to other patients. As the population has aged and the government has added people to their healthcare rolls, larger losses by the medical community must be transferred to the remaining health patients accelerating price increases.

2. Employer-sponsored health insurance also contributes to the market distortion for healthcare services as health insurance companies focus their attention on capturing the business of large organizations. This is unique in American insurance where policies are sold throughout the system to individual consumers allowing them to shop around. Compare other insurance needs, home, auto, life and liability. There are literally hundreds of insurance companies with numerous plans for each consumer to choose from. Not so for healthcare. Consumers who

do not have access to large organization health plans pay more and many have significant obstacles even accessing a plan. In most states, there are fewer than three companies selling health insurance. This is not the American way.

3. The fee-for-service model incentivizes providers to focus on services and tests to generate revenue instead of focusing on the desired patient outcome.

4. The litigation threat from tort lawyers adds unnecessary tests and services to patient care as providers do not want to be sued. While the direct litigation costs can be readily identified, the indirect litigation prevention costs of additional testing (defensive medicine) are estimated at $45 billion per year and included in the nation's health bill. (11)

5. The organization of individual providers results in each one doing only their portion of the care and then referring the patient on to another provider where many times the patient must begin a process of recording their history, medical issue and a new medical protocol is initiated. In an era of medical specialization, this structure inhibits the rapid search and identification of a solution to the patients' problem.

6. Out-of-network providers can bill patients at the highest sticker price because they are out of network, meaning they have not agreed to the price structure of the provider and insurance company. Hospitals must control their providers' billings to be the same as In-network charges.

7. The United States must negotiate trade agreements with their major trading partners that shares the cost of drug development. The United Stats is shouldering this burden alone as Americans pay the high prices for drugs while the E.U. countries negotiate discounts. (12)

<u>Example</u>

Let us use an example to illustrate the structure and operations of the U.S. healthcare system. It demonstrates how programs and costs of one group affect the cost of insurance for others who are not beneficiaries of these advantages.

Anytown U.S.A. is a fictitious town of 10,000 families. This town is far from a major city hospital center. The citizens decided that they should organize a healthcare system for their community. The cost is projected to be $15 million (10,000 times $1,500) or $1,500 per family per annum. This premium would cover preventive care at local doctors and hospital care at the trauma center to be built.

The facilities are built. The doctors are hired. Anytown has a functioning healthcare system. Residents are completely satisfied with the cost and level of care.

Several years have passed and the government has decided that the premiums are too high for retired people, and it decrees premiums for anyone over 65 be reduced to $750 per year. Ten percent of the town's population is over 65. The government also decrees that the poor should receive full healthcare and the government would reimburse the town for their medical care at the government rate, which works out to $500 per family. Ten percent of the town qualifies.

Senior medical payments for 1,000 families at $750 per year	$750,000
Government reimbursement for the 1,000 poor families at $500	$500,000
Sub Total	$1,250,000
Total healthcare cost for city	$15,000,000

Less premiums and reimbursement for seniors and poor remaining cost to city	$1,250,000
Remaining Cost Cost Per Family $13,750,000/8000	$13,750,000 $1,719

After the government decreed lower costs for seniors and the poor, the cost for the remaining families that are paying for healthcare has now increased by 15 percent to 1,719.

Anytown has three large businesses that together employ 50 percent of the town's workforce. They have watched as the government action has increased the cost of health insurance for themselves and their employees. They now argue that their employees should receive a discount because they represent so many employees. They ask for a 20 percent reduction of $300 per family. ($1,500-300=$1,200)

Recomputing the costs including the reduction in premiums for the three large companies' employees is as follows:

Total healthcare cost	$15,000,000
Less premiums for seniors and poor families	$1,250,000
Less premiums for large company employees (5000 X $1200)	$6,000,000
Sub Total	$7,750,000
Adjusted Premium for families not covered by any discounts	$2,583

The premium for the families not covered by the government plan and not covered by the large business discounts is $2,583, an increase of 72 percent over the original premium cost of $1,500, when every family paid an equal share. Government interference and large company domination significantly affect the costs paid by the families that do not have access to special programs and discounts.

The cost for those not on government programs is more rapidly increasing due to:

- Baby boom generation retirees increasing the number of seniors on Medicare.

- Continued increase in the number of Medicaid recipients 1) illegal aliens border crossing 2) reduced income requirements.

Other Issues

Comparative Shopping -- When people need specialists or surgeons, they usually ask the family doctor because they trust him or her. While other people are asked for referrals for products and services from auto dealers to contractors, the trust level is much higher with a doctor because a person is dealing with their body. They want a very competent physician, not just anyone who is advertising on the Internet or radio to be the cheapest. In a society where most people will drive well out of their way to save a few dollars and wait in long lines on Black Friday to get the cheapest price, shopping for a doctor is excluded from this ritual. This practice highlights one of the obstacles to shopping for lower priced medical care. It will be difficult to change.

Drugs

Drug Pricing -- The vilification of drug companies is one of the national pastimes in America, especially for politicians. Everyone should wake up every morning and thank God for the pharmaceutical industry, even with high prices and weird television commercials.

Developing new drugs is akin to drilling for oil -- a few gushers and a lot of very expensive dry holes. It costs on average $7 billion to develop a new drug and bring it to market. Therefore, the few gushers need to bring in billions to maintain the continuing drug research. Consumers complain bitterly about high-priced drugs, but in fairness "9 of 10 prescriptions in the United States are filled with generic drugs priced lower than in most other countries." (13)

For most every disease, there are many, many alternative treatments that are not expensive. Although the brand-new Rolls Royce treatment may be marginally better and significantly more expensive, it might also not work better for each person. Many times, patients are steered to the more expensive drug by advertising, but a conversation with the doctor may clarify the real difference and need for a more expensive drug. (Remdesivir versus Ivermectin)

The obstacles for operating successful pharmaceutical companies are daunting. They must hire and train a highly educated work force to research a variety of diseases and postulate a scientific and efficacious method to cure or at least improve outcomes of patients. They work on a variety of projects at the same time and most of them result in failure, but the costs remain. When they find a high potential drug, they apply for a patent and then continue through the de-

velopment and expensive human trials. They submit
this research to the FDA for final approval. The Patent
is for 17 years, but the clock starts when the patent
is approved, not years later when the FDA issues the
approval for sale. It may take six to seven years to obtain the final approval, leaving only 10 years of patent
protection to generate a return on the very large investment.

From the consumers' point of view patent-protected
products are the ultimate deal. The patent holder has
a monopoly for a few years, but when the patent protection expires, the product is now the property of
the world forever. The first patent, or monopoly, was
issued in Venice in 1474. However, the patent system
for protection of innovative NEW products was institutionalized in Great Britain in 1624 with the Statue of
Monopolies. This law provided patent protection for 14
years. America saw the benefit of this law and adopted
it. The law has been one of cornerstones of America's
industrial success because it provides the developer
the opportunity to generate wealth from their inven-
tion but makes the world the repository of the benefit
long term.

Unfortunately, government intervention in the pricing
of drugs while always "well intentioned", continually
creates unintended consequences that have limited
the availability of drugs due to the manufacturers dis-

continuing production, the inability to cover the cost of the drug by a provider or the lack of incentive to improve the efficacy of a particular drug. (14)

The Inflation Reduction Act enacted into law in September 2022 is another governmental misadventure. As usual, the label has nothing to do with the title (they never do). This law increases inflation. One of the provisions intended to reduce prescription drug prices will reduce pharmaceutical research and reduce the number of new drugs developed. Under this new provision, the Centers for Medicare and Medicaid Services (CMS) have the power to negotiate drug prices. If the company does not accept the CMS price, it will be taxed up to 95 percent on the Medicare sales revenue. This is just another short-sighted Democratic program that will allow them to tell their base they are helping them. Without patents to protect pricing of new drugs, many of the pharmaceutical companies will be unable to continue. When many of the patents expire, and/ or the government bureaucrats strip out the profits in the patented drugs, drug companies will begin to merge, close or be taken over by hedge funds to wring out the last bit of value. Who will develop the next generation of drugs? Who will develop a drug when the next COVID-19 hits the world? No one. Another great American industry will be destroyed by stupid politicians.

U. S. politicians are following the lead of their dumb E.U. brethren who have almost completely destroyed the pharmaceutical industry in Europe. Onerous price controls have reduced returns to a point where new investment and drug production is moving out of Europe and over to China and India. Price controls are also affecting supply. A European Public Health Alliance survey reported in 2019 that almost half of patients were unable to obtain a drug they needed. This is rationing of care. The government has X dollars allocated for healthcare. No more. Another industry will die in the developing countries and be taken over by an Asian country. (15)

Transparency is always a goal to set in any situation. Drug pricing, as a segment of the healthcare industry, is just as convoluted. First there are manufacturers, the drug companies such as Pfizer, Eli Lilly and Merck. Then the wholesalers and finally the drug stores who prepare the prescriptions for consumers. One of the practices that influence drug pricing is the use of rebates from manufacturers. Where these rebates finally reside affects the cost of drugs to consumers. The government tried to stop these rebates from being paid to the insurers, but they were stopped by insurers and their advocates. We are told that the rebates are used to reduce healthcare premiums, this does not help consumers who cannot afford high priced drugs. Rebate dollars make up approximately 33 percent of the cost of drugs. AARP, which professes to operate for the benefit of senior citizens, is reliant on commissions from these rebates from United Health Care (UHC) for over 50 percent of its corporate revenue. This is a clear conflict of interest and another example of the deliberate obfuscation of costs and profits in the U. S. healthcare industry. Drug costs are clearly separate from doctors and hospitals. The insurance plans are separate. (16)

Rebate dollars drive the choice of drugs by many health plans. The most expensive drugs have the highest total rebate dollars. These are the drugs chosen instead of more affordable substitutes. The result is that most healthy patients wind up paying a lot for co-pays and deductibles while the insurance company spreads the rebate throughout the system to lower premium costs. The rebate dollars should be allocated to these expensive drugs to lower the costs for patients with chronic conditions that cannot easily find a less expensive alternative and do not have insurance coverage. (17)

<u>Doctor Shortage</u>

Beginning in the mid 1960s, Medicare has been the primary funding mechanism for training new doctors under their residency programs. Economists and physician groups, alarmed that doctors' fees would be reduced and thus their incomes, decided that the best solution was to reduce the number of new doctors. At their urging, Congress passed the Balanced Budget

Act of 1997 and included a cap on Medicare-funded residency positions, keeping them at the 1996 levels. However, as usual this was short sighted at the least. Doctors' fees increased as the demand for service continued to increase, and the supply of doctors declined. At the same time hospitals learned they could generate more revenue if doctors were in the hospital, and they started buying up physician practices across the country. While each of these groups were busy interfering in the marketplace "doctors continued to age until now one-third of the approximately 900,000 doctors are over 60." Americans can now look forward to years of doctor shortages. (18)

Goals of a National Health Program

Before beginning to develop a program that will improve America's healthcare system, it is essential to list the objectives so that any proposal can be measured against the goals set forth

- insuring as many people as possible

- spreading the cost of care over the largest possible population

- reducing the number of special groups whose insurance premiums are subsidized by others

- a level of progressivity that makes higher income consumers pay more for health insurance coverage

- premiums (including deductibles) for regular care that can be affordable for a large percentage of working people

- patients keep their doctors, their access to local hospitals

- increase the number of health insurance companies in every State and the number of health insurance plan choices

- payments to providers that will provide good salaries for healthcare professionals and attractive ROI for other providers

<u>Singapore</u>

The United States wants to lower the cost of healthcare for its citizens and obtain better outcomes. While the United States spends 18 percent of its GDP on healthcare, Singapore spends 5 percent and has better healthcare outcomes. "What do they do that's so effective? A few things:

Price Transparency -- All healthcare providers in Singapore must post their prices and outcomes, so buyers can judge the cost and quality.

Health Savings Accounts -- Singaporeans are required to fund HSAs through a system called Medisave and to purchase catastrophic health insurance. As a result, patients spend their own money on healthcare and get to pocket any savings

A Limited but Effective Safety Net -- The Medi Fund program serves those people who, after exhausting their health savings and governmental subsidies, still need help paying their bills

"The combination of transparency and financial incentives has led to price and quality competition so intense that healthcare costs are 75 percent lower in Singapore than in the United States. Scripps College economist Sean Flynn estimates a heart-valve replacement costs $12,500 in Singapore ($160,000 in the United States and a knee replacement $13,000 ($40,000 in the United States)."

Could it work here? "It already has, if you consider the falling prices for Lasik and cosmetic surgery, neither covered by insurance. Transparency, competition and people spending their OWN money always produces smarter shoppers and lower prices. The Rand Health Insurance Experiment, the Dartmouth Atlas of Healthcare and similar research has proven that consumer involvement in price and treatment decisions results in savings and improved outcomes." If the United States wants to move to a better health system, then benchmarking the Singapore system would be a great way to start. (19)

One Solution

There is a solution that would solve most of the problems using the present system and without incurring the problems of a single-payer system:

It would require breaking down the healthcare funding into two parts. They are 1) regular care and 2) catastrophic care.

Under this structure all care would continue to be administered by the present healthcare companies and providers. Consumers would purchase healthcare policies from health insurance companies as they do now. Healthcare companies would be allowed to sell whatever types of plans they believed consumers would be interested in; including a) 100 percent coverage, no co-pays or deductibles or b) plans with co-pays and/or deductibles. They could operate in one state, a region or nationally without onerous State oversite. These policies would cover the cost of regular care with a ceiling of $50,000 per annum.

The catastrophic portion of the plan, all costs above $50,000, would be paid by a national healthcare premium of 1 percent (?) on all purchases. This is NOT a tax. It is each person's healthcare premium for catastrophic insurance coverage. The revenue would be collected by the state, kept in a separate fund (not pooled into a state general revenue fund) administered by the state, audited by independent auditors annually with a report issued by these private auditors published for the public. The states would offer insurance companies the opportunity to bid for the catastrophic policies in tranches of 25,000 to 50,000 individuals of all ages.

This program would work as follows. 1) Each consumer would be required to set up a Health Savings Account (HSA). This could be an individual or family account. The funds for this would be the present Medicare premiums paid out of each person's payroll. 2) next the consumer would purchase a healthcare plan from a health insurance company. Regular care expenses would be paid by the health insurance company. 3) If their medical bills exceeded the regular care threshold, let's use $50,000 as an example, the health care company would then bill the Catastrophic Plan for the cost of care exceeding the consumers 'regular care plan. The Catastrophic insurance plan would operate as a reinsurance program. (Reinsurance is a common occurrence in the insurance industry as companies offload the risks of coverage.)

<u>Price Transparency</u>

Under this structure, all providers would be required to post their prices and outcomes on a website for customers to review. Customers will then be able to shop for medical services based on the price and performance of the provider. The goal is to develop a system more like Singapore where the patient is in control of deciding which provider they will select.

The advantages of this type of reinsurance program would be as follows:

1. Primary care policies would be much less expensive because the health insurance company would only be covering primary care and not catastrophic care.

2. With lower premiums more consumers and companies would be able to afford health insurance. This would increase the number of people with health insurance coverage.

3. A nationwide health insurance premium would be paid by everyone depending upon their level of purchases. The wealthy purchase more, therefore they would pay more of the aggregate premium cost.

4. Our present healthcare network would stay in place to provide the high level of care Americans are used to having.

5. Consumers who refused to purchase primary care policies would be paying their share of the catastrophic coverage in the national health premium as they purchase goods. They also would be building up a fund in their Health Savings Account (HAS) to pay healthcare costs as the monies deducted from their check would be de-

posited in their HSA.

6. The plan would support the goal of increased preventive healthcare as the health insurance would be more affordable.

7. Eliminates bankruptcies caused by excessive medical bills.

<u>Pricing</u>

The pricing of healthcare is a significant problem because it is purposefully convoluted to hide and confuse anyone who attempts to compare prices. Currently, healthcare providers employ a system with an unconscionably high posted front-line price. This is called the "chargemaster" price. They then discount off this exorbitant price depending upon the policy the consumer has purchased, and the discount negotiated with the health insurance company. Consumers who do not have health insurance are asked to pay the chargemaster price without any discount. This results in exorbitant prices for these people. These are the very highest prices for health services in the country. If the people cannot pay for insurance, how can they pay for the inflated prices? This group features mostly low-income individuals, but it also includes individuals who are between jobs, self-employed, have limits on their health insurance coverage or feel they are very healthy and choose to pay cash instead of health insurance. On average, the fees for uninsured are 3.6 times the price charged to Medicare Advantage members. The hospital will provide care for the destitute and poor, then write off the cost of their care, using the highest prices, resulting in a large write-off offsetting their profits. Hospitals report that they have plans in place to "negotiate" these high prices with patients. However, many times, it is not true, and hospitals take a tough stand on their bills. These instances are the cause of many personal bankruptcies. They 1) want the money as these are very profitable patients and 2) they must keep up the frontline (chargemaster) price as a point of reference for negotiating with the insurance companies and the government. Hospitals argue that the money is needed to pay the cost of the poor. (10)

This high front-line price captures huge profits from all Workmen's Compensation medical billing because it is not covered by a health insurance policy, and therefore is not subject to any discounts. This type of billing system transfers the cost of medical care from government plans to private insurance and those without insurance who can pay, including the Workmen's Compensation insurance carriers who do not have health insurance plans.

An example of the present system is as follows:

Orthopedic surgeon replaces cervical disks

Posted price	$75,000
Billing for Workmen's Comp	$75,000
Billing for ABC health insurance basic plan	$50,000
Billing for ABC health insurance silver plan	$45,000
Billing for ABC health insurance gold plan	$40,000
Billing for ABC health insurance platinum plan	$35,000
Billing for Medicare	$15,000
Actual cost of procedure	$28,000

Under the new proposal, every provider would be forced to offer their services at the price they pay to everyone. Health insurance companies would then pay a portion of the bill depending upon the insurance plan purchased by the consumer.

An example of the proposed system is as follows:

Orthopedic surgeon replaces cervical disks

Posted price	$40,000
Billing for Workmen's Comp	$40,000
Billing for ABC health insurance basic plan ($3,000 co-pay)	$40,000
Billing for ABC health insurance silver plan ($2,000 co-pay)	$40,000
Billing for ABC health insurance gold plan ($1,000 co-pay)	$40,000
Billing for ABC health insurance platinum plan pay 100 percent	$40,000

Under the proposed system, Medicare is absorbed into the two-tiered system. Seniors, like everyone else, shop for and pay for their primary coverage policy. In most cases, it will be the same or less expensive than the combined Medicare premium plus the supplement insurance premium they are paying for now. (They pay for catastrophic coverage in their purchases.)

The primary plans will ALL be subject to minimum income protection. Those individuals whose earnings fall below the threshold will be able to sign up for a Medicaid-type of program at a reduced rate. However, because the insurance is for primary care ONLY the income thresholds will be higher for qualification and fewer people will qualify for a Medicaid program. Prescription Drugs are included in the plans.

<u>Disease Versus Illness</u>

The history of "modern medical practice" is the pursuit of science-based treatment for disease. By all measures, it has been extremely successful. Medical research has continued its quest to identify and successfully treat human diseases. The American medical system is recognized for its success, and patients who can afford treatment make the trip to American hospitals for treatment.

Unfortunately, the pursuit of "science-based treatment" may be coming to an end in America as the left is usurping the system with their familiar charges of systemic racism. In medical research "the National Library of Medicine database shows more than 2700 recent papers on racism and medicine, which purport to show physician bias leading to racial disparities in health outcomes." "The *New England Journal of Medicine* touts its "commitment to understanding racism" as a public health and human rights crisis." "Medical schools are increasingly preparing physicians for social activism at the expense of medical science." "Physicians are being pushed to discriminate. Hospitals, state health authorities and the federal government have all authorized race-based formulas for rationing COVID-19 treatments. Brigham and Women's Hospital in Boston (Harvard's teaching hospital) is moving toward "preferential care based on race across the board." As in every sphere of society, Democratic policies lead to the destruction of the systems that have been put in place to serve the people.

One area that needs improvement is the care of the illness. "The patients lived experience of pain and disability, suffering and symptoms and the management of that experience by them and their families, often facing conditions for which there is no pharmacological or surgical 'fix'." (20)

<u>The Future</u>

Considering the complaints and high costs of the U. S. healthcare industry, don't expect any real solutions. The providers are all making money. Doctors are in the top 1 percent of earners. Hospitals that can attract privately insured patients are making money (don't let the tax designation of Non-Profit fool you). Health insurers are very profitable. Drug companies are very profitable. Congress is receiving huge contributions from industry to maintain the present structure. It is not likely to change.

Footnotes:

1-"The False Promise of 'Medicare for ALL,'" Scott W. Atlas, *WSJ*, 11/13/2018

2-"The Middle Class Always Pays," Review and Outlook, *WSJ*, 11/29/2019

3-"Europe's Alternative to Medicare for All," Regina E. Herzlinger and Bacchus Barua, *WSJ*, 4/17/2019

4-"Stopping the Socialist Resurgence," Karl Rove, *WSJ*, 11/29/2018

5-Letters to the Editor, William Douglas, Jr., *WSJ*, 8/21/2019

6-"Bernie's Medicare for All Bailout," Review and Outlook, *WSJ*, 8/15/2019

7-"Europe's COVID Hospital Lesson," Review and Outlook, *WSJ*, 11/3/2020

8-"Public Option Kills Private Insurance," Scott W. Atlas, *WSJ*, 7/17/2019

9-"Single Payers Misleading Statistics," Scott W. Atlas, *WSJ*, 12/18/2018

10-"Hospitals Often Bill Uninsured the Highest Prices," Melanie Evans, Anna Wilde Mathews, Tom McGinty, *WSJ*, 7/7/2021

11-*Policy and Medicine*, May 2018

12-"How the GOP Can Win on Healthcare," Bobby Jindal, *WSJ*, 1/3/2020

13-"Expensive Medications Are a Bargain," Charles L. Hooper and David R. Henderson, *WSJ*, 9/14/2022

14-"Sometimes Drug Prices Are Too Low," David R. Henderson and Charles L. Hooper, *WSJ*, 11/1/2019

15-"The West's Drug Self-Sabotage," *WSJ*, Review and Outlook, 1/24/2023

16-"AARP's Interests Diverge from Its Members," Gerard Gianoli, *WSJ*, 8/30/2019

17-"Don't Blame Drug Prices on 'Big Pharma,'" Adam J. Fein, *WSJ*, 2/4/2019

18-Review and Outlook, *WSJ*, 1/5/2021

19-"Real Market in Medical Care? Singapore Shows the Way," George P. Schultz and Vidar Jorgensen, *WSJ*, 6/15/2020

20-"Treating Disease Is No Substitute for Caring for the Ill," Arthur Kleinman, *WSJ*, 11/30/2019

<u>References:</u>

"What is Universal Health Care?" Kimberly Amaded and Janet Berry-Johnson; June 27, 2021, The Balance.com

"Health Care Reform"; Mimi Chung; December 2, 2017; *Princeton Public Health Review*

"Understanding the Four Models of Healthcare and How they can Affect You"; Robert Kraft, Esq.; Kraft Elder Law.com

"Bismark or Beveridge: A beauty contest between dinosaurs"; Jouke van der Zee and Madelon W. Kroneman; BMC Health Service Research

"How Much Does a C-Section Cost?" Anna Wilde Mathews, Tom McGinty, Melanie Evans, *WSJ*, 2/12/2021

Chapter 7 Free Press Versus Media Propaganda

<u>Background</u>

The cornerstone of democracy is the basic goodness and common sense of the people. They alone have the power to support or reject government proposals to write and enforce laws, which affect them. For democracy to survive, it depends upon the people being educated and informed regarding issues and policies proposed by government officials.

Some elected officials have term limits, usually two terms in office. Many do not. Voters must turn them out of the office. The same is true for political parties. They may be in power for one term or more, but they can be replaced whenever the people determine they want to change and adopt the policies of another party.

The Founding Fathers believed that it was necessary for the people to be fully informed about the issues and that is why the First Amendment provides for freedom of the press. Simply stated, the media have been given the right to say whatever they wish without retribution or restriction by the government. But this "right" comes with a caveat, an implied responsibility, for the press to tell the people the truth. In effect the press is the people's watchdog on the activities of the government. They investigate government action, inaction, programs, policies, and the officials who are elected or appointed to manage these initiatives.

<u>This is an essential task in a democratic society.</u> The responsibility is great for every media group. In our society, it was not given to any one person, agency or group but to all those who set themselves up as a news agency. The task is spread among many news outlets with the expectation that different opinions will create a broader discussion and debate and help the people to determine the best course of action for the country for every policy proposal.

"In an advanced society, journalists have the vital job of keeping the citizenry well-informed so that the government can be held to account." (1)

Great news agencies continually deliver to the people accurate and unbiased coverage of local, national and world events. Their mission is to convey not only the facts but also the context for the story to create a more in depth understanding for their customers, the American people. Over the years there have been many news outlets in various forms whose work has been exemplary. Americans have relied on these organizations for highly accurate news coverage and intelligent opinion pieces since our inception.

America, like other countries, has had news outlets that fomented hate, attacked individuals or organizations, distorted the facts, and engaged in propaganda instead of reporting the news. As far back as George Washington's first term in office, pamphlets appeared under innocuous names such as Cicero, viciously attacking President Washington personally, citing his bad judgment and mistakes in policy, especially for his lack of support for France in their war against England. One must wonder what type of people enter this industry. It is certainly not always the finest.

And so, the die was cast. The range of coverage, the quality of coverage and the accuracy of coverage spanned the entire gamut from the worst to the best. Personal attacks, cartoon characterizations, hyperbole and downright lies became common in the press. Sensationalism sold and the business model was to sell more lies to increase circulation/viewers and as a result their revenues. Presidents were the biggest targets and when under stress for policies that were not working received additional criticism. Early in the Civil War, Lincoln was viciously attacked by numerous newspapers daily, including the *New York Times.* Caricatures appeared daily exaggerating the size of his ears and other facial features, ridiculing the president. No one apologized when Lee surrendered.

<u>News Model</u>

News in the early 20th century was mostly conveyed to Americans by newspapers, then radio and TV. Newspapers had followed a formula for many years wherein they printed the stories on the front pages of the paper, bigger on the front (to attract purchasers), gradually declining in newsworthiness in the following pages. The newspaper would present their opinion on the editorial page with commentary about the issue written by the editor or a senior staffer. This format was not adopted by radio or TV newscasters as it did not fit in their formula for news, which had to be summarized and delivered quickly. TV supplemented this coverage with in-depth coverage of major news stories, interviews, and occasionally they would read a formal editorial on air to voice their networks' opinion.

Traditional TV news coverage with morning and evening news reports was the norm until CNN began 24-Hour news coverage in 1980. For years, it was the only 24-hour news station, but as TV viewership declined and cable expanded, more and more cable and legacy outlets began 24-hour news networks. This fundamentally changed the news and the media in the United States. For years, the average American came home from work ate dinner and watched the local and then the national news and tuned into their favorite TV programs broadcast that night. Watching the news was more of a transitional event between dinner and the real programs of interest to the TV viewer. The TV anchor covered the high points of news and if you wanted to know more, you could read the newspaper.

The 24-Hour news stations needed viewers to watch longer, not just tune in for some news and leave. They could not attract the advertisers and generate the revenue needed to make news more profitable with viewers who tuned In and out after 30 to 60 minutes. The news formats of the 24-hour stations changed. Their response to the challenge was to introduce separate news shows every hour hosted by a different anchor and focusing on portions of the news. Panels of talking heads were hired to supplement the anchors who repeated droning reports of the events, each one providing their insight into the event. To add drama, there were breaking news intrusions all day into these programs, either by an anchor or reporter, or flashed across the TV screen. These news panels had 24 hours to examine the news, the interviews and statements by individuals and press releases. They examined and analyzed every word, parsed the sentences, and squeezed out every bit of inuendo, intended or not. The panel would re-examine and regurgitate a new perspective. The so-called "experts" would be called upon to provide analysis. Much of the information was derived from "sources" with no names. News became TV gossip to raise ratings. These stations began to massage the facts somewhat to sensationalize the news into more provocative stories of intrigue, more akin to novelettes than factual news coverage. The news was carefully crafted to represent the opinions and biases of the uninformed audience. The nightly TV news, based on fact was now the hourly novelette, focused on an audience who already had been indoctrinated to believe something. Facts were not required, but to make the novelettes appear credible, an occasional fact was introduced into the storyline. Welcome to the new age of media. American propaganda had replaced the hard news on cable news channels and on the legacy networks, the former homes of Walter Cronkite, Chet Huntley and David Brinkley and of course the icon of TV journalism, Edward R. Murrow.

The next incarnation of news became the politicization of every news story. The news outlets picked winners, liars, grievance groups and victims. A steady drumbeat of hate and division rose from their anchors. A day of news became 24 hours of hate, disinformation, misinformation, division, and attacks on every individual or organization that did not subscribe to the point of view championed by the news outlet. False accusations became the norm. Sources consisted of liars, leakers, whistleblower wan-a-bees, or just program directors residing on another floor who rewrote the story to increase its salaciousness. Former government officials from the FBI, CIA and Congress were hired to give these reports a patina of respectability. Lawyers were added as anchors to increase the attack intensity without stepping "over the line."

No longer is there any pretense of actual factual sources of news for many of these network newsrooms. They slant the story against the accused party then hype it up with the continual introduction of talking heads and breaking news updates, which are mostly old news rehashed.

In our modern world, newspapers have been joined by radio, television and now social media news outlets all of whom purport to cover the news and opine continually. This has created a cacophony so large, loud and unending that the average person is overwhelmed. There is simply too much news all the time. Unfortunately, a larger and larger portion of the media coverage is just plain unadulterated garbage, consisting of lies, personal attacks and propaganda, posing as professional, reliable, accurate news reporting. Americans laugh when TV anchors maintain they are professionals. (Maybe professional disseminators of hatred and lies). The media news anchors today more closely resemble Lord Haw-Haw (William Joyce) and Axis Sally (Mildred Gillars) both propaganda broadcasters for the NAZIs than Edward R. Murrow. Each year, a larger percentage of the American people realize the truth about these news organizations and tune them out. Unfortunately, they still have the ability to mold public opinion for millions.

If anything, the Trump presidency demonstrated that the behavior of most media outlets deteriorated significantly from their already low base. Gone was any pretense of honesty, accuracy, unbiased coverage of news. Personal attacks on this president, made those of any other public figure, pale in comparison.

The media engaged in a continuous conspiracy together with the Democratic Party to vilify the president. This began with the fake Russian election meddling charges and subsequent staged investigations and special prosecutor appointment. The media hired two of the ringleaders of the hoax, John Brennen and James Clapper, to beat the drum nightly and attempt to legitimatize the false charges and investigation leaks. American media truly reached the nadir of their existence.

<u>Propagandists</u>

We have reached a point where the media, the leftist media to be specific, has aligned itself with the Democratic Party to transform American into a one-party Marxist/communist state. These organizations are no longer news outlets. They are propaganda stations brainwashing Americans into believing Marxist/communist policies enacted by the Democrats are beneficial to the country.

What is so scary for Americans is that propaganda works. It is very successful in forming long-lasting opinions on issues. It also is very difficult to change the mind of a person who has been inoculated with propaganda even when presented with the facts. Paul Podolsky, an American journalist married to a Russian woman, tells the story of his mother-in-law, who completely believes the stories she sees on Russian state media. She supports Putin and the Russian media's account of the Ukraine war as a fight against the Nazis. She steadfastly refuses to believe her daughter, her son-in-law and even her sister who live in Ukraine. Is she any different than the liberals who quote CNN or the New York Times and turn a blind eye to the facts that refute the American propaganda? (2)

<u>What's Next?</u>

Here we are, a large minority of 75 million Republican voters being marginalized by fake news reports demonizing us. If you are a Republican, conservative, religious or an American patriot, maybe you are feeling helpless, confused, defeated or deflated after an election that was at best controversial and at worst stolen through Democratic corruption.

Speeches are nice but people want action, leadership and a plan moving forward to combat and defeat the enemies of freedom. So, what to do to restore news to it proper purpose of assisting the American people through honest presentation of the facts.

First, the media must be evaluated and rated in a systematic, non-political manner on a continuous basis. This should be accomplished in an unbiased manner using the journalistic principles they ignore daily. Evaluating and grading the integrity of their reports on selected major and minor news stories. An apolitical organization like *Consumer Reports* or J. D. Powers, but for media companies, should be formed exclusively for this purpose. Currently, the Society of Professional Journalists, the main professional organization for journalists, has issued ethical principles that all organizations and individuals should follow. The Ethics Committee issues reports of companies that violate those principles. However, most organizations ignore them because SPJ does not have any means of sanctioning journalists.

The organization tasked with monitoring news reports should receive contributions to fund its activities. There should be limits to ensure a lack of influence and coercion. Staff should be a mix of industry and academics who commit to reviewing media reporting in an unbiased manner. Reports to be issued to the public every 90 days with supporting rationale for the rating provided. Using a simple rating system to assign a grade to the coverage of the outlets media coverage of story selected for evaluation. The media companies, including social media, should be evaluated and rated on a four-point ranking system rating media on its level of integrity: excellent, good, poor or unacceptable. A small staff would be required to gather the media reports for presentation and review by the evaluators. Ratings would be released to the public on the organizations' website and through press releases.

As the quarters pass and it becomes clear to the public who the transgressors are, the public would decide for themselves which outlets to use for honest news. Hopefully, the public would reward the organizations with the highest integrity scores and punish those with the lowest.

CNN, ABC, CBS, NBC, FOX, Newsmax, OAN, *New York Times, Washington Post, Los Angeles Times, USA Today, Wall Street Journal, NY Post,* Google, Facebook and Twitter would be included in the ratings.

Second, consumer groups must become more vocal during the license renewal process of the TV and radio affiliates of the organizations with poor integrity ratings. For example, if the TV station in Lexington, Ky., is an affiliate of CBS and CBS has continually unacceptable integrity scores the public must pressure the local station to change its network affiliation or protest the renewal of its license to operate.

Third, local patriots should organize boycotts of legacy network affiliates to force them to improve their integrity ratings or end their affiliation with the legacy news organization. Local boycotts are more effective as they can influence local advertisers to transfer their advertising to another station.

<u>Other Actions</u>

It appears that Republicans and conservatives are intimidated by big tech and the media. They feel helpless to fight against the organized level of propaganda, misinformation and outright lying by these companies. No one ever expected a U.S. corporation to have the audacity to restrict free speech for political reasons and to cancel the accounts of people and organizations who are political adversaries. The left feels emboldened to act in any way it wishes. The recent manifestation of this began with the IRS denying tax-free status to conservative organizations. It continued with social media companies operating beyond the protection of rule 230. The ultimate slap in the face of the American people was the cancelling of the account of a Republican president of the United States.

These companies regularly flout Congress and other regulators and do whatever they wish, aided by vast troves of money that is liberally distributed around Washington through lobbyists to politicians forever needing election contributions to remain in power.

It is obvious that the solution lies outside Washington. Florida recently passed a law allowing those cancelled the right to sue for damages. The downside of this approach is that most of the individuals harmed do not have the financial wherewithal to slog it out in court with a mega wealthy corporation. States should be exploring legislation to punish every company who restricts any individual's rights guaranteed by the federal or state constitution. Large fines (starting at $50 million) that double for each infraction would be the best method of punishing big tech for their malfeasance.

Another possible solution to reign back the power of BIG Tech has been proposed by Barak Richman and Francis Fukuyama in their article "How to Quiet the Megaphone of Big Tech." (3) The authors state that the core issue is the oversize power of Twitter, Facebook, Amazon and Google to "amplify certain voices and exclude others." Their solution is to require dominant platforms to allow users to select their own output from the algorithms. This would require the development of a new kind of "middleware," that would be "a filtering agent on the big platforms."

The question is whether an organization can impose limits on individuals in violation of their constitutional rights. Legal challenges, such as that of President Trump, will begin to work their way up through the courts.

Twitter banned President Trump and closed his account after the Jan. 6, 2021, riot. Republicans moved on to Parlor to continue their dialogue, but it was destroyed completely in three steps:

First, Apple blocked it from its App store

Second Google blocked it from its App store

Third, Amazon Web Service withdrew access to its cloud network

This is the first time in history that business has united to shut down the free speech of a U. S. president and American citizens with different political ideologies. At no time in history have a few companies had so much power over free speech in the United States.

There is a continual movement of powerful tech companies to participate in the censorship of opinions that do not support their far-left political ideology. The erosion of free speech, in the form of an open Internet, one of the hallmarks of democracy, does not bode well for the continuation of democratic governments around the world. (4) Congress must pass strong legislation to codify all social media as speech covered under the First Amendment, not subject to any private company decisions to restrict speech on their platforms. In essence they will be public utilities to be used by ALL to say whatever they wish, just like the free press. There is no reason to debate Section 230 of the Communications Decency Act or amend it in any way as that only opens the questions of what is decent and what is not and another round of questions of who will decide. Free speech for everyone is the order of the day for ALL social media. Back when the Internet was in its infancy, the Supreme Court ruled that the

Internet was more like a town hall environment where everyone had a right to speak, than a broadcast station. At the time, the Supreme Court was encouraging open debate.

<u>Unethical Tech</u>

Some tech companies are unethical and use their wealth and power to steal technology from smaller companies. Below are some examples:

1)-Amazon's investment in Defined Crowd Corp. through its venture capital arm allowed it to gain access to its confidential information. Several years later, Amazon's web service offered an identical service called A21. This is only one example of many companies who have filed complaints against Amazon for stealing their technology through their venture capital investment arm to launch competing businesses.

2)- "In 2016, Amazon's Alexa Fund bought a stake in Nucleus, a company that made a home video device that integrated with the Alexa voice assistant. After gaining access to its plans and technology Amazon introduced ECHO Show device and Nucleus sales plummeted."

3) "In 2010, Amazon invested in Living Social. Amazon requested company financials, pricing and customer lists. A short time later, customers called telling them

Amazon was selling a competitive product at a lower price."

4) "Leo Grebler created a voice-activated device called Ubi that had much of the functionality of Amazon Echo, and he got it on the market well before the Echo was introduced. Gruber signed a non-disclosure agreement with Amazon and provided a lot of proprietary information during their meetings. Amazon introduced ECHO shortly thereafter copying many of the features of Ubi. Gruber consulted a law firm regarding a potential lawsuit, but he did not have the funds to fight Amazon, David vs. Goliath."

"Amazon's *modus operandi* is to find technology it thinks is extremely valuable and seduce people to engage with it, and after it learns as much as it can while giving the impression it is serious as a buyer or investor, it will cut off communication and use the technology in one of its products," says Alfred Fabricant, an attorney for Vocalife LLC. The more one learns about Amazon the more evidence that it is a corporate predator, preying on the smaller, financially weaker companies. (5)

Communications Decency Act

Google, Facebook, Amazon, Twitter and other social media companies were given an exemption by Congress of parts of the Communications Decency Act in 1996. Section 230 provides an exemption for these companies, specifically, immunity against certain legal claims. The purpose of this special legislation was to encourage the growth of the Internet as an open forum for free speech without the legal liability entailed by being a publisher for the content on their sites. In exchange for this exclusion, the companies would moderate indecent content. However, social media companies have violated this agreement. They want both: 1) the power of a publisher to regulate whatever is on their sites and 2) the immunity of a non-publisher to continue to be immune from lawsuits.

Numerous independent journalists, academics and legislators have analyzed the content that is restricted and for the most part, it is political speech of the Republicans. Social media companies, which are mostly headquartered in California and Washington, are run by Democratic activists. They do whatever they can to promote the Democratic agenda and stifle the Republican Party and its conservative allies.

Surprisingly, there are many Republicans who continue to support the status quo and are loath to change the present exclusion in Section 230. Their argument is that these companies are private, and they should be able to decide what they wish to publish. As an outside observer, one must wonder why people would act in violation of their own party's best interests. It makes no sense. Unless these members of Congress have been paid to support this position. It is common knowledge that Silicon Valley provides more money to Washington lobbyists than any other group. Hopefully one of the investigative reporters can follow this story and prove or disprove it. (6)

Congress should have never provided the Internet companies with an exclusion. What they should have done and should do now is to use the same standard that was enacted for radio in the 1927 Radio Act and Communications Act of 1934.

<u>Modern Monopolies</u>

When Congress grilled the chief executive officers of Apple, Alphabet, Facebook and Amazon about anti-competitive practices and market abuses, it concluded by stating that the anti-trust laws don't work in the digital age. Our historic anti-trust legislation was written to stop companies limiting consumer choice and being subject to predatory pricing. The modern digital powers are not fixing prices. They are in the business of "idea fixing," which forces consumers to conform to the ideas the companies believe are acceptable. (7)

A recent severe example was Apple's decision to restrict access to the Air Drop app that Chinese protesters were using to organize. They purposely co-opted their technology to suppress Chinese people and the voice of America.

"On the premise of 'social responsibility,' Google's

subsidiary, You Tube, recently decided to remove videos it deemed untruthful. The site has taken down videos that were critical of COVID-19 lockdown policies in certain states, stifling discourse about the most important scientific and public policy debate of the year." (7)

"Facebook has created a corporate politburo of so called 'experts' to determine what types of speech are acceptable on its site." For example, Facebook will take people's money but not show their Christian ads because Facebook believes they are too "controversial." This stifled the debate about the efficacy of face masks. As science progressed, the debate was shut down by its so-called experts. For experts and ordinary folks alike, history proves that many of our current beliefs will be proved false, and determinations of truth are always conditional and probabilistic. Unfettered dialogue isn't a liberal-arts luxury, it is necessary for science and democracy." (7)

Facebook is now using these fact checkers to suppress articles that do not match the company's ideology. They attacked the book written by Steven Koonin, a renowned climate expert, with this headline "*Wall Street Journal* article repeats multiple incorrect and misleading claims made in Steven Koonin's new book, *Unsettled.* The left will not allow anyone to challenge the climate narrative it has introduced as it will endanger the support of liberals for the Green New Deal legislation. (8)

"This problem extends beyond Big Tech. Take Goldman Sachs, a leading member of the small cartel that enjoys 'toll booth's status as a gatekeeper for companies seeking to raise capital, go public and acquire other companies, thanks to archaic securities regulations. CEO David Solomon announced that he will refuse to take any company public that doesn't have one 'diverse' board member. Here Goldman is the sole arbiter of who counts as diverse." Of course, it will be blacks, gays and women. All other groups have been cancelled and no longer exist. More and more corporations are abandoning their historic role of being neutral in political battles and are taking positions where they are betting their businesses on a particular political ideology. Disney's decision to go woke and insert sex into its various media offerings to young children is the latest example. Parents will not take this well and the blowback will be devastating for a company with a mission to sell escapist entertainment to children. (6) It has backfired for Disney as more and more of its movies are not doing well at the box office or on streaming services.

"America has a strong tradition of separating spheres of society to preserve the integrity of each. Separating capitalism from democracy is no less important than separating church and state. By using market power to exercise undue social, cultural and political power, today's corporate leaders violate this fundamental American principle. It is time to resist this ideological cartel that now represents an existential threat to the American public and our basic freedoms." (7)

In the *Wall Street Journal* article, "End the Media's Campaign Privilege," the authors David E. Rivkin and Lee A. Casey, point out the media's new role as advocate of a particular candidate or political party. "Such organizations are regulated by campaign-finance statutes. So are other corporations, for profit or non-profit, that engage in electioneering speech. But those laws exempt media organizations, provided they are not owned by a political party, committee or candidate." The legacy media organizations in the United States operate under the umbrella of the First Amendment and parry any criticism of their publications with that defense. The introduction of social media and the growing politicalizing of the media have demonstrated that many media companies regularly cross the line from observer and commentator to partisan advocates of one side. Television media are blatant violators as many newscasts on different media outlets present stories with almost the exact same headline, lead-in and talking points as if they had each received a communique from a central source advising them what to say on air. Do they?

The Supreme Court in *Citizens United vs. Federal Election Commission* (2010) stated "we have consistently rejected the proposition that the institutional press has any constitutional privilege beyond that of other speakers."

The authors suggest that media companies should be prosecuted under the ban on "coordinated communications." They cite the current law allowing corporations and other independent organizations to have the right to speak for or against, but they are forbidden to develop messages "in cooperation, consultation or concert with, or at the request or suggestion of, a candidate, a candidate's authorized committee, or their agents, or a political party committee or its agents." Congress needs to investigate this.

The article continues to describe the collusion between a *New York Times* writer and the Hillary Clinton campaign. Of course, many are familiar with Donna Braziles admission that she gave Hillary Clinton some of the questions in advance of the presidential debate with Donald Trump, when she worked for CNN. Despite this breach of journalistic ethics, FOX hired her for the 2020 election season as a commentator.

It is obvious that the left continually crosses the line using their media power to influence political events and when challenged, hides behind the first amendment. The law needs to be tightened and the perpetrators need to be punished. But they won't. Democrats will never attack an ally and Republicans lack the guts.

<u>Social Media</u>

Social media sites were designed by companies to be addictive. They want you to keep checking your app for updates. You see people at the gym, in restaurants or driving their cars, constantly looking for a new message. You wonder if they are waiting to be hired or find out if they won a prize or had a loved one undergoing surgery. Their body language displays a certain intensity that is completely different from a person answering their phone.

Let's face it, do you have "friends" whom you have met on the phone? Can you call them to fix a flat or take you to a doctor's appointment? Will they come over and prepare dinner for you when you are bedridden?

Social media have some benefits, but they also are a place of hate. People feel they can project their uncontrolled anger at others when they are not present. Do you want to support a community that engages in this type of behavior? Would you move to a place like this?

Facebook algorithms are focused on keeping people on their site. They do this with inflammatory content and algorithms that keep you connected in a silo to others who share your views. Instagram focuses on children to develop online versions of themselves who are "better" than the real version. Unfortunately, this fantasy destroys the self-esteem of these children, mostly young women. The crime is that these things are done purposely to make money. Depressed, suicidal and dead children are just the casualties of war. (9)

<u>Big Tech Censorship</u>

Tech companies are attempting to have it both ways in their avoidance of government regulation as common carriers. On one hand they wish to be treated like publishers and be able to censor whatever information they desire (usually conservative/Republican speech). However, they refuse to then be accountable for the speech on their platform by stating it is the speech of others. A newspaper is not a common carrier as it conveys its own speech and of course decides what that speech is. If that speech harms a person or business, the newspaper is then liable for damages. A tech company is not acting as a publisher, it is solely a common carrier of the speech of others, attempting to limit what it does not like and using the First Amendment right to free speech as a shield.

Tech companies qualify as common carriers in two ways. First, they offer their services to the public for the purpose of conveying speech, just like a bus company that offers its service to anyone who wishes to ride the bus along its service routes. Second, they provide market dominance, which means they hold a monopoly or quasi-monopoly for the use of their service in the communication method they offer.

The famous section 230 (C) (I) of the 1996 Communications Decency Act distinguishes between information provided by an interactive computer service and "information provided by another information content provider." Section 230 also protects tech companies from being treated as "the publisher or speaker of any information provided by another content provider. In other words, big tech platforms are conduits for information. Therefore, they serve as common carriers. As such, they have been given immunity from traditional publishing liability. (10)

The problem with Section 230, is that it provides privileges to the companies for serving as a common carrier that no other common carrier possesses. It can discriminate against any speech that it does not wish to carry. They do not like Republican/conservative speech, so they ban it whenever they wish. Back to our bus company example, a bus company cannot deny transit to anyone based on political beliefs, sexual orientation, gender or ethnicity, but social media companies can.

What seems at first glance to be an insolvable problem can in fact be addressed if we go back into our history and learn the lessons it is always anxious to teach us. One hundred years ago, when radio first was being mass marketed, society faced the same questions of the effects of a small group of people reaching and influencing a mass audience. This new medium had the power to influence public opinion quickly to incite riots, protests and civil disorder.

The government brought together leaders from Congress, radio executives, radio listeners and technology experts to discuss the concerns. The result was the Radio Act of 1927 and the Communications Act of 1934. "These laws defined broadcasting as a privilege not a right. They required radio stations (and later television stations) to operate not only for their benefit but also for the public interest, convenience and necessity. The Communications Decency Act of 1996 included a provision to let social media companies escape any accountability. That was a mistake. They must be reclassified as broadcasters, not technology companies and required to apply for licenses and operate under the auspices of the Federal Communications Commission. (11)

The Supreme Court held in *Norwood vs. Harrison* (1973) that the government "May not induce, encourage or promote private persons to accomplish what it is constitutionally forbidden to accomplish." But that is exactly what Congress has done by passing section 230 of the 1996 Communications Decency Act which permits tech companies to censor constitutionally protected speech and immunizes them from state liability if they do so." "Prominent congressional Democrats have issued severe, explicit and repeated threats to retaliate against social media companies if they fail to remove 'hate speech' and 'misinformation' from their sites. These threats have worked, and the speech Democrats labelled as offensive has repeatedly been removed. All of it being Republican/conservative. The government using its power to have private companies censor speech becomes an actor in this event." (12)

Because it's online, it is somehow "forgiven," but much of the hatred and anger sticks with many of the people caught up in these social media communities. Are they responsible for the increased crime? The mass shootings? Never had them before?

Finally, the fact that social media companies feel that it is their "right" to limit the constitutional rights of citizens they do not like is unconscionable. No U. S. corporation should have the power to restrict any citizen's rights. Where is the Justice Department? Where is Congress?

YouTube censored a discussion of eminent scientists "because it included content that contradicts the consensus of local and global health authorities regarding the efficacy of masks to prevent the spread of COVID-19." This public policy roundtable hosted by Gov. Ron DeSantis of Florida reviewed the studies by several countries regarding the transmission of the disease by children and the wisdom of requiring children to wear masks. This is another example of the Democratic Party's obsession with controlling the narrative on COVID-19 and refusal to allow any contrary opinions. (13)

The first step is to shut them down. Cancel your account and improve your life. (14)

When it started at the turn of the century, Google adopted the motto, "Don't Be Evil." Unfortunately, it has NOT lived up to its goal. Social media outlets continually participate in disinformation, misinformation, deliberate polarization, ideological bias, data harvesting, deliberately addicting users, acquisition and sale of personal information, pornography and interference of elections, among other crimes. Its technology is advanced to the point where legislators do not understand it or control it. These companies may be able to justify everything when dealing with adults, but when children are being affected negatively by their products, it is appropriate for parents and the government to stop them. After the testimony of Frances Haugen, a former Facebook employee in which she produced evidence that the company is aware of the specific harm to children, including eating disorders and suicidal thoughts, Congress was infuriated. In her article, "Can Anyone Tame Big Tech," Peggy Noonan, a *Wall Street Journal* columnist suggests an age limit of 18 for social media participation. This is a quick, easy solution to preventing harm to children. It will never pass because of the wealth of these companies. They will throw money at Congress to water down any proposals to become ineffective claptrap.

The Corrupt Media at Work

Perhaps the most infamous example of the media's suppression of "important news" from the American people was the Hunter Biden laptop story. Several months before the 2020 election, the *New York Post* reported the discovery of a laptop belonging to Hunter Biden that contained information that confirmed the son of a presidential candidate was selling political influence to Russians. The story was immediately expunged from all legacy media companies and social media websites. "The media and tech companies that colluded together to kill the story were given cover to do so by a letter that appeared quickly alleging the *Post*'s story was a Russian disinformation." This letter was signed by 50 former National Security Agency experts and thus, it had the weight of their combined reputations. Fast forward 18 months. The *New York Times* admitted that the laptop was in fact genuine. *Mea culpas* from other media outlets followed and as the story continues to play out, they hid the news because they wanted Biden to win. The 50 signers, attesting to the fact the laptop story was fake, were contacted by the *New York Post*. None offered any contrition. These are the people who run the nation's spy services. They took an oath to support the Constitution and thus our democracy. Their actions are more like those of commissars in the KGB. This is another concrete example of a government bureaucracy that is out of control. Are they National Security Agency experts or Communist party moles? (15)

<u>Freedom of Religion</u>

The Founding Fathers' vision of America was shaped by their religious faith as they interpreted the Bible's lessons tempered with the enlightened reasoning from the great thinkers, Locke, Rousseau, Montesquieu and Voltaire. This vision became the template for discussion and debate of the issues and challenges facing America. But social media changed this template. They have used their power to censor religious speech using a variety of reasons or no reason at all, just their power to shut down programming on their sites. "On matters ranging from foster care and education to gender ideology and the family, this new fundamentalism is displacing the moral convictions that once grounded U. S. culture." Social media have replaced the traditional media outlets, print, radio and television as the predominant communications venue for debate in America. Unfortunately, the companies who control the public square are untethered to the moral history of America, unregulated by Congress and Communist ideologs. This has resulted in their imposition of a new morality and censorship of all who disagree with their ideology. The new ideology of "killing freedom in the name of A New Freedom is the new Orwellian dream of the fundamentalists who run the social media companies." (16)

Unfortunately, the American people are seeing first-hand exactly what the "New Freedom" vision entails. It is a monolithic government controlling every aspect of individual life, complete control over the means of production, censorship of all speech, monitoring all activities, support of criminal life, open borders, degradation, eventual elimination of the military, repression and elimination of all who do not yield.

Religious speech is necessary in every democratic country as religious beliefs act as a check on government excess. Social media companies and their acolytes are godless people who want no check on their dogma. (16) However, there are signs of hope. The podcast industry is exploding with differing viewpoints. Sites like usa.life and frankspeech.com are trying to counteract the issues associated with social media that are banning speech. People are waking up to the negativity from corporations by not using Amazon to shop, not using Facebook, avoiding Disney movies and refusing to give money to these organizations.

There still is a long way to go. Media outlets' misuse of power is shown clearly in the myths being discussed about the environment and climate change, which we discuss in the next chapter.

Footnotes:

1-"Woke Universities Lead American to a Primitive State," John M. Ellis, *WSJ*, 11/3/2020

2-"My Russian Mother-in-law Believes Putin, Paul Podolsky," *WSJ*, 5/27/2022

3-"How to Quiet the Megaphone of Big Tech," Barak Richman and Francis Fukuyama, *WSJ*, 2/13/2021

4-"Jack Dorsey Has Second Thoughts," *WSJ* Review, 1/15/2021

5-"Amazon Wooed Startups, Then Competed with Them," Dana Mattioli and Cara Lombardo, *WSJ*, 7/24/2020

6-"Don't Let Google Get Away With Censorship," Dennis Prager, *WSJ*, 8/7/2019

7-"Anti-Trust Can't Bust a Monopoly of Ideas," Vivek Ramaswamy, *WSJ*, 8/6/2020

8-"Facebook's Book Banning Blueprint," Review and Outlook, *WSJ*, 5/8/2021

9-"We Also Need to Change Ourselves," Sherry Turkle, *WSJ*, 10/30/2021

10-"On Censorship, Big Tech Has It Both Ways," Philip Hamburger and Clare Morell, *WSJ*, 8/1/2021

11-"Social Media Should Be Treated Like Broadcasting," Nicholas Carr, *WSJ*, 10/30/2021

12-"Trump Can Win His Case Against Tech Giants," Vivek Ramaswamy, *WSJ*, 7/12/2021

13-"Masks for Children, Muzzles Fox News," Jay Bhattacharya, *WSJ*, 4/14/2021

14-"Quitting Facebook," Dalvin Brown, *WSJ*, 5/3/2022

15-"Hunter Biden's Laptop and America's Crisis of Accountability," Gerard Baker, *WSJ*, 3/22/2022

16-"Social Media's Threat to Religious Freedom," Archbishop Salvatore J. Cardileone and Jim Daley, *WSJ*, 8/13/2021

Chapter 8 The Climate Change Myth

<u>Background</u>

The world is now engrossed in a debate about the causes of climate change. Alarmists claim that, if ignored, it will result in apocalyptic changes that threaten the continued existence of humans. Climate changes will melt the polar ice caps, raise sea levels, inundate low lying coastal communities, bury islands, lengthen droughts, and increase the frequency and power of cyclones and hurricanes.

The moderate climate scientists are more cautious regarding their projections for the future. They argue that climate science is extremely complicated, and as of today, there are more unknowns than knowns. Although politicians, the legacy media and some less-than-honest scientists claim the science is settled, it is NOT.

Our purpose is to separate the truth from the media hype and help the reader better understand the issues.

<u>History</u>

Apocalyptic predictions, affecting humans, have been made for over 2000 years. None have come true. Most of these predictions were related to Biblical accounts of the Rapture, Great Tribulation, the Last Judgment and the Second Coming of Christ.

However, since the 1960s, there have been an increasing number of predictions of doom by the climate *cognoscenti,* **none of which have come true.** A few of these are listed below:

YEAR	PREDICTION
1970	Ice Age by 2000
1970	Nitrogen buildup will make land unusable
1970	Oceans dead in a decade
1970	Water rationing by 1974
1970	Food rationing by 1980
1972	Oil depleted in 20 years
1978	No end in sight for 30- year cooling trend
1988	Maldives Islands under water 2018
1989	NYC highways under water by 2019
2008	Ice Free Arctic by 2013
2012	The Mayans say the world ends

As one can see, the climate alarmist hysteria has shifted from Ice Age doom and gloom in 1970 to Global Warming in 2020. Leonard Nimoy narrated a sober documentary on the coming Ice Age in 1978. This followed the coldest winter in 100 years in North America. This history is precisely why a more measured approach is required. Unfortunately, in our modern super communication age of cell phones and social media, the narrative is "The Science" and all other voices are cancelled. Be skeptical.

Using temperature proxies, such as wormholes and tree rings, scientists have determined the Earth has experienced periods of rapid warming and then slower cooling. Much of this is attributable to slight changes in the Earth's orbit, specifically the tilt angle. Warmer temperatures were replaced around 1000 and led to the Little Ice Age from approximately 1450 to 1850. This was followed by a warming trend that continues today. These historical data highlight the dilemma of comparing the changes to a fixed starting date. For example, if we begin measuring temperature on Jan. 1, by April 30, we could conclude the Earth is warming. If we begin Aug. 1st, by Nov. 30, we could conclude the Earth is becoming cooler. Scientists studying global climate change are using a limited number of years in their analyses. Are natural forces at work? The historic temperature changes do not support the claim that the 1.8 degrees F rise in the Earth's surface temperature since 1880 was caused by humans. The honest answer is that **we do not know for certain** what part of this temperature change was caused by human activities.

Climate vs. Weather

It is important to differentiate between climate and weather. Everyone watches the weather reports for the day, week, month or even season. Meteorologists may announce that the current year has the wettest spring, hottest summer or coldest winter in 20 years. Each of these observations is about "The Weather." Climate is defined by the U.N. Meteorological Society as "the average of the weather over 30 years." It is NOT what is reported in the evening weather report. There is also a difference between "climate change," which refers to a change in climate attributable to human activity, and "a changing climate," which is natural changes in the climate. As the reader can readily see, even the language is confusing for the average person.

During the past 20 years, climate change has evolved into a major international political and social issue. Climate change is the current edition of the doomsday chronicles. "The world is coming to an end," a continual line of soothsayers prophesying fear, death and destruction. The soothsayers' strategy to insert fear into the populace always contains the same three elements.

- First, a cataclysmic event will occur.

- Second, the event will occur on a future date

when a large portion of the present population will be alive and thus affected. The fear of your death is thus inserted into your consciousness.

- Third, this event can be prevented, IF you do exactly what THEY say.

The result is to transfer to the soothsayer an enormous degree of power and influence over the decisions made by the political leadership. Now, more than any time in the past 100 years should democratic countries be alarmed about this type of prognostication as they have recently lived through a similar experience with COVID-19. During the COVID-19 pandemic, much of what "the experts" told us was either wrong through inadvertence or purposely inaccurate to maintain their control over the situation. Ask Dr. Fauci.

Citizens of developed countries are already living under the mandates of government due to the fear of mass extermination. It is ALL false propaganda to destroy the economies of Western countries.

<u>Scientific Integrity</u>

Scientists are ethically bound to the scientific method; this means telling the "whole truth." Unfortunately, their activism has clouded their judgment and destroyed their moral compass. In their zeal to "persuade" others they are correct; they have resorted to reporting only parts of the data that support the popular narrative and justify this by claiming that it is necessary to save humanity. A few examples are highlighted below:

"It doesn't matter what is true. It only matters what people believe is true," Paul Watson, Co-Founder of Greenpeace (1)

"We have to ride this global warming issue. Even if the theory of global warming is wrong, we will be doing the right thing in terms of economic and environmental policy". Timothy Wirth, president of the U.N. Foundation (2)

"Some colleagues who share my doubts argue that the only way to get our society to change is to frighten people with the possibility of a catastrophe, and therefore it is all right and even necessary for scientists to exaggerate. They tell me my belief in open and honest assessment is naïve." Daniel Botkin, former chair of Environmental Studies, U.C. Santa Barbara (3)

"Inaction will cause, by the turn of the century (2000), an ecological catastrophe that will witness devastation as complete, as irreversible as any nuclear holocaust." Mostafa Tolba, former Executive Director of the U.N. Environmental Programme (1982) (4)

"Within a few years, winter snowfall in the United Kingdom will become a very rare and exciting event. Children are just not going to know what snow is." (5)

Climate alarmists love to use the example of Greenland's ice sheet shrinking at the fastest rate in history. The result would be constantly rising sea levels swamping coastlines around the world. The truth is somewhat different. Although human influences in the climate are 10 times now what they were in 1910, the actual data show large swings in the loss and gain of ice with the present loss being the same as it was during the 1930-1940 period. It seems that "natural cycles in temperatures and currents are responsible for the majority of the ice changes." (6)

<u>Fear</u>

The media have done a remarkable job of fear-mongering the public and the political class while most scientists stay on the sidelines, allowing the media to distort their scientific conclusions. The media have claimed forest fires, hurricanes, floods and droughts have all increased due to climate change.

To set the record straight, the U.N. Intergovernmental Panel on Climate Change (IPCC), which is the authoritative body on climate, stated the following in their *AR5WGI* report:

- No change has occurred in the frequency of floods.

- No change has occurred in droughts or dryness.

- No change in the frequency or intensity of cyclones and hurricanes.

- No change in the frequency of storms.

These conclusions are quite different from the usual media spin after every weather event where the media report, with absolute certainty, that the weather event followed the trend of increased severity as a direct result of climate change.

The media have invented "event attribution studies," a combination of false weather modeling and selected historical observations to prove that humans are responsible for the climate change that resulted in the specific weather event. However, the World Meteorological Organization does not agree with this methodology. They state, "any single event, such as a severe tropical cyclone (hurricane or typhoon), cannot be attributed to human-induced climate change, given the current status of scientific understanding."(2)

Add this to the continual use of the scariest terms, such as "climate emergency," "climate crisis" and "climate catastrophe," and we have a world in fear.

Unfortunately, fear mongering has been extremely successful. "A 2019 poll found that almost half of the world's population believes climate change likely will end the human race. In the United States, 40 percent of the people surveyed believe global warming will lead to mankind's extinction." (7)

What Do We Know?

Science says that most extreme weather events show no long-term trends that can be attributable to human influences on the climate. (8)

The average coldest temperature in the United States has increased since 1900 while the average warmest temperature is about the same. (8)

The IPCC report *AR5*, issued in 2014 states that even a 1.5 percent additional rise in global temperature by 2100 will have a minimal net economic impact. (9)

The 2021 IPCC report states there is "low confidence that the Antarctic-sea ice will melt."

There is "low confidence in long term (multi-decadal to centennial) trends in the frequency of all-category tropical cyclones." (10)

"Heat waves in the United States are no more common today than they were in 1900." (8)

"The warmest temperatures in the United States have not risen in 50 years." (8)

Ninety percent of the Earth's heat is contained in the oceans. The ARGO Ocean measuring system data indicate that the oceans are warming modestly; a few hundredths of a degree Celsius per decade. (8)

Natural disasters are NOT increasing in intensity or frequency. (11)

<u>Incorrect or Misleading</u>

The *2017 Climate Science Special Report (CSSR)* issued by the government made an error in stating that record warm temperatures are occurring more often. The actual data clearly show that the warm temperatures have stayed at the same level since 1910. Therefore, we are NOT experiencing more weather extremes.

2016 National Climate Assessment issued by the government (NCA2014). It reads:

"The intensity, frequency and duration of North Atlantic hurricanes, as well as frequency of the strongest (Category 4 and 5) hurricanes, have all increased since the early 1980s. The relative contributions of human and natural causes to these increases are still uncertain. Hurricane-associated storm intensity and rainfall rates are projected to increase as the climate continues to warm." Accompanying this report, was a graph that begins in 1970 showing a rising incidence of hurricane power dissipation (actual number of hurricanes adjusted for intensity). However, if one does some additional research and adds the years 1945 to 1970 to the graph the conclusion is very different. In the corrected graph, the numbers begin high then drop around 1970 and then rise again to the level at the beginning of the graph in 1945. The conclusion is one of variability not absolute increase. This is another example of skewing the numbers to arrive at a specific conclusion to support the false narrative that climate change is leading to more and stronger hurricanes.

"The Intergovernmental Panel on Climate Change (IPCC) issued a new report in 2021 entitled *AR6*. The Summary for Policymakers section says the rate of global sea-level rise has been increasing for the past 50 years. It doesn't mention that it was increasing almost as rapidly 90 years ago before decreasing strongly for 40 years." (9)

The Lancet report concludes that "rapidly rising temperatures have increased annual global heat deaths by 68 percent in less than two decades." "The U.N. Secretary-General Antonio Guterres tweeted a link, with a grave comment of his own, "The Climate Crisis is Killing Us. The Annual Global Climate Summit (COP27) must deliver a down payment on climate solutions that match the scale of the problem." Annual heat deaths have increased significantly in people over 65, but that is because the population of those 65 and over has increased by 60 percent or more over this same time period. Despite requests to adjust the data to account for the higher population of elderly, no adjustments were made, and the false narrative continues to be reported by news agencies around the world. (12)

"In fact, these data are also misleading. Around the world, the cold kills many more people than heat. "In the United States and Canada between 2000 and 2019, 20,000 died from heat while 170,000 died from cold."

The exclusive focus on heat is very misleading. "Low temperatures are much more dangerous than high ones. Half a million people a year die from heat, but more than 4.5 million die from cold."(13)

<u>Why Are Climate Scientists Lying to the Public?</u>

Mostly because they work in universities or governmental agencies and are fearful of losing access to grants, promotions, or being cancelled or fired. They must support the narrative or be punished, and obviously they are afraid.

The Paris Climate Agreement

The Paris Climate Agreement is a non-binding agreement by 194 countries to reduce their carbon dioxide (CO2) emissions over time. The goal is to ensure the global temperature does not rise by more than 2 degrees C (3.6 degrees F). (Where did this number come from?) Unfortunately, there is no agreed upon baseline figure, so measuring achievement will be subject to interpretation. Some scientists do not agree that a small amount of warming will be detrimental, citing the improvement in agricultural yields, reduced heating costs and the reduction in deaths due to cold weather in the northern hemisphere. "The International Renewable Energy Agency estimates the world will need to invest $115 trillion through 2050 to limit global warming to 1.5 degrees C." (14)

This informal agreement has been the source of much consternation since its goals and commitments were published. Maybe the most controversial issue was President Trump's renouncing the U.S. commitment (reversed by President Biden). Trump was the only leader with the courage to call out the big lie of climate change. The fact that this is an agreement and not a treaty means that it lacks complete support in the United States and other nations. The goals are strictly voluntary and there is no enforcement mechanism. In fact, there is no official consensus of what the accord will achieve.

The goal is to limit the rise in global temperature to 2 degrees Celsius (3.6 degrees Fahrenheit. The more ambitious goal is 1.5 degrees Celsius (2.7 degrees Fahrenheit)

This agreement is the third, behind Rio De Janeiro (1992) and Kyoto (1997), and neither of these two prior agreement goals were achieved by any of the major countries. The chart below highlights the vast difference between the promises made and the reductions in CO2 required to achieve the goals.

<u>Paris Climate Agreement</u>

Year Promised, Reduction	Promised Reduction (In billion tons)
2030	64
2100	540
Reduction of emissions needed to achieve 3.6 degrees F	5,340
Reduction of emissions needed to achieve 2.7 degrees F	6,410

Source: Bjorn Lomborg 2020

The difference between what was promised and what is required to achieve the goal is so vast as to be insurmountable. However, what is even more troubling and frankly irrational is the result. If the Paris commitments are fully achieved, the reduction in global warming will be 0.05 percent. This modest reduction is certainly not worth the trillions of dollars spent to achieve it. This should serve as a wake-up call, that this approach is not the best possible plan. This Paris Agreement was a kumbaya moment and a photo op for all the leaders to show solidarity with the climate change movement. These accords support the shallow analysis and policy solutions put forth by politicians. The truth is that in a world where 80 percent of the energy is produced by fossil fuels, **it is not possible**

with present technology to replace fossil fuel with renewables.

Some western industrialized countries however have thrown themselves into the fight against CO2, spending huge sums of money to "transition" their economies to net carbon neutral, regardless of the cost, damage to their economies and the absolute futility of their goal. Bank of America estimates that achieving net zero by 2050 will cost $150 trillion, more than ALL countries spend on education. This money will be taken away from investments in defense, agriculture, technology, education, infrastructure and science, all of which are needed to accelerate the weak growth of the industrialized West and to find new, clean and cheap sources of energy.

Solyndra has become the poster child for the massive spending on poorly thought-out investments in green energy. Solyndra cost the U. S. taxpayers $535 million. It seems there is a new and larger boondoggle champion called Tonopah Solar Energy. With technology that could not attract any private investment, (wonder why?), the government stepped in to provide $737 million in guaranteed loans. It filed for bankruptcy. Thank you, President Obama. This is another example of why government should not be involved in picking winners and losers or funding for any technological innovation. (15)

The constant media drumbeat has led politicians and bureaucrats to rush to enact poorly thought-through policy initiatives around the world. The wealthy countries' response has been to spend, like drunken sailors, as much money as possible and tell the people the problem will go away. The poor countries do not have the option of deciding for themselves what to do. Their options are more limited and controlled by the money purveyors, namely the United Nations, World Bank, Greenpeace and International Monetary Fund. These wrong-headed bureaucrats have added climate goals to all their development programs as an additional condition to receive aid. The results of these ivory tower ideas have been a disaster. A few of these are highlighted below:

Greenpeace decided that they would use Dharnai, India, as a model of renewable development. Dharnai would be the first city to be powered exclusively by solar power. They proclaimed it would not be victimized by the fossil fuel trap: buy, burn and then suffer the consequences of fossil fuel. They set up a solar-powered micro-grid to serve this city exclusively. The batteries drained quickly and there was barely enough power to light one lamp in a home. The people were stuck with burning cow dung to cook and no refrigeration. The people's dream of a reliable electric source for refrigerators and cook stoves was gone. They organized a protest and after some time the government agreed to hook them up to the main power grid, which is powered by cheap, reliable, fossil fuel.

In Fiji, the government and a Japanese company collaborated to build a solar grid for the town of Rukua. The residents were excited and many bought refrigerators. When the system was installed, it was unable to power more than three homes at a time. Several of the frustrated residents decided they had enough of the fake promises and bought diesel generators. This is what will occur around the world if governments insist on replacing reliable fossil fuel electricity generation with unreliable renewable generation equipment.

"Sri Lanka is the epitome of elite environmentalism gone wrong. Pushed to go organic by activists and the World Economic Forum, the government banned synthetic fertilizers in April 2021. Food production cratered and the economy collapsed. Hungry and outraged citizens launched protests, overran the presidential palace, and forced the government to resign *en-masse* and the president to flee the country." (16)

<u>The Green Mirage</u>

The International Energy Agency (IEA), the leading authority on energy, issued a report entitled *The Role of Critical Materials on Clean Energy Transitions* in May 2021. The report states clearly that the transition to clean energy requires a massive increase in mining and infrastructure. "Demand for key materials, such as lithium, graphite, nickel and rare-earth metals would explode, rising by 4,200 percent; 2,500 percent; 1,900 percent; and 700 percent respectively by 2040." In effect, they made it clear that the transition to clean energy sources is a transition from a "fuel-intensive to a material-intensive energy system." This means a shift from fuel and gases whose environmental footprint is relatively light, and whose transport is cheap and efficient to big footprint mines and the energy-intensive transport of large quantities of rocks that need further chemical processing and refining. The IEA data show that, depending on the location and nature of future mines, the emissions from obtaining energy transition materials (ETMs) could wipe out much, or most, of the emissions saved by driving electric cars." The real problem however is the source of these materials. Oil and gas are sourced around the world while ETMs are concentrated in China. (17)

"This green fantasy would require more turbines, batteries and solar panels than the world has raw materials to make. All the mines that exist in the world today for critical minerals like graphite, cobalt, vanadium and nickel produce only one-third of what is required to achieve the green transition, according to the International Monetary Fund." (18)

What is missing in this one-sided "discussion" is the voice highlighting the benefits that fossil fuels have provided to humanity since the discovery of oil in 1870, in Titusville, Pa. "Fossil fuels let people heat their homes in the winter, reducing the risk of death from exposure. Fossil fuel-based fertilizers greatly increased crop yields, reducing starvation and malnutrition. Oil- and coal-burning transportation opened up access to education, commerce, professional opportunities and vital services such as medicine. Fossil fuels are used to produce plastics which reduce the need to destroy forests for wood. Climate activists worry about an "existential crisis," decades down the road, but poor people, really poor people, face an existential crisis every day." Reduced access to cheap and abundantly available fossil fuels will significantly impact the development and prosperity of poor and developing countries. ([19])

<u>Climate Models</u>

Scientists continually make presentations that begin with the phrase "the model says," which projects an authority like God giving Moses the Ten Commandments on Mount Sinai. Honestly, a model is no more than a fancy and very expensive calculator. The scientist inputs the information, and the calculator calculates the result. George Box, a University of Wisconsin statistician said, "All models are wrong, but some are useful." That is because gaming various scenarios helps understand the parameters of a problem and its ossible solution.

The real obstacles to good modelling of the climate are:

- Our lack of understanding of the dynamics of the Earth's weather patterns.

- Developing the data for a starting point.

A model of the Earth's climate is developed by dividing the Earth's land and atmosphere into grid boxes. Land boxes are 60 miles square with 10 to 20 layers on top rising into the atmosphere. The ocean grids are 6 miles square with 30 layers of atmosphere above. Measurements include temperature, carbon, wind, humidity and cloud cover among other things. There are more than 1 million grid boxes and to start the model this information must be measured for each grid box at the same time. It is not possible to measure each of the required inputs and because the scientist must enter something into the computer model, they make up information. The result? The model is inaccurate at the start. Models are tested by feeding historical data to determine if the model can retroactively forecast the weather that has already occurred. None of the 40+ models in use today have been able to pass this basic test and therefore their ability to predict future climate changes years in advance is suspect at best. None of the models can explain the rise in global temperatures from 1910 to 1940 when the world population was much lower. This is why people worldwide should be very, very, very skeptical of scientists and/or politicians who lecture us with certainty about the climate cataclysm that is about to befall humanity.

<u>The California Model</u>

California has positioned itself as the most progressive state in the country. Everything is better in California, and its governance is the best of any state, according to their officials. High taxes, wildfires, unaffordable real estate, overcrowded highways, store looting, carjacking, robbery, homelessness, rampant drug addiction, and the growing exodus of people and businesses are all overlooked in its self-congratulatory bromides.

The California vision for fighting climate change begins with the conversion of the primary power grid from fossil fuel power to complete reliance on wind and solar power. The problem with this dream is that sometimes the wind does not blow and for 50 percent of the day, or more, the sun does not shine. Therefore, the state needs a backup source of power, and the primary backup is the fossil fuel power generation system at present, although the goal is to completely shut down all fossil fuel power stations and replace them with renewables by 2050.

Solar Panels

Californians have been encouraged by massive financial incentives to purchase solar power systems for homes and businesses. Many have, but not everyone can afford these systems. Home solar power is still expensive even though the price continues to fall. It is an option only for the affluent in California. Even though the government (federal, state and local) assists with purchasing these systems, the rebates come after the homeowner has shelled out the upfront cost. The cost for a 3,000 square ft. home is as follows:

3,000 square foot house requires 1840 kWh per month

The system loss adjustment (-23%) 1840 X1.4 =2576 kWh per month required

Multiply by 12 Months   2576 X 12 = 30,912 kWh

Divide by the irradiance factor for your local city (San Francisco is used for this example).

(Irradiance is the number of peak sun hours per year)

San Francisco irradiance is 2089.1

30,912/2089.1 = 14.8Kw or 14,800 watts required to electrify home

14,800/ 300 (watts per solar panel) = 49.3 panels

Rounded up to 50 panels at 2.50 per Kw cost = $37,000

Example Source: Business Wire

In addition to the individual residential and commercial systems, California has large commercial solar farms that sell power to the utility companies. They presently produce so much power during peak sunlight periods, the state must pay neighboring states to take the excess.

With federal and state tax rebates for the solar systems, the actual residential consumer cost is closer to $18,000, very close to the price of a back-up generator. Each has its advantages. However, the cost of both is beyond the means of millions of California families, so in effect the state is subsidizing the affluent to purchase solar panels so that they can save money, using the tax money of the poor.

Over 230,000 homes have been fitted with solar panels for a total investment of $8.5 billion (230,000 X 37,000).

<u>Generators</u>

Other homeowners have decided to purchase fuel-powered back-up generators to provide power during blackouts. According to the policy consulting group M. Cubed (10/6/21), the number of permitted residential generators in the Los Angeles metro and San Francisco metro areas are 23,507 of which 90 percent are diesel-powered. This relatively small number of generators has a power equivalency of 15 percent of the total grid. Sales of these back-up generators are increasing at 20 percent per year. At that rate of growth in 10 years the total number of generators will exceed 145,000 and be equivalent to 92 percent of the entire state grid power.

Non-residential back-up generators (most of which are diesel powered) are also being installed throughout the state for data backup, medical facilities (mostly hospitals and surgery centers), government agencies including police and fire, manufacturing, commercial and retail businesses.

Diesel engines burn a low grade, dirty fuel that emits a plethora of harmful byproducts and a plume of black smoke. Will the total pollutants emitted by the generators offset most/all of the savings from the green initiative?

<u>Conclusion</u>

California is replacing its reliable fossil/nuclear fuel (coal, nuclear, natural gas, hydro) electric grid with a multi-layered, unreliable grid consisting of the following layers of electric generating capability and storage:

<u>Wind and Solar</u>

- Parts of the old fossil fuel grid

- Privately owned (residential and commercial solar)

- Back-up generators (residential and commercial)

- Battery storage (both private and utility systems)

Will this new electric "grid" be as reliable as the one it is replacing? How much more expensive is the new grid than the "old reliable" grid (natural gas, nuclear and hydro)?

<u>Trade-Offs</u>

We touched on how the cost of solar panels makes a complete transition to solar power impossible. However, let us consider another trade-off. When you use acres of land for solar farms, you are reducing the amount of land that could provide crops, homes or businesses for jobs.

Wind power has its share of trade-offs too. For example, NIMBY comes into play with wind power. That stands for "Not in my Back Yard." Many years ago, Sen. Ted Kennedy rejected a plan to build a wind farm in the waters off the coast of Cape Cod. He didn't want the eyesore ruining the view from the Kennedy family Hyannis Port compound.

A major problem with wind farms is bird deaths as they fly into the propellers.

While hydro power is not being considered for California even though it is a renewable energy, it also has trade-offs. The fish can't get upstream to spawn because of the dams. When a lake is low due to drought as in the case of Lake Meade, it is hard to generate enough power. Ocean power technology has not been perfected yet to be useable.

<u>Electric Vehicles</u>

California is also transitioning its automobile industry into an all-electric fleet. There are 29 million vehicles registered in California and they will all need to be replaced by EVs. (Maybe the older cars can be sold to the stupid states that do not mandate electric vehicles?) To keep electric vehicles on the road, the state plans to install 1.2 million chargers by 2030. This will also result in the closure of the majority of the 10,000 gas stations in the state, although some will remain open serving as convenience stores without gas. (20)

If California proceeds with its goal to be 100 percent fossil free, then they will need to add to their renewable electricity generation capabilities. To get some idea of the scope of this change, the following illustration is presented:

<u>Electric Grid Example</u>

For this example, the daytime demand, when everyone is working is designated as D, (7 a.m. to 7 p.m.) and the nighttime demand, when people are home, most businesses are closed (or open part of the time), and the electric vehicles are being charged for use the following day as N (7 p.m. to 7 a.m.).

The state would need:

- a renewable grid large enough to power the daytime requirements (D).

- a renewable grid to generate electricity during the day (no nighttime sunlight) to satisfy the electricity requirements for the nighttime (N).

- a renewable grid to generate electricity during the day for days when the sun is not shining. No sun days. (NSD). Also, for days when the wind is not blowing. (The wind turbines will generate power both day and night (when the wind is blowing) but solar will not).

- 4- Battery storage (B) to store the power for the N grid and the NSD grid.

<u>Residential Segment Renewable Energy</u>

There are 14.5 million(mm)homes in California. The goal by 2045 is to provide 80 percent of the power through wind and solar and 20 percent via hydro, biomass and geothermal. This does not include future homes to be built.

Renewable Power

80 percent X 14.5 = 11.6 million homes to be powered by wind and solar

Assume 50/50 split between wind and solar

Solar Analysis

11.6mm X 50 percent = 5.8 million homes to be powered by solar

32-acre solar farm is required to power 1000 homes

5.8 million/1000 = 58,000 solar farms

58,000 X 32 = 1,856,000 acres

One acre of solar panels = 43,560 panels

1,856,000 X 43,560 = 80,847,360,000 panels

The useful life of a solar panel is 25 years. Energy efficiency degrades 0.05 percent per year.

The residential sector uses approximately 33 percent of the electricity in California (Statista.com/energy), commercial and industrial use the remaining 66 percent. Therefore, to find the total state requirements for solar panels we multiply by three.

Residential Sector	All Sectors (Residential x 3)
58,000 solar farms	174,000 solar farms
1,856,000 acres	5,568,000 acres
80,847,370,000 panels	242,542,080,000 panels

Wind Analysis

5.8 million homes

17,000 turbines power 500,000 homes

1 turbine powers 29 homes (500,000/17,000)

5.8 million/29 = 200,000 turbines needed to power residential homes

200,000 X 3 = 600,000 wind turbines required for all three (3) sectors.

One turbine contains:

900 tons of steel

2,500 tons concrete

45 tons plastic (usually nonrecyclable fiberglass)

Wind turbines life span is 20 years.

<u>Other State Obstacles</u>

The reliability of renewables was put to a real-world test by Winter Storm Uri, which hit Texas with severe temperatures. The result was that electricity generated from renewables declined by 52 percent while natural gas generated electricity increased 72 percent. Federal regulations over the past decade, specifically federal tax subsidies accounted for the poor investment decisions in renewable capacity. For every 39 cents invested in the oil and gas industry, $18.86 was provided for wind subsidies and $82.46 for solar subsidies. Lots of money spent, lots of capacity added, but not enough energy because the capacity added was unreliable. This will be the continual story of the transformation of the electric grid. Massive government incentives to build unreliable power generation resulting in frequent brownouts and blackouts. This is how the government wastes trillions of dollars of taxpayer money. (21)

Many other large states do not have the same level of sunshine as California (Illinois, Massachusetts, Michigan, New York, Ohio, Pennsylvania, Wisconsin and other northern states) and will require a considerably larger number of solar panels and wind turbines to generate electricity and a very, very large battery storage system for the many days with little or no sunshine. In many states, they have insufficient wind or land to make turbines viable. Another challenge for the colder states is the fuel requirement for heating. Electric heat is expensive and doesn't work well and heat pumps do not provide satisfactory levels of heat in very cold areas. Do these customers add wood or coal stoves to supplement the inadequate electric heating? If they are cold, they will.

<u>Vehicles</u>

Type	Number
Cars	16.1 million
Light trucks	12.7 million
Medium/HD trucks	1.0 million
Motorcycles	0.9 million
Total	28.8 million

Requirements	Amount
Two vehicles per household	14.4 million households
Two chargers per household	28.8 million chargers
28.8 million chargers x $600	$17,280,000,000

If we combine the total of cars and light trucks and assume they are mostly personally owned, we have a total of 28.8 million personal vehicles. Using an average of two vehicles per household, we need two chargers per household or 28.8 million personal charging systems. These cost $600 each or $1,200 per household for a total expenditure of $17,280,000,000.

California has set a goal of having 1.2 million charging systems installed statewide. These commercial charging stations are larger and more expensive than a household system. The costs vary depending on the size and the power of the system. The 240V system is estimated between $2,500 and $5,500 each. The more powerful 480V systems cost $40,000 per stall and charge a car in one hour. Many people outside their homes do not have eight hours of free time to charge their vehicles, although one can argue that overnight hotel stays and charging stations at work can accommodate a longer charge, if not the full eight hours. For the purpose of this example, we are assuming a 50/50 split between the 240V chargers and the 480V chargers.

Charger Type	Amount Needed	Cost
240V	600,000	$ 4,000
480 V	600,000	$40,000
600,000 240V	X $4,000	$2,400,000,000
600,000 480V	X $40,000	$24,000,000,000
1,200,000 total chargers		$26,400,000,000

Vehicle Emission Comparison

A gasoline-powered car emits 34 tons of carbon dioxide over its useful life of 10 years. An electric car emits 26 tons of carbon dioxide over the same period. Electric cars use more CO2 in their production and are charged by electric grids that continue to be powered by some fossil fuel. (22). This is a 25 percent reduction. Is this worth all of the money invested, and CO2 produced to completely change the automobile industry from one that relies on American energy sources to battery and renewable generating components from China? Scientists say yes as electricity generated from renewables produces less CO2. The questions that remain from this transformation are a) the reliability of these power sources and b) the environmental impact of all the toxic materials used to produce and then recycle batteries c) the total CO2 used to produce the other materials used in wind turbines and batteries. (23)

The Drivers Conundrum

With all the news and political hyperbole surrounding EVs, it appears that the actual experience of drivers has been forgotten. Below is an example to better understand what will occur.

Example:

Drivers in southern Florida travelling north will need

to refuel or recharge somewhere around Atlanta. For gasoline powered vehicles, they just find an exit, get-off drive a short distance to find a gasoline station and then fill up. Five minutes at the most but for EV owners, they need a charging station. While it is expected that highway signs will provide charging station locations to drivers, the entire experience will be much more challenging.

<u>Auto Refueling</u>

Average car length	15 feet
Safety distance from next car	90 feet
Total space at 60 mph	105 feet
Maximum number of cars per mile	50
Average number of cars per mile depending on traffic	25
Adjust for three lanes	75
75 cars per minute reach a given point	
50 percent need gas	
Cars needing gas in Atlanta each minute	38

Gas Station Capacity:

Eight exits (four south and four north of city)

Four stations per exit (two on each side within .5 mile)

16 pumps per station (four bays four pumps in each)

Four gas stations per exit X 16 pumps per station = 64 pumps per exit

Eight exits X 64 pumps per exit = 512 pumps

38 cars X 5 minute refueling time = 190 cars refueled every five minutes

Pump utilization at average traffic 190/512= 37 percent

<u>Electric Vehicle:</u>

Assume 30 minutes of charging time for an electric vehicle.

38 cars per minute need	30 minutes of charging
Chargers and space needed	1,140
Square feet in an acre	43,560
30 percent access roads	13,068
Usable land for parking	30,492 sq. ft.
Parking spot size 9 x 18	162 sq. ft. per spot
30,492/162	188 parking spots per acre
1,140/188	6.06 acres required for chargers

The example above demonstrates that gasoline powered vehicles have no problem with refueling (we see that every time we drive along an interstate and need to fill up.) The EV charging problem will be occurring throughout the United States at major cities and other driving destinations.

The electric vehicle presents more problems for refueling(charging). Vehicle charging stations will require a substantial amount of land for the number of vehicles that require charging. The capital cost of the land, fast chargers, real estate taxes, operating expenses and a profit will be added to the actual electricity costs. Charging may become more expensive than originally estimated. Charging stations must be added along all interstates (and other state roads) to handle peak traffic days.

Currently, the biggest draw on people's electricity usage is the air conditioning/heating units. California already has rolling brownouts due to usage and the inability to keep up with demand for electricity. When everyone is required to drive electrical cars, the EV's will be the largest draw of electricity usage. There will not be grid capacity to handle all of it.

<u>Questions</u>

At this point, it is wise to pause and ask a few questions about the climate plan. The goal of this entire endeavor is to reduce CO2, the human contributing factor to climate change from fossil fuels.

1- What is the total cost of this massive transition? Taxpayers have a right to know.

2- How much CO2 is being generated by the production and installation of the renewables and EVs, from the mining of the ore, processing, transportation, installation, energy production to the dismantling, removal, recycling of waste and replacement that is required every 20-25 years?

3- What is the impact on the environment of solar farms, wind turbines, EV charging stations, production and disposal of toxic chemicals? How many new Superfund sites will require expensive cleanups? We know toxic chemicals will leach into the water table from the solar farms. How many people will develop cancer from these toxic chemicals? How many dead whales from the offshore wind farms? Dead birds?

4- In short, is the "cure" more destructive than the illness?

Maybe an honest scientist can examine these questions to assure the public that the government's policy cure is better than a simple cure of:

1) converting the electricity generation to natural gas and nuclear and

2) transitioning the transportation sector to hybrid vehicles.

National Impact

Because California is the leader in the transformation to renewables it is helpful to review its progress and problems to help understand the issues for other states. The first thing one cannot fail to understand is the enormity of the project involved. The cost is astronomical, and the amount of mining, manufacturing, construction and land required is only comparable to our effort to supply the allied armies during WW2.

Net Zero

"Net Zero by 2050 is more than a slogan of climate activism. It has become a chief organizational principle for multinational corporations and the Black-Rock led cartel pushing (ESG) environmental, social and governance investing. Mentioned in over 6000 filings with the SEC and adopted by the Securities and Exchange Commission as a goal requiring corporate reporting on their progress."

"The Electric Power Research Institute, (EPRI) the research arm of the U.S. electric utility industry, released a report titled *Net Zero 2050: U.S. Economy-Wide Deep Decarbonization Scenario Analysis.* The EPRI report concludes that the utility industry cannot attain net zero. This study shows that clean energy plus direct electrification and efficiency are not sufficient to achieve net-zero economy-wide emissions."

"In other words, no amount of wind turbines, solar panels, hydropower, nuclear power, battery power, or electrification of fossil fuel technologies will get us to net-zero by 2050."

"The North American Electric Reliability Corp. (NERC) is a government-certified grid-reliability and standard setting group. NERC concluded that fossil-fuel plants are being removed from the grid to meet electricity demand and putting the country at increasing risk of blackouts." (24)

The American people are being asked to cede control over the economy to progressives, who have proven that they cannot run anything properly. They cannot run cities. They cannot run schools. They can't manage the border or COVID-19. Their two skills seem to be spending and lying, neither one conducive to building a strong economy.

<u>Less Developed Countries</u>

The less developed countries (LDC) countries will be unable to meet any of the climate goals set forth in the Paris Agreement. The reasoning is simple, they are engaged in raising the standard of living for their people. In Africa, there are millions who live in mud or thatch huts without running water, electricity or sanitation. In India, millions live without electric power. They use animal dung for cooking. These people deserve the opportunity for a better life, and a better life means a life with more energy. According to the Organization for Economic Cooperation and Development (OECD) the population of the developed countries is 1.3 billion and the population of the LDC is 6.5 billion. The combination of population growth and industrial development in the LDC world will require a **50 percent increase** in energy generation capabilities by 2050. China has already signaled that it is not committing to any reductions in CO2 emissions. "India says it will move toward net zero if the rest of the world pays it one trillion by 2030." Without these two countries serious commitment to net zero, the goal of reducing CO2 emissions globally is unattainable. This begs the serious question, why are the western countries destroying their economies for an unachievable goal?(25)

These two countries (China and India) are the major causes of rising CO2 levels among developing countries due to their 1) rapid industrialization and 2) large populations. China, the second largest global economy, once again managed to out-negotiate the weak western countries and claim a considerable dispensation on CO2 reductions as a "developing economy." They can increase emissions until 2030. This is ludicrous. Coal accounted for 64 percent of Chinas power generation in 2021. Since signing the 2015 Paris accord it has increased its coal-fired power by 185 gigawatts while the United States has reduced its by 80 gigawatts. (One gigawatt powers 770,000 homes). Obviously, the Chinese priority is economic growth while the feckless

American and European politicians' priority is destroying their economies. Climate change is only an excuse. (26)

In his book, *Cobalt Red*, Siddharth Kara gives the reader a detailed description of the cost of cobalt on the thousands of poor people who actually do the physical mining of cobalt. Cobalt infused lithium batteries power all the portable power tools and now the 1000-pound EV batteries. They have driven the demand for cobalt from 20 kilotons to 140 kilotons. It is expected to exceed 200 kilotons by 2026 when the EV mandates begin to take effect in the developed countries. The author describes the thousands of men, women and children as they dug, shoveled, scraped and toted the raw ore in open pit mines. All of this under the watchful eyes of armed guards. There are no human rights here or child labor laws. Just the dirty secret is exposed while the major corporations hide behind their anti-child labor policies in their supply network. Thousands are sickened and die from exposure to these toxic chemicals. Once veins of ore are identified they dig down deep into the ground to extract it. Children are sent into these narrow tunnels that can go 40-50 feet into the ground. When it rains the earth softens and the tunnels collapse, the people who die are the lucky ones. Many are maimed; have broken ribs, pelvis, arms or legs and then suffer in agony. There are no doctors or hospitals. No medical care whatsoever and the villagers can do very little. When they cannot work the family has lost a contributing member who earns money to pay for food. There is no one to replace him and less food to share. This is commercial slavery. Conveniently, enforced slavery operates around the edges of "their supply network." This is the real cost of the Green New Deal. Environmentalists in the wealthy countries can preach about how they are saving the world when, in fact, they are just exporting the dirty, environmentally destructive mining of battery materials to poor countries and then in the future will ship the toxic dead batteries and spent solar panels back to these same countries for disposal, killing thousands more. Some things never change. Maybe if Tim Cook, Elon Musk, Larry Fink or John Kerry worked In the mines for a week themselves their vision of a battery powered world would change. Of course they will never get near these mines. (27)

Carbon Tax

The generally accepted method for reducing fossil fuel use around the world is the enactment of a carbon tax on the purchase of all fossil fuels. Higher prices, it is postulated, will reduce demand. Therefore, a carbon tax is the most efficient and most effective method of reducing fossil fuel use and saving the human race from extinction. The problem with this solution is that the tax burden is regressive and falls most heavily on the poorest people in the developed and certainly less developed countries. They pay the cost of the climate policies enacted by the wealthy countries.

A much better method of reducing fossil fuel use is to eliminate activities in which the **overuse** of fossil fuel is for the benefit of a very small group. That would entail the following:

1-complete elimination of the use of private jets.

2-mandate that all pleasure boats over 40 feet be totally powered by wind.

3-Assess a progressively increasing carbon tax on the cumulative square footage of homes owned of over 4000 square feet. For example, if a person owns three homes with a total of 30,000 sq. Ft. in size, they accrue a progressively rising tax on 26,000 sq. ft. (30,000-4,000).

A carbon tax is not a deterrent to using fossil fuels for the wealthy. Money is not an object for them. A ban is the only measure that will reduce their overuse of fossil fuel. They can fly commercial and wait in the airports, be groped by TSA agents like all the peasants. A penalty for the CO2 used to build their mansions is appropriate. This forces the wealthy activists (John Kerry, Al Gore, Leonardo DiCaprio, Larry Fink, and the Davos crowd) to make sacrifices instead of preaching to others to sacrifice while they continue to use enormous amounts of fossil fuel themselves. Al Gore's home in Tennessee uses more electricity than any other home in the state. <u>The estimated carbon savings would be 3 percent to 5 percent of total U. S. emissions.</u>

<u>What Have We Learned?</u>

- The climate is warming.

- Humans have some responsibility but precisely how much is not certain.

- The problem is not existential.

- Models that "predict" the future are **unreliable**.

- The "cure," namely solar panels and wind turbines, produce as much CO2 (or more) to manufacture and recycle as the fossil fuels they replace. They cause toxic waste to eliminate and are eyesores.

- We cannot achieve net zero in 2050.

- The United States is reducing the generating capacity of its grid by retiring fossil fuel plants, increasing the unreliability of the grid, especially during bad weather. The unreliable grid causes consumers to purchase diesel powered generators which pollute more than the original fossil fuel grid.

- Less developed countries will NOT agree to re-

ductions in low-cost fossil fuel electricity generation.

- "If every country achieved its stated electric vehicle targets by 2030, the world would save 231
million tons of CO_2 emissions. Plugging these
savings into the U. N. Climate Panel model the
reduction in temperature would be 0.0002-de-
grees Fahrenheit by the end of the century."
This modest improvement is NOT worth all the
cost involved. (28)

- Achieving the goals of the Paris climate accord
will result in a minor reduction in the earth's
temperature, if any.

The present situation and proposed solutions do not
appear to be feasible, but the politicians and U.N. scientists do not want to admit it. Their intransigence is a
product of hysteria and fear, drummed up by misleading information generated by the scientific community
and the media. Any good CEO would have approached
the problem of global warming more intelligently.

1. Identify the underlying cause(s).

2. Identify viable solutions.

3. Choose the most cost-effective solution.

4. Implement the plan.

Instead of a rational process, the climate *cognoscenti* has jumped from problem, (Global warming), to cause (human use of fossil fuel) to solution (ban all fossil fuel).

The question to be addressed is whether CO_2 is the underlying cause of the human portion of global warming? Here, we rely on guidance from Socrates, who never stopped asking the question WHY, to discover the root cause.

Why do we have CO_2?

Because we burn fossil fuel.

Why do we burn fossil fuel?

Because we need food, clothing, shelter, transportation and jobs for each person.

CO_2 is a result, not the cause of global warming. Excess population is the primary cause of global warming. The Earth now boasts 8 billion people, and they all require energy to survive. During the past 80 years the problem of global warming has increased as:

1) the world population continued to grow at an unprecedented rate and

2) the developing countries accelerated their industrialization, using more energy in the process.

This is a very unpopular conclusion to present to politicians. In the developed countries, politicians depend on ever increasing populations to pay for their Ponzi type entitlement programs that are sold to the people with low-ball estimates, but soon find them perpetually underfunded. In the developing world, politicians do not have the resolve to control population growth. Even China had to abandon its one -child policy due to political pressure. The alternative is to continue to increase the population to a point where nature begins to fight back, killing plants, animals and humans.

The present plan to address global warming is a very poor plan because the "solution" will require as much or more CO2 and other harmful elements to be released into the environment. Discarded solar panels contain cadmium and arsenic and when sent to landfills leach into the water table. It is not profitable to recycle the panels because the elements recovered are worth about $3 but the cost to recycle them is between $12 and $25 per panel. Thus, they are discarded into landfill. According to hazardouswasteexperts.com, solar panel waste is 300 times more toxic than nuclear waste. Many of the panels are collected and shipped to developing countries where they are dumped into their landfills after they are scavenged for any valuable metals.

"A major new study published in the *Harvard Business Review*, finds the waste produced by solar panels will make electricity four times more expensive than the world's leading energy analysts thought" due to the massive cost of the toxic waste. The EPA should get ready for another Superfund initiative just like the Comprehensive Environmental Response, Compensation and Liability Act of 1980. (29)

The $150 trillion price tag will destroy the economies of the western democracies. China will take over the world without firing a shot. A better plan would include the following elements:

- Add nuclear and natural gas to the list of renewable sources of electricity.

- Tap the methane in landfills around the world and deliver it to the closest utility for an electric generation source. Wastewater treatment plants and landfills have been capturing methane to power their plants for years. They are quite successful.

- Replace coal-fired-electricity-generated plants with natural gas plants.

- Replace residential communities' oil-fired heating with natural gas.

- Add small nuclear power stations (similar to those powering naval vessels) to the grids.

- Increase the Earth's reflexivity of the sun's heat

by replacing dark roofs with light roofs and dyeing black asphalt roads a light color. Roof gardens also will help.

- Plant two acres of trees for each acre cut.

- Accelerate tree planting everywhere.

- Replace gasoline vehicles with hybrids.

- Increase the required efficiency ratings of new A/C and heating units for both residential and commercial applications.

- Provide government tax credits for insulation, A/C and heating efficiency upgrades and energy audits.

- Eliminate tax credits for EVs and renewable sources of electricity as they are inefficient sources of energy.

- Explore and frack everywhere to increase the supply and lower the cost of natural gas.

- Ask every government to add a sourcing requirement to all purchases verifying the product was manufactured in a plant where electricity was NOT generated by coal, effective in 2030. This will force China and other intransigent nationals to join the effort and eliminate coal fired generation.

- Ask families to adhere to a two-children goal.

<u>Developing Countries</u>

- Increase the availability of birth control measures throughout urban and rural areas. Smaller families will slow population growth and increase living standards as there will be fewer people to feed in a family.

- Replace coal with natural gas for electric generation.

- Explore and frack for natural gas everywhere.

- Expand highway and rail systems to improve the transport of products to shipping points for sale.

- Adhere to a two-children goal.

The problem was created over decades. The solution will take time.

<u>Final Thoughts</u>

While the world has embarked on its nonstop transformation from gasoline-powered automobiles to electric vehicles, very few people have stopped to question whether this is a good decision. It is just "assumed" to be the single most important method of fighting climate change and therefore absolutely no comments that question this transformation are allowed. The orthodoxy, like so much of what is practiced by the left, is unquestionable by mere mortals. So, just shut up.

But there are some voices out there who dare to speak up. The Ifo Institute in Germany is one of them. According to Ifo, the carbon emissions of battery-electric vehicles are "slightly higher than those of a diesel engine" in the best-case scenario.

This "transition" to clean energy is a purposeful war against America's fossil fuel industry and its automobile industry. An American electric automobile industry will be a weak competitor because it depends on rare materials that are primarily available from Chinese companies. This places the Chinese government in the catbirds seat, perfectly positioned to provide preferential treatment to their battery and automobile companies and control another major industry.

So why the religious fervor for a solution that is not a solution? Those TV detective stories always tell us if we want the perpetrator of a crime, start by asking who benefits.

<u>In this instance:</u>

- China benefits from the increased use of solar panels as they are the world's largest producer.

- China benefits from the increased use of wind

turbines as they are the major supplier.

- China benefits from the transition to EVs as they refine 70 percent of the world's lithium, cobalt, manganese and nickel, the world's battery building minerals. (30) They also control most of the mines.

- China also dominates the market for the parts that go into the batteries, such as cathodes, anodes and the batteries themselves.

- China benefits from converting the world from gasoline to electric battery vehicles as it transfers dependence on energy to China.

- China is already the largest exporter of EVs, and its lead seems to be growing according to the International Energy Agency.

- The Democratic Party and OPEC+ (include Russia) benefit from the destruction of the American oil and gas industry. The Democrats from the 1) reduction in wealth of the red states and subsequently their support of the Republican Party and 2) OPEC+ from the elimination of a major competitor whose goal is "lower" prices. (31)

Because the modern Democratic Party is now a mix of Socialist/Marxist/Communist ideologies, it is kissing cousins of Chinese and Russian communists. It is not surprising that their economic goals are congruent.

The climate hysteria started with the United Nations and was supported by American universities. Add in the fact that China is doing almost nothing to transform its economy from dependence on coal to clean energy sources and any intelligent observer must wonder if this new climate religion has in fact been orchestrated by the Chinese government. Everyone knows they have tremendous power to mold opinion in American universities and the United Nations. (32)

Footnotes:

"The Not So Peaceful World of Greenpeace," *Forbes*, 11/11/1991

"In Their Own Words, Climate Alarmists Debunk Their Science," *Forbes*, 2/6/2013

"Global Warming Delusions," Daniel Botkin, *WSJ*, 10/18/2007

"U.N. Parley Opens Amid Gloom," Philip Shabecoff, *N.Y. Times*, 5/11/1982

"Snowflakes are now just a thing of the Past," CharlesOnians, *Independent*, 3/20/2000

"Greenland's Melting Ice is no Cause for Climate Change Panic," Steven E. Koonin, *WSJ*, 2/18/2022

Bjorn Lomborg, *False Alarm*

Steven L. Koonin, *Unsettled*

"Climate Change Brings a Flood of Hyperbole," Steven L. Koonin, *WSJ*, 8/11/2021

IPCC 2021 Report

Dr. John Christy, Climatologist, University of Alabama

"*The Lancet*'s Heat Death Deception," Bjorn Lomborg,

WSJ, 11/5/2022

"How the Climate Elite Spread Misery," Bjorn Lomborg, *WSJ*, 7/22/2022

14-"Climate Goals Carry Big Costs," World News, *WSJ*, 4/26/2021

15-"Another Green Subsidy Bust," Review and Outlook, *WSJ*, 12/12/2020

16-"Sri Lanka's Green New Deal Was a Human Disaster," Tunku Varadarajan, *WSJ*, 7/15/2022

17-"Biden's Not so Clean Energy Transition," Mark P. Ellis, *WSJ*, 5/12/2021

18-"Biden Should Quit Putting Green Energy Fantasies Ahead of America's Families," Senator Bill Hagerty, *Grassroot Quarterly*

19-"Climate-Change Solutions that are Worse than the Problem," Jason De Sena Trennert, *WSJ*, 4/7/2022

20-Energy.ca.gov

21-"Texas Blackouts Blew in on the Wind," Wayne Christian, *WSJ*, 3/20/2021

22-International Energy Agency

23-"The Electric Vehicle Push Empowers China," Robert Bryce, *WSJ*, 12/24/2021

24-"A Quiet Refutation of Net Zero," Steve Milloy, *WSJ*, 12/29/2022

25-"Today's Soaring Energy Prices are only the Beginning," Bjorn Lomborg, *WSJ*, 1/6/2022

26- Review and Outlook, *WSJ*, 9/13/2022

27-"The Human Price of Cobalt," Mark P. Mills, *WSJ*, 2/2/2023

28-"If Electric Vehicles are so Great, Why Mandate Them?" Bjorn Lomborg, *WSJ*, 9/10/2022

29-"The Dark Side of Solar," Michael Shellenberger, *Forbes*, 6/21/2021

30-"Alternative Energy," *WSJ*, 11/14/2022

31-"AmericaCan't Depend on China for its Cars," William P. Barr, *WSJ*, 11/22/2022

32-"Electric Vehicles Dirty Secret," Lauren Silva Laughlin, *WSJ*, 10/12/2019

Chapter 9 How to Trade With Allies, Enemies

<u>Background</u>

Politicians and economists in the United States agree that trade is good for America. Therefore, if trade is good, more trade must be better. Trade is growing globally. Trade provides benefits to all countries. Trade improves the standard of living for both wealthy and poor countries. Trade provides consumers with the lowest cost of goods.

Trade is good and free trade is better, end of story. Why do you keep asking?

If free trade is good, then why have 77,000 U. S. manufacturing plants closed?

If free trade is good, then why has the United States lost more than 1 million manufacturing jobs since the North American Free Trade Agreement was formed in 1994?

The trade issue is complex and can be confusing. Media outlets write stories and provide some factual backdrop, but many times without the proper context. This chapter will explore and discuss some major trade issues.

<u>History</u>

One of the cornerstones of modern free trade is the theory of comparative advantage first proposed by the economist David Ricardo in 1817. His theory states that a county should purchase products from another country who is a more efficient producer of the product. A good example of this is Switzerland purchasing wheat from Australia. Switzerland has a cold climate and mountainous terrain, both not conducive to high yields per acre of wheat. The Swiss, in turn, sell pharmaceuticals, time pieces and their famous cheese to Australians.

Australia by comparison has large areas of fertile plains with a climate that is suitable for grain production and is flat and expansive enough to allow for extensive mechanization. The result is high yields per acre and large total crop yields that exceed the country's food requirements.

Countries that can produce products using less land, labor and capital than their trading partners enrich themselves and their trading partners as they use fewer resources to produce a product or service.

Below is a hypothetical example to demonstrate the theory:

Resources required to produce 1000 bushels of wheat

	Country A	Country B	Extra Re-sources Needed by B
Land needed	40 acres	400 acres	360 acres
Capital needed	$10,000	$20,000	$10,000
Labor needed	100 hours	500 hours	400 hours

In country A, it takes 40 acres of land, 100 hours of labor and $10,000 of cash to produce 1000 bushels of wheat. In country B, it would require 400 acres of land, 500 hours of labor and $20,000 of capital. When you compute the cost of the land/labor and capital required to produce 1000 bushels of wheat in country B, you quickly realize that the cost is significantly higher than the cost to produce the wheat from country A. The conclusion is that country B should not produce wheat but purchase it from country A and redeploy their land, labor and capital into production of a product that can be produced more efficiently versus other countries.

This is the economic theory that drives globalism. It postulates that if each country would focus on the production of products where it is most efficient, then the world's wealth will increase.

Of course, this theory assumes that the trade platform everywhere is equal for all participants with freight costs being the only variable.

The theory sounds wonderful. Each country specializes, and the world gets wealthier. However, when there are many countries that have the resources to produce the same products, as many countries do, trade becomes much more complicated. For example, Germany, Japan, South Korea, Sweden, the United Kingdom and the United States all produce quality automobiles. If you are the premier of Germany, should you open your market for all imports? The result would be a loss of German car sales in Germany, and unemployment of German auto industry workers. This is not a politically acceptable option, and therefore Germany imposes a 10 percent import tariff for U.S. cars.

Should the Germans shut their factories and import cheaper cars from other countries? No, and this is where the problems arise.

Free trade is not good for everyone in every circumstance. To better understand the issue, it is necessary to look at what happens to the parties involved in global trade. Only by understanding the actual winners and losers, and how they win or lose, can the policy makers develop a strong and fair policy for the country and negotiate "good" trade deals.

<u>Tariffs</u>

Most countries have tariffs. They are established to protect industries that have lobbied the government for protection from other countries who can supply equivalent or higher quality products for the same or lower prices.

Farm tariffs are very common as the farmers in almost every country are a powerful political force. Politicians cross them at their peril. Farmers want their farm products protected from imports so they can earn higher profits. Most of the industrial countries have extensive farm support and protection policies. Many of these are holdovers from the 20th-century due to food shortages caused by drought and war. The global economy has negated the need for many of the support programs because the diversity of growing regions usually means droughts in some growing areas are offset by bumper crops in other regions. Staples such as corn, rice, wheat and soybeans can be easily shipped long distances. Of course, the local farmer earns nothing from products purchased from another country. Therefore, they are against purchases of foreign farm products.

When there are many countries producing the same products, the competition can get fierce. Every country is under immense pressure from various constituents for some form of protection for their industries in the home market.

The World Trade Organization (WTO) was formed to reduce barriers to trade. It has been very successful in lowering trade barriers and increasing world trade. However, there are winners and losers in this open trade environment. The winners and losers consist of countries, industries and individual companies. Some countries will sign onto the WTO program, and then encourage or look the other way when their companies sell into the world market at below cost pricing. This is called dumping and creates complaints, bad feelings, mistrust, and reciprocal dumping by other countries. China encourages dumping as it believes in doing whatever it wishes without consequences. To the Chinese, winning is everything. Rules are for fools.

Unions support tariffs because they want the well-paid manufacturing jobs to stay in the country. There is always a country that can produce equivalent products at lower cost.

Company owners want tariffs. They want protection from:

- More efficient manufacturers in other countries,
- From foreign companies that compete unfairly.
- From companies in low wage countries

With all this pressure from inside a country, it is surprising that tariffs have been reduced at all. (1)

GATT and the WTO

In 1947, the General Agreement on Trade and Tariffs (GATT) was established. This agreement established the trade rules until 1995 when the WTO was formed. The problem with GATT was the lack of an enforcement mechanism. WTO has an enforcement mechanism to mitigate the weakness of GATT. However, it has been unable to cope with the difference between global businesses and domestically oriented businesses. The WTO, with its flaws, operated successfully until 2001 when China joined. China was a different type of economy that was able to circumvent the system. With government-controlled companies, it was able to skirt many of the rules that applied and were measurable in a market-based system. Government incentives, such as free land, low-interest loans, subsidized utility rates and discounts on raw materials purchased from other government-owned companies made it difficult to develop apples to apples comparisons on which to file complaints. Where skirting the rules did not work, China just disregarded the rules completely. The major complaint was its requirement for all companies to share technical information with the Chinese government as a condition for market participation. This requirement was illegal under WTO rules, but the other members were afraid to complain about the bullying tactics of China and be punished by reduced trade with China. Is this fair trade?

When Trump was elected president, he no longer wished the United States to play by these unfair rules. Thus, the evolution of the Trump tariffs to make the playing field for many domestic industries level.

<u>Non-Tariff Barriers</u>

When a Japanese automobile company wants to sell a

new model in the United States, it submits one of the cars to Environmental Protection Agency (EPA). The car is tested. EPA then certifies the sale of all cars of this specific model type into the United States.

When a U.S. automobile company wants to sell a new model in Japan, it ships over a model for the Japanese government to inspect. This vehicle is tested and eventually approved.

The difference is that the Japanese government inspects each individual vehicle that is imported. While the Japanese car company can ship an entire cargo ship full of car models that have been approved by the EPA and land them on the dock knowing they are all pre-approved. The American car company can ship a few cars, wait for the Japanese to decide to inspect them, (and they are in no hurry), before they can be moved to dealers. Flaws can always be found by the local inspectors anxious to demonstrate to their superiors they are doing a conscientious job.

This difference in inspection protocols is a purposeful impediment by the Japanese government designed to prevent the U. S. auto industry from establishing itself in Japan. Is this fair trade?

The biggest barrier is the requirement that all corporations have 51 percent ownership by Japanese. In the United States, Japanese companies can set up a U.S. corporation without a U.S. partner. Is this fair trade?

<u>Value Added</u>

One of the most important issues in trade that is never discussed in the media or by economists is the concept of value added. Many readers will not have ever heard of this concept applied to trade or may confuse it with a value-added tax used in Europe to tax goods.

Value added in this context is the value added to materials by workers. For example, let's take a house. To understand the value added, we would list the individual materials purchased to build the house including wood, cement, electrical wiring, fixtures, components, roofing materials, bricks, cement, wall board, piping, and flooring.

For this example, let us assume the cost of the materials is $225,000 then add the building lot at $50,000 for a total cost without labor of $275,000. The value of the home when finished is $550,000. The value added is the difference between the material/land cost and the selling price of $325,000. The value-added component is then computed as $325,000 divided by $550,000 or 59 percent. The labor adds $325,000 in value to the cost of the components.

To calculate the hourly wage for building this house, divide the value added of $325,000 by the number of hours required to build the home. In this example, 1,000 hours is giving us an hourly value-added wage of $32.50.

In the case of automobiles, the calculations for value added are also very impressive. Building an automobile requires steel, aluminum, glass, plastics and other raw materials. The finished car raises the value of these components. However, each of these basic ingredients is in itself a value-added industry. Glass is made from sand; steel comes from iron ore; aluminum comes from bauxite; and plastic comes from oil. These industries pay workers high wages to transform the basic ingredient into a finished product ready for manufacture into an automobile.

This value-added calculation is the key to understanding the difference between good trade and bad trade. President Trump focused on the balance of trade differences. This is a good start to understanding trade but only the outside layer of the onion. To understand whether you have good trade or bad trade, one must compute the value added of the trade for each of the products traded. (2)

What we are measuring by computing the value-added percentage is the value of labor. When the labor rate is high, the product creates wealth for the company, and therefore the country. This relative wealth equals the salaries of the labor required to design, manufacture and sell these products plus the company profit.

When we use the balance of trade as the standard for fair trade, we miss the concept of good versus bad trade. The following example is used to further illustrate this concept.

Let us propose the United States purchases $1 billion of automobiles from Japan, and Japan purchases $1 billion of chicken parts. Everyone is happy because there is a balance of trade. Unfortunately, this is a bad deal for the United States and a great deal for Japan. Why? The U.S. workers who raise chickens and cut them into the parts are earning $18 an hour. The workers in the Japanese auto industry earn wages comparable to U.S. auto workers at $80,000 per year ($38.50 per hour).

In this example, the Americans are enriching the Japanese. The Japanese standard of living will rise because higher wages lead to more wealth creation as the Japanese have more disposable income for purchases of homes, automobiles, leisure and investments. This is how wealth is transferred from country to country over time. The U.S. workers in the chicken parts company work for wages that allow them to exist at the poverty level. Many are able to obtain additional government benefits. The cost of these programs is an additional cost in computing the benefits of trade. This is a bad trade deal for America. Unfortunately, due to political demands by the farm belt and/or the state department or just plain old bribes, there are many trade agreements that continually suck the wealth from the United States in favor of the trading partner.

Let's take another example from the British colonization of India. The British would buy land in India and force the tenant farmers to grow cotton that the British would buy at low prices. The cotton would be shipped to British mills for processing into clothing to sell back to Indians at a profit. Wearing European clothes was in fashion, and Indians accepted this practice. When Mahatma Ghandi spoke in public, he criticized this as exploitation and urged Indians to buy homespun cloth, not as fancy, but woven in India, to keep India's money in India. The transition of cotton into cloth was a value-added event that made the British wealthy and made the Indians poorer.

When we examine the most successful countries of the past 50 years, we see the same pattern. They select products to sell where the value added is high and focus on selling these worldwide. These countries have been among the most successful economic stories. They place tariffs on imports of these products to the home country. In many cases, the products are sold at higher prices in the home markets, which further subsize the international sales and marketing efforts. Germany, Japan, South Korea and Singapore are the best examples. China is somewhat different. It wants to produce everything. It has basic raw materials and began by producing low value-added products and continued to move up the food chain to produce high value-added products. However, where Japan moved up the food chain by producing higher value-added products over time and jettisoning the cheaper products, the Chinese keep the markets for all goods, low tech and higher value. Every job they steal from the United States and Europe adds more wealth to China and removes it from Europe and the United States.

Let's look at this example:

One U.S. automobile worker loses his job:

One German worker gains the job:

U.S. Worker	German Worker
-80,000	+80,000

<u>U.S. government gain/loss of tax:</u>

Social security (6.5%)	-5,200	5,200
Employers' portion (6.5%)	-5,200	5,200
Medicare (1.45%)	-1,160	1,160
Employers' portion (1.45%)	-1,160	1,160
Federal tax (20%)	-16,000	16,000
State tax (4%)	-3,200	3,200
Total U.S. tax loss/Germany gain	-31,920	31,920

U.S. employees gain/loss after taxable income	-54,440
German employees gain/loss after taxable income	54,440

To determine the value of this single salary to the economy, economists use a velocity of money calculation. It measures the impact of one person earning a salary and then spending, saving or investing his/her earnings. The long-term multiplier factor of the persons distribution of the annual earnings is computed by economists by country. The long-term U.S. Factor is approximately 1.8 times. For our example, the value to the U.S. economy of the loss of this job is $54,400 x 1.8 = $97,920. If the taxes were the same for Germany, (German taxes are higher) the gain for the German economy would be $97,920.

Therefore, when a U.S. automaker closes an assembly plant employing 2,000 people in Michigan and moves it to another country, the U.S. economy loses $195,840,000 (2,000 x $97,920). Yes, this is real money and certainly worth our government fighting to keep plants here.

The Chinese government has some of the most stringent trade requirements in the world.

Foreign companies are required to have a Chinese partner who has 51 percent control. Most of the time, the partner corporation is partially owned/controlled by the Chinese government.

Foreign companies are required to relinquish their proprietary technology to the partner (the Chinese government) (this is a violation of its WTO membership, but it does it anyway because the other members do not complain lest their companies get punished by China) for the right to sell products or services in China. All technology owned by business is shared with the Chinese defense department for military applications.

The U.S. government does not impose a local ownership requirement nor relinquishment of proprietary technology as a condition to operate here.

China and other countries subsidize domestically owned companies in various ways to increase exports. These subsidies include:

- Low-cost or interest-free loans to build a plant or provide working capital.
- Subsidized electricity from the government-owned utility.
- Subsidized raw materials from government-owned suppliers.

In many instances, the delivered price to U.S. customers is lower than the American competitors' cost of production. It is sometimes difficult for the non-Chinese company to understand the costs of the Chinese company or to file a claim with the WTO because so many of the costs of production for a Chinese company are purposefully obfuscated by government ownership of suppliers.

The Chinese government will also encourage dumping products overseas. Because the government's goal is a strong economy with high employment for the Chinese people, spare capacity must be fully utilized. Products are sold overseas at whatever price they can command and are subsidized by the government.

These trade barriers are prohibited by the WTO. China does not care. The stupid countries in the European Union and the United States let China into the WTO, and China completely disregards the rules. The foreign companies were lured in and told of the vast opportunity they would have in China to make money. Some have made money but at the cost of losing their technological advantage.

Unfortunately, this was another Trojan horse. China, a backward Third World country when it entered the WTO (thank you again President Clinton) is now a global powerhouse who has violated every trade agreement and stolen, and continues to steal, all the technology it can. Their rapacious trade policies and blatant violations of WTO rules have enabled China to leap ahead of E.U. countries and now only has the United States ahead of it technologically.

The offshoring craze that started in the 1980s has now reached almost every industry. Companies are now transferring their product development to China to be closer to the manufacturing center. New product development and production improvements are developed better in a manufacturing environment. As manufacturing leaves, so does product development and engineering expertise. (3)

Unless it is stopped, within 30 years all high-tech products will come from China. The western countries will be significantly behind technologically. With a commanding lead in these technologies and the ability to manipulate trade around the world, the Chinese will dominate the world's economy; become fabulously wealthy; and arm the largest and most powerful military in the air, space, land and sea.

What is fascinating about this is the obvious lack of resistance by the U.S. government, the European Union and even the companies that are having their technology stolen. Somehow, they have all been brain-washed that someday, China will wake up, reform and play by the rules and we will all live together in a Hans Christian Anderson fairy tale world. President Trump has been viciously attacked by leaders worldwide because he is not naïve about the real China threat.

One example of the methods used by the Chinese to steal technology is the story of Steve Saleen, a car manufacturer who entered a joint venture with the Chinese city of Rugao, in 2016. Rugao did not have the expertise to build a factory to produce cars. The deal commenced with Saleen bringing his experience, design, engineering and related technologies while the city would bring $500 million in capital and another

$600 million in subsidized loans to the venture. During the initial years, Saleen designed three cars as working models for production. While he was busy meeting his requirements under the agreement, the Chinese had taken his engineering and designs and applied for more than 500 patents, never crediting him with any of the patent fillings, thus stealing his expertise. The government claimed his contributions were overvalued and based on false information. Any Chinese citizen willing to attest to this conveniently disappeared. (4)

<u>Impact of Global Sourcing by U.S. Retailers</u>

China was admitted to the WTO in 2001 with the encouragement of President Clinton. That means they were given most favorable trade status and were allowed to sell into the United States and other member countries all products with the minimum duties/tariffs as a favored partner. Immediately large retailers (like Walmart) began to build supply chains by contacting Chinese officials to introduce them to manufacturers for a wide variety of goods. As the Chinese companies provided price quotes for products, the U.S. retailers would contact their current American suppliers and ask them if they could meet or beat the price. The U.S. manufacturers' choices would be:

Meet the price and earn little or possibly lose money to keep the customer.

Set up their own supply chain to manufacture the product in China, saving costs and hopefully saving the large volume customer's business. (This would be a short-term fix as the customer would eventually want to deal directly with the Chinese manufacturer and capture every dime of the cost savings)

Close their U.S. manufacturing plants and open in China with a Chinese partner, which requires that the partner be given the technology unique to producing the product.

Downsize and operate a smaller company with the smaller customers

While the U.S. manufacturers are dealing with the Chinese competition, they are also losing non-Walmart customers. Whenever Walmart opens a store, it sucks the air from the area. Walmart's strategy of opening stores in the counties between towns allows them to pull customers from a larger area. The variety of stores in each town, women's clothing, shoe stores, furniture stores, pharmacies, grocery and hardware. Each lose a significant percentage of their sales to Walmart. Consumers shop at Walmart for lower, or perceived lower, priced goods of the same quality. Chinese goods do not always meet this criterion of being of equal quality. Of course, Walmart has the buying power to obtain better deals on name brand staples, such as toothpaste and laundry detergent. These easily comparable items reinforce to the consumer that everything at Walmart is priced lower and therefore they save money by shopping at Walmart.

Many of these locally owned stores, usually family-owned, slide into financial difficulty. The owners in many cases lose their business. Many of these stores were passed down by parents and grandparents, but now they are worthless. Some store owners also own the building and that also becomes part of the bankruptcy because potential new tenants understand that that the commercial center has died and been removed out to the new hub in the suburbs where Walmart has its shopping center.

Most of these small businesses have revenue of $250,000 to $2 million, depending on the size of the town. The value of these businesses is in the range of $150,000 to several million. This equity is lost to the owners. Many of these stores will have been sold to the present owners. Financed by the prior owner, a bank or the Small Business Administration, the buyer in these situations is required to provide some form of collateral and a personal guarantee. For these small business owners, not only have they lost the business, but also other personal assets. This may mean their homes.

As these small stores (non-Walmart customers) close, there are fewer and fewer non-Walmart customers for the regional manufacturers. Back when these manufacturers first received an order from Walmart, (or another big retailer) they were ecstatic as it added volume to their manufacturing plant, which lowered unit costs. Profits exploded even though they sold to Walmart at a lower price and profit margin. But now, without their small town regular (higher margin) customers and the volume from Walmart, they have nothing left. The Trojan horse was installed; the plot hatched; the retail stores were put out of business; and the regional manufacturers followed shortly thereafter. Walmart, a company that used to advertise its "Buy American" credo (refer to Sam Walton's book) to its customers has sold out America to increase its own profits.

The small retail stores supply jobs for the family, father, mother, kids and grandparents. The income for the family probably ranges from $60,000 to $500,000. These are middle-class incomes. With the loss of their businesses, their employment choices are limited. Bankruptcy has depleted their savings, ruined their credit and virtually eliminated their ability to borrow money, but they can always work for Walmart for $15 an hour.

Let's look at the loss of wealth to the small store owners. For this example, we will use a median revenue of $400,000 per store with a 20 percent pre-tax profit of $80,000. At a three times multiple, the business is worth $240,000. We do not know the exact number of retail stores Walmart put out of business, but we will use several scenarios in the chart below:

Number of Stores Closed	Total Equity Lost
100,000	$ 24,000,000,000
500,000	$120,000,000,000
1,000,000	$240,000,000,000

One million may sound like a high figure, but it could be low. A small Walmart store with a revenue of $40 million would need to steal the revenue of 100 retailers if we use an average revenue of $400,000 per retail store. Of course, some stores suffered reduced revenue and stayed open. Reduced revenues equate to a loss of value, and these partial losses of equity must be considered as well.

We should note here that the Walmart concept is to steal the sales of other retail stores. They advertise lower prices and consumers shop at Walmart to save money.

When Walmart opens a store in a county, it already knows the demographics of the area. Walmart knows within a tight range what the first-year sales will be and from prior experience the store sales growth trajectory as their small-store competitors continue to die and the field of competition is reduced to a few hard-core survivors.

The loss of the small retailers' equity is only part of the story. Now let's consider the regional manufacturers. These are the companies all over the United States that sold to the non-Walmart stores in every city and town, mostly within their region. These are men's,

women's, children's clothing, food, beds, sheets, pil-
lows, blankets, hardware and furniture.

The Republicans used a figure of 77,000 manufacturing
plants lost from the inception of NAFTA to the 2016
election. For our example, we will provide a range for
the reader. The revenue of these regional plants was
probably in the range of $2 million to $200 million. We
will use a median figure of $7 million for the average
plant. Using a pretax profit margin of 12 percent, our
median profit per plant is estimated tobe $840,000.

Number of Plants Closed	Total Equity Lost
10,000	$ 8,400,000,000
20,000	$16,800,000,000
40,000	$33,600,000,000

When the U.S.-based manufacturer closed, the staff
lost their jobs. This includes management employees,
technical specialists as well as the rank-and-file production staff. For a production worker earning $50,000
a year plus benefits, finding a job paying an equivalent wage is very difficult. In a production setting,
line employees have unique skills that are valuable
to that type of manufacturing and maybe that specific plant that justify their salary. The same is true for
the management staff. Employment is specialized,
and employers want a person who has experience in
the same industry, product, production processes and
maybe specific machinery. A steel company will look
for a cost accountant who has experience in the steel
industry. Companies believe that hiring within an in-

dustry eliminates most of the learning curve, and the employee can contribute on day 1. This is common not an exception.

When the U.S. company in your industry closes due to products being purchased from a foreign source, most likely the same challenges are facing other U.S. companies in the same industries. They are under duress and certainly not hiring more staff. The result is that the employees cannot find comparable jobs and will in most instances only be able to find unskilled positions in non-manufacturing companies with lower salaries. This is particularly true in the smaller communities without many other manufacturing facilities. Older workers are hit the hardest because they may have worked at a particular company or industry for 20+ years and built-up specific skills or been promoted from a machine operator to a supervisor or foreman based on their expertise. With the industry shrinking, due to the transfer of production to China, the prospect for employment elsewhere is nil. We have used the example of an unskilled worker above, but the same problem exists for management. General manager, engineer, Occupational Safety and Health Administration manager, personal manager or controller face similar issues. Fewer plants equal fewer jobs.

Many of the line employees, being unskilled, wind-up working retail and earning $15-18 per hour. Most work 29 hours per week at their main job, thanks to the President Obama mandate for the employer keeps the hours below 30 so no benefits are paid. The employee then pieces together one, two or sometimes three more jobs working 50+ hours a week to barely scrape by earning $750 a week at 50 hours, as opposed to $1,000 a week for 40 hours. Now the employee must pick up the $750 per month health insurance policy (employer is required to pay 50 percent if the employee works more than 29 hours per week).   The comparison is as follows:

Annual salary comparison

Factory worker who lost their job

Work at plant	Retail employment	Difference
40 hours per week	50 hours per week	+10 hours per week
$52,000 salary	$37,500 salary	-$14,500
$1,500 401K match	$0 401K match	-$1,500 401K match
$4,500 health insurance	$0 health insurance	-$4,500 health insurance
$2,000 paid vacation	$0 paid vacation	-$2,000 paid vacation
$28.85 hourly wage	$18 hourly wage	-$10.85 hourly wage
Total $60,000	$37,500	-$22,500

In this example, the employee loses $22,500, or 37.5 percent of income while working an additional 10 or more hours per week.

One of the criticisms leveled against many workers in industries that have shed jobs due to plant closing is that they never move. Why can't a steel worker move to Texas and become a roughneck? One major reason is that now their home has lost 50 percent to 80 percent of its value. Even if you could sell it to anyone, there are few jobs in a small city where a major plant has closed.

Walmart aired a long-standing advertisement highlighting the fact that buying at Walmart will save the average family $2,400 per year. The hypothetical savings of $2,400 are more than offset by the loss of $21,000 in wages and benefits. The argument that free trade helps consumers is clearly not evident to these people.

During the 2016 election, the Republican Party quoted a figure of 77,000 plants closed since the passage of NAFTA in 1993. In total, more than 2 million people lost their jobs. That computes to $45 billion of lost wages. The larger cost is the loss of the American dream for most of these families. With a loss of $22,500 in income per family per year, the majority of these families cannot buy a home, take a vacation or send their children to college. No wonder there is a significant rise in depression, divorce, domestic violence and drug use.

The Walmart story is a classic case that shows how political decisions can transfer wealth from one group to another. The Walton family who owned Walmart financed Bill Clinton's political career. When he was able, he paid them back by providing China, a communist country, most-favored nation status. An enemy is a favored trading partner. Really? Now the United States and many of our allies are dependent on China for many products. This is the equivalent of Britain closing its steel industry and purchasing steel from Germany in the 1930s.

<u>Better Trade Policy</u>

The United States and European Union have transferred a significant portion of their consumer and industrial product sourcing to China and away from domestic suppliers. The rationale has been twofold. First, lower prices for consumers increase their standard of living. Second, bringing China into the global community reduces potential conflict. Both rationales are somewhat suspect. First, consumer prices will be lower, but what about the cost to society of all the U.S. companies that go out of business as orders are transferred to Chinese firms. That is a hidden cost that consumers do not readily see. Some social costs for welfare, Medicaid and food stamps will be evident in higher taxes. Again, these are hard to identify for most taxpayers. Second, hoping communists change their ways is like hoping a leopard will change its spots. There are no examples of this happening although U.S. and E.U. leaders continue to "wish it so." Not one autocrat has changed their behavior in response to the "be nice to autocrats" strategy. China, Cuba, Iran, North Korea and Russia continue their hostile ways. Vladimir Putin made both President Obama and Angela Merkel look like novices when he invaded Ukraine. Both of these "statesmen" thought they had a "good relationship" with Putin. However, the Chinese communists are the masters of duplicity. They will smile and say yes to everything. Then, they turn around and do what is in their best interests, giving some lame excuse as to why they never agreed to anything else.

While the western countries trade to make money for the industries that the politicians want to help, the communists understand it is a weapon of war, and maybe the most important. China has used the money it made from producing western goods to build the second most powerful military machine in the world. Soon, it will become the most powerful from money the stupid countries gave it. The western countries now have a second major enemy. They will need to increase military spending much more to offset this additional power. Where are the consumer savings now?

A better trade policy would be to resign from the WTO and ask our friends to do the same and create a new trade paradigm. Just divide the countries into three groups:

> Friends

> Enemies

> Other

Friends would be given the most favorable trade status although individual trade deals would be necessary in each case.

Enemies would be the most limited trade partners where trade would be made based on need, maybe for specific materials unavailable elsewhere. We must have tight controls and government approval for each individual transaction. The other group would consist of perpetual neutral nations, soft enemies, soft friends and others who wish to chart a middle ground between the western democracies and the communists.

Footnotes:

"Give Trump Tariffs a Fair Test," Peter Navarro, *WSJ*, 1/14/2020

"U.S. Misses the Point in Trade Negotiations," Jon Sindreu, Heard on the Street, *WSJ*, 1/22/2020

"Innovation Should Be Made in the U.S.A.," *WSJ*, 11/16/2019

"How Chinese Companies Hijacked My Company," Steve Saleen, *WSJ*, 8/1/2020

Chapter 10 What Do Superminorities Mean for America?

<u>Background</u>

In the previous chapters, we have discussed how political issues are turned into ways to help a few. In this chapter, we discuss those few groups.

Sometime in the 1990s, the Democratic Party recognized that it had to decide regarding their support of constituencies to continue their dominance of the American government at the federal, state and especially local level. For the past 100 years, its base of support has been working people, especially union workers and newly arrived immigrants like the Irish and Italians. After the Democratic Party decided to support globalism and the benefactors of globalism in America, it began to lose the support of the non-municipal union and blue-collar workers who were losing their jobs to China, Mexico and other countries. Globalism decimated the jobs for these constituencies and therefore, the Democratic Party had to reinvent itself.

It chose to become the party of the "aggrieved" but run by the ruling class. It proceeded to organize the groups that it claims were aggrieved by "white men."

These groups include black Americans, LGBTQ groups and women (except when Medically Modified (trans-people) are involved they move up in the pecking order above women).

At the same time, Americans were introduced to the "new idea" that these specific groups must be represented equally in all facets of American society for the country to be "truly diverse." All the other groups in America, the 100+ other ethnic groups, races and religions were purposely excluded from the "quest for diversity." There is no longer any reason for Italians, Irish and Vietnamese immigrants to be part of the quest for diversity. Forget about Muslims, Mormons, Hindus, Sikes, Buddhists and the many other religious groups. These groups do not have enough "grievance" credentials and maybe some are, God forbid, Republicans. The connection between the new Democratic Party of the revised definition of diversity is to extend Affirmative Action to these groups as a reward for their unerring support of the Democratic Party. These new converts needed to have their grievances continually reaffirmed, and nothing is more reaffirming than "special treatment", provided with any type of cover story (lie) that is convenient. As a result, these groups enjoy privileges that are denied to other Americans. These privileges include; preferred access to government contracts, preference for civil service jobs, preferences for admission to elite high schools and colleges, special loan programs, preferences for jobs at elite high schools and colleges, preferences for corporate jobs, corporate board seats, preferential treatment for medical graduates for prestigious residency appointments, gerrymandering voting districts to ensure black candidates win, Black Caucuses in legislative bodies, establishment of Diversity, Equity and Inclusion (DEI) departments in colleges and corporations run by highly paid black Americans and laws that make any speech against them a hate crime. They were given additional federal holidays, including Martin Luther King Day and Juneteenth and public celebrations, such as Black History Month and Pride Month. More recently, the Democratic Party has offered a variety of reparations programs in blue states and court awards for claims of racism for not passing civil service type exams. TV commercials almost always have black actors, even though blacks comprise only 13% of the population. Very few Asian actors even though they comprise about the same percentage of the U. S. population as Blacks. Democrats can never do enough to buy black votes.

<u>Ethnic</u>

First, let us define the word ethnic to clarify the topic being discussed. Websters defines it as "designating a population subgroup having a common cultural heritage or nationality as distinguished by customs, characteristics, language and common history."

The United States, being the great melting pot of the world, is comprised of many ethnic groups. In the 2000 census, the largest 15 were identified as follows:

German	15.2 percent	42 million
Irish	10.8 percent	30.5 million
Black	8.8 percent	24.9 million
English	8.7 percent	24.5 million
American	7.2 percent	20.2 million
Mexican	6.5 percent	18.5 million
Italian	5.6 percent	15.6 million
Polish	3.2 percent	9 million
French	3 percent	8.3 million
American Indian	2.8 percent	7.9 million
Scottish	1.7 percent	4.9 million
Dutch	1.6 percent	4.5 million
Norwegian	1.6 percent	4.5 million
Scottish-Irish	1.5 percent	4.3 million
Swedish	1.4 percent	4 million

The U.S. Census Bureau no longer refers to these groups as ethnic but has changed the name to ancestries. The practice of changing definitions is common for the communist left. The term ethnic has been redefined to include only the groups the government has deemed "special enough" to merit this classification. This is an important distinction because following this reclassification has come the affirmative action (DEI) programs for these "special groups." According to our government, affirmative action is a policy or program providing special advantages for people of a minority group who have traditionally been discriminated against. Therefore, reverse discrimination against other groups is now legally the official remedy.

According to the democratic narrative, blacks have the greatest grievance against the United States due to their slave history. According to their narrative, Black people lived in harmony with each other in bucolic unspoiled Africa. It was the Americans who captured them and enslaved them and brought them to the United States to work on the cotton and tobacco plantations. A review of the history tells a different story.

<u>Black Slavery</u>

Portugal was the first country to establish an African colony at Elmina, which is present day Ghana, in 1471. It found that slaves were available for purchase there from the black coastal tribes.

The Africans didn't see anything wrong with slavery. "Buying and selling human beings had been a part of many African cultures, as a form of serfdom, long before the first white man landed on our shores. If anyone asks me for reparations, I will tell them to follow me to my backyard so I can pluck money from the tree there and give it to them. The Europeans couldn't have gone into the interior to get slaves themselves." (1)

In his book titled *In Defense of German Colonialism*, historian Bruce Gilley dispels the often-told myth that indigenous African people were innocent people living in harmony with each other and nature. "Human sacrifice was common among at least one of the tribes of Cameroon. Slavery was common across both Namibia (Southwest Africa) and the German Colony of German East Africa (present day Tanzania, Rwanda, Barundi and part of Mozambique). The Nama and Herero peoples were engaged in a bloody, genocidal war. The Herero raided native Damara and Saan villages, killing all but the young and strong whom they exploited as slaves. Many of these people escaped to the Germans for protection."

King Ghezo of the Dahomey people had a strong relationship with the European slavers. He was an ally of Francesco Felix de Souza, a Brazilian who emigrated to Africa. He became a respected man in the Kingdom of Dahomey, an honorary chieftain. He helped Ghezo overthrow his predecessor King Adandoan to expand the slave trade. After the coup, Dahomey became very militaristic, raiding its neighbors for the best slaves. Ghezo was a monarch whose whole existence depended on the slave trade. (2)

In the 15ᵗʰ century, black slaves were initially brought to Portugal to work on the farms and plantations. Demand for slaves was high and Black slavery was then expanded to Spain and the Mediterranean. Blacks were found to be especially hardy and able to endure the heat and the other colonial powers (Dutch, English, French, Spanish) began to transport them from the African coast to work the spice plantations in the Caribbean. America was added to this list by Great Britain in the early 17th century as they needed workers for the tobacco and cotton plantations in the southern colonies. At the conclusion of the American Revolution, there were 700,000 black slaves in the 13 colonies. By 1860, this figure had grown to 4 million. In 1863, President Lincoln issued the *Emancipation Proclamation* freeing all slaves, which came to fruition when Gen. Robert E. Lee surrendered to Gen. Ulysses S. Grant on April 9, 1865.

Part of the political narrative in the United States is that the country is bad because it fostered slavery. But history shows us that slavery has been part of human history since the beginning of time. The Egyptians had slaves. Approximately 30 percent of the population of ancient Rome consisted of slaves. "The Court of Cordoba, Spain had 13,000 slaves in 961. Ninth century wealth in Europe was supported by the slave trade. Viking and Russian merchants sold slaves to Muslim buyers in Spain. Irish and Flemish men women and children were brought to Marseilles to be sold. By the mid 10th century, Prague was a major trading center with Viking, Russian and Muslim traders buying and selling slaves. Jewish merchants exported adult slaves, boys and girls to Arabia castrating men on arrival. Muslims raided Slavic bands from eastern Iran with captives turned into eunuchs who were highly valued. Muslim traders also actively traded Northern European slaves in Marseilles. Irish and Flemish slaves were sold in Rouen, France." Slavery was an established international institution BEFORE the United States declared its independence. (3)

The Spanish conquistadores enslaved and eventually killed millions of native peoples in Central and South America, but the Spanish are not vilified, only the Americans are vilified regarding its slave history. This is because its good politics to arouse the blacks every election cycle and blame slavery on the Republicans, although it is the Democrats who enslaved blacks.

Under the leadership of the Republican Party, three amendments were added to the U. S. Constitution -- the 13th, 14th and 15th -- to clarify and codify the freedoms guaranteed black slaves. Unfortunately, the Democrats in the Southern States enacted laws that denied these rights to blacks. While no longer slaves, blacks continued to suffer the indignity of being second class citizens in the former Confederate States. The Civil Rights movement in the 1960s added federal Legislation to supersede the state laws. During this prolonged fight for equal rights, blacks were subjected to discrimination, beatings and sometimes death at the hands of the democratic ruling class.

<u>The Big Lie</u>

The greatest scam perpetrated on the American people in the 20th century was the concept that all white people are homogeneous. In other words, they have the same cultural attitudes toward black people. Let us examine this idea more closely. The white population emigrated from Europe to the United States beginning in the 17th century. First, the Dutch and English came. They were followed by Germans, Scandinavians, French and Spaniards. Later waves included Irish, Italians, Poles, Hungarians, Russians, Chinese, Greeks and various others.

The history of Europe is certainly consistent in one measure. That is, many of the groups identified above have fought each other since the beginning of recorded history. Greek city states invaded north, east and west. Rome invaded Spain, Greece, Britany, Germany and France. The French fought the English the English the Germans, Austrians and of course the Russians. The Russians fought the Germans, the Poles, the Swedes and the Finns. The Germans fought the Russians, British, French, Dutch and Norwegians. The Spanish fought the English.

How many millions of men and women were killed

during all of these wars? How many trillions of dollars were spent on arms for war? How many trillions in property damage ensued?

But now suddenly, we are all to believe that these groups, now settled in America, are culturally homogeneous in their attitudes toward black people and other "people of color" as the new phrasing suggests.

<u>Italians</u>

What about the Italians? They are now included in the white category, but their story is hardly without suffering. "Italian immigrants, most of whom came from Naples and Sicily, faced severe discrimination in the 19th Century. They were called WOPs, which stood for without papers. They were heavily exploited, and in some instances, they were paid less than "white" and "colored" labor. For instance, in the work on New York's Croton Reservoir, says Seton Hall historian William Connell, author of *The Routledge History of Italian Americans.* That wasn't the worst of it. In 1899, the *New York Sun* described the unwritten law of the south, under which, white men could not be lynched-with the exception of the Italians. Italian-Americans were the target of the largest single lynching in American history in New Orleans in 1891. After the police chief of New Orleans was shot, hundreds of Sicilian immigrants were rounded up without cause, and nine were tried for murder. The jury acquitted them, but Mayor Joseph

A. Shakespeare organized a mob of 20,000 people who stormed the prison and murdered the nine men and two other Sicilians who were being held for unrelated charges. A future president was among those cheering on the mob. "Personally, I think it rather a good thing," Theodore Roosevelt wrote to his sister. *The New York Times* editorialized, "These sneaking and cowardly Sicilians, the descendants of bandits and assassins, are to us a pest without mitigations." In 1920, Nicola Sacco and Bartolomeo Vanzetti were executed for an armed robbery in which there was no evidence, except the publicly held belief that because they were anarchists and greasy, sinister looking, they must be guilty. In 1927, a statue of Columbus was erected in Richmond, Va., to the consternation of the Klu Klux Klan. In June 2020, Black Lives Matter protestors toppled the statue, spray painted it and threw it in a lake. These are two groups of racists, both loyal to the same party. (4)

Asians

"The NAACP says that systemic racism is embedded in laws, policies and institutions that uphold and reproduce racial inequities." This sounds very much like what Asian Americans are facing currently, especially in education. Students work hard to obtain the grades, standardized test scores and community service credentials necessary to gain admission to the "select" colleges. Then, they are refused admission because the university believes, equity and diversity, is more important and so blacks are admitted in place of the Asians, which are a "minority," but as they learn when a university denial letter arrives, not a "super minority." Maybe, if they marched, burned and looted stores, they would get more respect and more acceptance letters to Ivy League universities? (5)

Fox news reported on Jan. 16, 2023 that high schools in Northern Virginia failed to notify students of their National Merit Scholar status. The notifications were purposely held up until after the students sent in their college applications. This action negatively distorted their application and opportunity to gain acceptance to highly rated colleges. The rationale was "to not hurt the feelings of those students who did not win." Most of the students impacted were Asian as the left continues their racial assault on Asian Americans. Every adult involved must be terminated, lose their license to teach and be blacklisted nationwide to never be involved or employed in education. It is time to call the Tort lawyers. However, these are Asians. Nothing will be done to punish the school administrators.

In San Francisco, the school board has extended the lottery system it has substituted for the merit- based entrance for Lowell High School, the crown jewel of its public high school system. The school had 82 percent minority student body, but these were not black students, they were Asians. The school board wants more black students in Lowell and so the Asians lose out. Whatever system adds blacks at the expense of other more qualified students is selected by the Board of Education. This is a modern replay of the "Asian Exclusion Act," laws to limit Chinese immigration to America in 1882. But ironically, it is supported by the DEI party. (5)

This all sounds like an extension of the racism against Chinese that has been evident in the policies of the United States for more than 100 years. Chinese were unable to become citizens, they could not testify in court against white people, which made it impossible to seek the assistance of the courts for crimes against them. It was also common for Chinese women to be sold as slaves after the *Emancipation Proclamation*. Their story is never told by the fake media.

<u>Jews</u>

What about the Jews? Even today, Jews are victims of the most hate crimes of any group in the United States according to the FBI. However, there are no preferences for Jews in high school or college entrance evaluations. No government agency checking to see if Jews are present in sufficient numbers in every corporation.

In America, the "white people" include a fisherman from Maine, a Jewish merchant from Brooklyn, peanut farmer from Georgia, a Baptist coal miner from Kentucky, a roughneck from Louisiana, a cattle Rancher from Montana, a corn Farmer from Kansas, a wildcat oil driller from North Dakota, and a gay mayor from California. We are to believe that this groups cultural attitudes are homogeneous toward people of color.

Unfortunately for Americans, this lie was sold, lock stock and barrel to the politicians and courts and resulted in the codification of racism in America. Ever since, Americans have been forced to complete all applications and information forms with the race identity box checked. Human beings are classified not by sex, male and female but by race. The federal, state and local governments collect this information, analyze, sort and conclude by whatever means that "racism" exists in America. The proof of course is that black people are not evenly represented in all areas of society, such as housing, college and professions. But is this a fair way to analyze and evaluate racism? Have we checked other groups to see if they are "fairly represented" in all areas of society? What about people of Polish decent in America? What about Portuguese Americans? Vietnamese Americans? Or let's look at another bodily feature, what about people with blue eyes? Another way to look at this issue is to analyze professional sports. Are there enough Philippine Americans, Mexican Americans, Jewish Americans playing football or basketball or are these racist games, dominated by black Americans? Yes, there are numerous ways to split up a population of humans and analyze and sort it so that you prove the answer you wanted in the first place.

The result of this mistake was the introduction of affirmative action for blacks. In plain language, quotas were "in." The government would investigate companies and educational institutions to ensure blacks were present in sufficient numbers. Children had to be bused to schools many miles from their home to achieve an "acceptable" racial balance. Civil serve exams now had to be "adjusted" by a points system to allow blacks to "pass" to get jobs. Colleges lowered their academic standards to admit blacks as they could not attain the necessary scores on standardized tests like SAT or ACT. If you recall, these tests were originally instituted to eliminate the differences in high school grading and rigor, across the country and around the world. Now the very tests are accused of being "racist." The justification for these special preferences is that blacks were disenfranchised, and it affects their ability to take these tests. Many asserted that the test itself was "racist" because the questions were about white topics. The Supreme Court stepped in to give affirmative action their stamp of approval. Americans were told by Sandra Day O'Connor in the 2003 Supreme Court decision *Gruther vs. Bollinger* that "We expect that in 25 years from now the use of racial preferences will no longer be necessary". That was the justification for a Supreme Court decision that had NO BASIS in law. If anything, racial preferences are growing. Companies have special programs to help finance minority candidates for franchises. (6) This means black candidates. What about Italians, Irish, French, Vietnamese, Chinese, Polish or Filipino Americans? Some companies have specific programs to attract Black candidates. Racial preferences are a powerful tool to affect elections and reward those in power. The truth, however, is simple, preferences for one group constitute discrimination against another. Authority for affirmative action legislation is not in the Constitution. In fact, the Constitution states that all people are equal under the law, the very opposite of affirmative action.

Now that the Supreme Court has changed its mind and ruled against affirmative action in *Students for Fair Admissions Inc. vs President and Fellows of Harvard College,* you can expect to see a tacit change in behavior. However, Harvard is wedded to pushing blacks forward by any means necessary. It will circumvent this decision by changing admission policies. It could be as simple as requiring a photo be sent with your application.

The racial divisions in America reached a crescendo with the death of George Floyd. "This type of social unrest has long been nurtured and exploited by black leaders and their political allies, who have turned the hallowed civil rights movement of the 1960s into a lucrative racket today. These efforts have been abetted by Supreme Court decisions that hem and haw over the legality of racial preferences. The Civil Rights Act of 1964 plainly mandates equal treatment of individuals regardless of race. In its earliest iteration, affirmative action in practice meant an outreach to low-income blacks. Over time, however, quotas and set-asides replaced simple outreach, and racial double-standards in college admissions were defended on the grounds that they enhanced "diversity" on campus. What about adding more polish Americans, Italian Americans, Greek Americans, Indian Americans, Native Americans, Brazilians and Vietnamese to enhance diversity? Don't be ridiculous.

The left asserts that the growing black middle class is a direct result of these policies. However, "the progress toward equality for black Americans didn't begin in 1965, writes Harvard political scientist Robert Putnam and his co-author, Shaylyn Romney Garrett, in the book, *The Upswing*. By many measures, blacks were moving toward parity with whites well before the victories of the Civil Rights movement, despite the limitations imposed by Jim Crow laws. Moreover, after the Civil Rights movement, that longstanding trend toward racial equality slowed, stopped and even reversed. In the 1940s and 1950s, the black/white gaps were shrinking in income, educational attainment, home ownership and other measures. The gaps were shrinking at unprecedented rates that have never been repeated even during the subsequent era of affirmative action. If anything, the evidence shows that racial preferences have coincided with slower black upward mobility." (7)

The media are the culprits for much of the racial narrative in America. Face the facts, hate sells newspapers and TV news stories increase viewership. Stories about whites killing blacks are the best and most profitable for the media. White on white does not have much media interest and black on black crime has NO INTEREST WHATSOEVER. White on black crime is always good for four to eight weeks of stories that regurgitate slavery, Jim Crow and everything that was unfair about black life in America, the pathologies of high unemployment, poverty, poor schools and high crime rates. This results in a knee-jerk reaction for an immediate remedy, usually money. It is at this point that the switch comes, these funds are usually spent on the black-educated class in the form of new or expanded poverty programs (additional jobs or higher wages) as funding for the poor increases. The money never reaches the people who are unemployed in the form of better jobs or more police to reduce the high crime rates or school vouchers to enroll poor children in schools that educate them.

The Race Industry

It is essential for every American to keep in mind that racism is a huge industry in America. Yes, an industry. Just like poverty is an industry. The government bureaucrats are assiduously keeping track of the racial component of every citizen's birth, education, housing, transportation, participation in every activity, marriage, procreation, health and death. The purpose of this is to provide continual reports on how unequal the country is. Of course, this is only accumulated for the specific super minorities. No one cares about what happens to the hundred or so non-super minorities. Because of this fanatical focus on racial equity, America IS a racist country, and the government bureaucracy works hard every day, in every way to keep it that way. America should follow the example of the French. In this instance, the French have transcended this issue by not keeping any records of a person's race. Therefore, France is NOT a racist country. Chief Justice John Roberts agrees, stating "The way to stop discrimination on the basis of race is to stop discriminating on the basis of race." Perhaps, the entire question is moot when so many marriages are now inter-racial (using the governments definitions), "a larger and larger percentage of children are inter-racial so asking the question on census documents, school or work applications does not truly reflect the precise status of the person." (8)

Racial hatred is a subject continually revved up purposely by the Communist Left who run the Democratic Party. The purpose is only for political gain whether to extort money from the federal government to fix racism or to arouse a group into action by demanding racial equity. Should Pakistani Americans riot, burn cars and buildings, and loot stores to gain racial equity because they are under-represented in many companies and industries and probably in government jobs. What about Brazilian Americans? Of course, this is a ridiculous suggestion. But is it? Black people do it regularly and very successfully.

When an Italian American marries, and Argentinian American is that really an interracial marriage? Yes and no. It depends on who sets up the definitions. The government has not included these two ethnic groups in their super minority list, and so it is not officially a racial event and not worth recording in the racial archives of America. Remember Washington is almost entirely run by Democratic Party bureaucrats, so their philosophy always prevails.

If we could evolve to be like France, a country that does not collect racial information and therefore is not racist, we could save ourselves so much time, money and hatred. But this will never happen because racial hatred is a strong political issue that drives donations and voter turnout for Democrats. It is the one issue that keeps 90+ percent of blacks voting for Democrats. The Democratic Party is betting Racism is its ticket to a ONE-PARTY SYSTEM. After all, it only needs a few more states to assure perpetual control of the presidency and the Senate.

The Oregon legislature believes math is racist and ended a high school requirement for proficiency in math to graduate. Advanced math courses were cancelled because of the low number of black students. Good-bye to merit. Hello to false justification to support preferences by the "super minorities." A squared times B squared equals C squared. Euclid was a racist.

After more than 50 years and the expenditure of trillions of dollars on affirmative action programs, the country remains racist according to the experts on these matters. This is the rationale for increasing the effort to eliminate racism against the Democrats grievance groups, namely blacks and gays. This is done by increasing racism and discrimination against white men and Asians.

Let's try to understand who exactly these hard-core white racists are. Obviously, they cannot be people who support blacks. This excuses the Clintons, the Kennedys, Nancy Pelosi, Chuck Schumer, President Biden and the Democratic Party leadership. Of course, the followers of these people are also excused from being racists because they all embrace black people and hew to the party line. We see them on television at Democratic rallies hugging and kissing black leaders everywhere. So, where does this leave us if all white Democrats are absolved from being racists? It leaves the Republicans, conservatives and the independent voters as the guilty, the true American racists.

Is this true? Are Republicans the racists they are accused of being?

A little history is in order to help us gain some perspective on this issue:

- DEMOCRATS imported black slaves to the southern colonies to work on their plantations.

- DEMOCRATS organized the Confederate States of America (CSA) to maintain slavery.

- DEMOCRATS financed the CSA and started the Civil War.

- DEMOCRATS were the political and military leaders of the CSA. Jefferson Davis, the president of the CSA was a Democratic senator from Mississippi.

- DEMOCRATS enacted a variety of Jim Crow laws after the Civil War to deny blacks the opportunity to purchase land, homes, vote, attend schools and obtain jobs.

- DEMOCRATS organized and financed the KLU KLUX KLAN to intimidate, punish and kill blacks.

- DEMOCRATS fought the enactment of Civil Rights legislation.

- DEMOCRATS disallowed black WWII veterans' education benefits from the G.I. Bill

- DEMOCRATS recruited black women with children to apply for welfare across the country leading to the establishment of present day black inner-city ghettos entrapping them in perpetual poverty.

- DEMOCRATS enacted urban renewal laws that allowed the federal government to use eminent domain to confiscate land, homes and businesses in black inner-city neighborhoods to build highways and housing projects, which destroyed black neighborhoods and further destroyed black communities.

- DEMOCRATS support open border policies that allow illegals to bid down labor rates for unskilled labor and shutting out blacks for these job opportunities.

- REPUBLICANS under President Lincoln fought the Civil War to end slavery. Three hundred sixty thousand, mostly white, Union soldiers died to end the scourge of slavery in the United States.

- REPUBLICANS enacted the 13th, 14th and 15th constitutional amendments to assure blacks equal standing with whites.

- REPUBLICANS fought unjust Jim Crow laws in

southern states to exclude blacks from voting.

- REPUBLICANS supported President Lyndon Johnson's Civil Rights legislation.

- REPUBLICANS support a closed border and the removal of Illegals who take American jobs (mostly from poor blacks).

The evidence completely absolves Republicans from the charge they are racist and raises the question: "Why does any black person support the Democratic Party?" Supposedly because the Democrats championed Civil Rights legislation in the 1960s. Blacks started migrating to the Democratic Party when they were awarded freebees from FDR. Here, the evidence again needs to be reviewed. More Republicans voted FOR Civil Rights legislation than Democrats, so why are Republicans accused of being racist, and the Democrats continue to have this charge, supported by the evidence listed above, exonerated? Frankly, because 1) Democrats control the media and 2) Democrats have bought off the new black leadership.

The Diversity Illusion

"Give them an inch and they'll take a yard" is an old saying, and it is certainly true of the Diversity Police who now are a growing segment of the faculty at the prestigious Dalton School in New York City. While this school has been run in recent years by liberal N.Y.

Democrats who have children of this same group, the ever-increasing demands of the Diversity Police are starting to rankle even this leftist group of parents. "The recent racist demands from 120 teachers included the following:

- Expand the Office of Diversity to at least 12 staffers.

- Reroute 50 percent of the school contributions to the New York City Public School System

- Compensate any black student or student of color who participates in antiracism initiatives

- Require courses in Black Liberation and challenges to white supremacy and yearly antiracist training for employees, trustees and Parent Association volunteers

- Ensure that there is no correlation between a students' racial background and their ability to be successful at Dalton." (9)

Maybe, the school should change, admit only black students and just give them a diploma recording an A in every class while not requiring the students to attend any classes.

President Biden has promised "the single most diverse cabinet based on race, color and gender that has ever existed in America." After two years of this diversity

cabinet, Americans see it for what it is -- less competent than the Keystone Cops, and they (the cops) knew
they were trying to be screwballs. Biden's cabinet is
without a doubt the least-qualified, least-experienced
collection of fools that has ever been assembled in
the White House. The border is open, the Consumer
Price Index is indicating 8 percent inflation and fore-
casted to continue to increase. Inflation may continue
for years. A banking crisis, in which three of the four
largest bank insolvencies in history, have occurred.
The problems are caused by 1) overspending by Congress, 2) overstimulation by the incompetent Federal
Reserve Chairman, Jerome Powell and 3) the War on
Energy by the Biden administration that has decreased
supplies of oil and natural gas in the United States
and increased prices.4) regulatory policies that are
anti-business and anti-the American people 5) Lack of
proper oversight of banks as long as they espoused the
DEI and ESG manifesto. Every problem is addressed by
spending more money. The fact that the country must
borrow the money is of no consequence to the Biden
administration or any Democrats.

The Biden administration has two gods -- climate
change and diversity. Every decision made in the
White House is first passed through a screen to assess
the impact on their gods. They truly believe the diversity cabinet is a major achievement. (NO Italians, No
Native Americans, No Chinese Americans, No Pacific
Island Americans, No Greek Americans, No Vietnam-

ese Americans, No Pakistani Americans on the diversity cabinet). The American people want a cabinet of competent people with a leader, Biden has delivered neither. Virtue signaling to his base just cannot get the job done. Although it is evident from the interviews that Biden and his staff just do not care about the problems and obstacles of the working- class Americans. They could fix the problems (high gas prices), but they won't because high gas prices make the climate change god happy. The American people are not stupid. They have seen other administrations at work. The Biden administration is more incompetent than the Carter administration and even worse than the Obama administration.

The government will continue to coerce the education, military, government and business sectors to follow the WOKE policies and pay homage to their twin gods. Unfortunately for America, these policies will ultimately destroy the country as they work together to defeat the primary strength of America, the merit system. "Continuing to give jobs to a selected group of minority candidates, even though they are not the most qualified candidates cannot bring these super minorities equality." These can only be obtained by hard work and individual achievement, just like other people. (10)

"Diversity has become the most powerful word in higher education today." At most universities, a huge bureaucracy has been institutionalized to ensure the diversity goals are achieved and that anyone caught violating the diversity creed is at least cowed and most probably severely punished (cancelled or expelled) for his or her infraction. Every activity in the university is subject to the test of whether it meets the ever-more strict guidelines of diversity and inclusion. Looking in from the outside, one sees a cult with the fervor of a mob during the French Revolution, constantly searching for "Republicans" to try to send to the guillotine. Yes, the analogy is so appropriate. (11)

To those who can see through the entire Diversity movement, it is very clearly a political action by the Democratic Party to increase the power of the party by increasing the power of their favorite grievance groups at the expense of all other groups of Americans. The big lie here is that these are the only minorities, that we have previously discussed in length that no other group in America has any grievance. Once again, do Jews, Italians or Chinese Americans have grievances? Of course, they are not agitated and organized to seek reparations in the form of special privileges. Why don't ugly fat men and women get high paying jobs as TV anchors? Shouldn't they organize and have a grievance? What about 5'5" Filipino Americans who cannot get a high paying job playing in the NBA? Shouldn't they organize and express their grievance? Many people have grievances about a system that they believe is not fair, but only the Democratic Party Super minorities are allowed to voice their grievances and gain politically. Law firms have weighed in to offer "diversity audits" to ensure they pass the smell test for numbers of "diverse" people. (12)

In a recent call for "diversity," black activists are calling for more black people on the boards of corporations. This has spawned a new industry to "prepare" black people for board membership. Board members have historically been selected from pools of retired chief executive officers and presidents because their role and value to the company is to advise the CEO on strategic issues. Individuals who attend "prep" classes are NOT QUALIFIED because they do not have the experience but because they are black, they receive special consideration. What about Italian, Polish, Mexican, Vietnamese board members? These groups each have less ethnic representation in the U. S. population than blacks and therefore are mathematically more entitled to the term minority. Sorry, these groups are not part of the Democratic Party's super minorities group. And so, when the CEO of a multinational confronts declining sales and profits in ALL business units, is he/she going to ask the new black board member who recently graduated from Board Prep school for advice? Don't bet your lunch money. (13)

The establishment of the DEI Police across the country in every institution is essentially a "soft" introduction of a secret police organization into the United States. Under the false banner of doing good for mistreated minorities, the police will slowly expand their power to force conformity to the communists' ever-increasing rules of behavior. They will systematically destroy the constitutional rights of Americans. Freedom of speech, freedom of the press, freedom of assembly, the right of self-defense, freedom of religion, freedom from unreasonable search and seizure of property and the right to a speedy trial already are disappearing. When Amazon decided that certain books were racist and refused to sell them or libraries removed books from shelves, the First and 14th Amendments were violated. The Biden administration has violated every one of these rights since taking office. Unfortunately, the Republican politicians and conservative media have done little to fight back.

The Melting Pot

America, unlike most countries, is a melting pot of hundreds of ethnic and religious groups from around the world. Many of these "newcomers" were not always greeted with open arms. They were "different" and people were wary of "different" people. The sole purpose of the Diversity movement is to brainwash thousands of young, impressionable students to support their individual grievance group, which, in turn, supports the Democratic Party. This party wants to build a one-party Communist country that it will run using the same playbook used at colleges. The fact is that the Diversity police in colleges treat everyone who is not a super minority like second-hand citizens with no rights, much like the treatment of Jews in Nazi Germany.

What is discouraging about today's academic culture is the unprecedented weight that these grievances are given by teachers, students and administrators alike. Even raising them puts one on high moral ground that requires all other considerations to be put aside until the grievance has been assuaged by an appropriate act of contrition: apologize and reform or face the consequences. This is like the cultural revolution in China where people were forced to conform to the new orthodoxy or face the punishment to be identified, called out and then to lose your job, friends or be cancelled. Many were separated from their families and sent to "re-education" camps (prisons) by the government. What is so ironic about this movement <u>in the universities across the United States is that the movement is based on a lie and the administrators and faculty, who consider themselves "the smartest people in the country" are being used as pawns to perpetrate this lie.</u>

"It is hard to see how we can address social disparities if we can't have honest conversations about what's driving them. A Georgetown University law professor was terminated for musing aloud that year after year, many of her black students tended to have the lowest grades. A University of Pennsylvania law professor expressed a similar sentiment and was reprimanded for her remarks. They were attacked as racists for something that is well-known among academics at elite institutions but that you are not allowed to discuss." Black and Hispanic kids are admitted to elite universities for diversity reasons, and they are poor students. (14)

"What happened in higher education after racial preferences were introduced is what social scientists call "mismatching." Black students were admitted to schools with academic credentials far below those of the average student in attendance. Subsequently, these black students struggled academically, dropped out at higher rates, or were more likely to switch to an easier major than they originally intended to study. They were set up to fail because the institution wanted to promote diversity." (15)

"Peter Arcidiacono, an economist at Duke University, and two of his colleagues, Ken Spenner and Esteban Aucejo, published an academic paper in 2012 on how racial preferences affect the number of science and economics majors at elite universities. They found that while 76 percent of black applicants chose a major in economics or a hard science, only 35 percent went on to receive a degree in one of these fields. They found the attrition rate of 41 percent was due to the difference in admission test scores." Thus, the admission of less qualified students to inflate the school's DEI credentials does not help the student succeed. It also supports the fact that so many students graduate with lots of debt and degrees in soft subjects that do not lead to well-paying jobs. (16)

If you support the Diversity movement, you, in fact, support the Communist takeover of America and the loss of your personal freedom. First the freedoms of the "Republicans" will be eviscerated as they are forced into submission then you will be next when the government finds some other excuse to persecute you.

Americans must fight the DEI movement in every place they find it. It is not so easy now. School administrators are attempting to persecute 8th graders for not using the correct pronouns. Employees are afraid to speak up because they may lose their job. "State Universities in Virginia make DEI ideology a veritable requirement for employment." Unfortunately, history is filled with examples of individuals who were threatened by totalitarian regimes, whether government or other institutions to conform. The name of one of those individuals was George Washington. Tyranny is tyranny is tyranny. Never accept it. (17)

<u>Racism</u>

"A belief that race is the primary determinant of human traits and capacities and that racial differences produce an inherent superiority of a particular race."

Websters Dictionary.

When you read the definition carefully, it certainly describes Hitlers Master Race theory of the German people but does not apply to America in 2022. "The power of the word racism -- always cocked, aimed and ready to fire -- makes it impossible to say anything outside the most obeisant praise about black culture, black politicians, black entertainers or black anything." This present situation is the opposite of the life blacks lived in the South 100 years ago where they were systematically oppressed and made to feel inferior in nearly every way possible. The Woke culture and Diversity police have now flipped the script and treat anyone who does not prostrate themselves on the altar of their beliefs as racists while in effect they are the true racists. (18)

America went through something very similar in the 1950s and early 1960s, but not as pronounced when any criticism of Jews was met with the response you are antisemitic. Fortunately, this was short-lived as Jewish people realized that criticism was part of the give and take of ideas. They realized that being so defensive had more downside than advantages. The same is true now because there can be no serious discussion of the problems facing black Americans. Racism is used to deflect any criticism of policies developed by Democratic white and black politicians to improve the lives of black citizens. The policies are a dismal failure. The old expression "the best defense is a robust offense" applies here. The more the Democrats spew out racial hatred against Republicans and apply charges of racism to everything they do not agree with, the less attention is directed at their failure. The ever-increasing crime, poverty, drug addiction and hopelessness of poor blacks living in Democratic run cities. The purposeful poor teaching by the teacher's union to keep blacks uneducated and poor. The inconsolable pain and grief of black mothers in these cities who have lost their children to gang violence.

"The best solution, perhaps, is for black Americans to cease thinking of themselves as victims and to recognize that the real racists in this country are those who insist blacks are permanent victims and always will be so in what they claim is an irretrievably, hopelessly racist America." (18)

Racial discrimination is no longer the most significant factor in the advancement of blacks economically. This is the conclusion of William Julius Wilson's book, *The Declining Significance of Race* published in 1978. While white racism in its new form of "systemic racism" is a major component of every Democratic election, every speech by a Democratic governmental official and a talking point in every Democratic fundraiser, the facts are not supportive of the false assertion. The Democrats will continue to label everyone with a different viewpoint on any number of issues a racist. So what else is new? "Evidence of racial bias in the past is not proof that racism is responsible for current social disparities. The pathologies seen in low-income black communities are not confined to those communities." (19)

"Black poverty and employment are more a function of family formation than of white racism. For more than 20 years, black couples have had poverty rates in the single digits and black married men have had a higher labor force participation rate than unmarried white men." John Iceland of Penn State University has concluded that "Differences in family structure are the most significant variable in explaining the black-white affluence gap." "Liberal politicians and activists have little interest in addressing ways in which black behavioral choices impact inequality. It's easier to turn out voters and raise money by equating racial imbalances with racial bias." (19)

Critical Race Theory

Critical Race Theory refers to an idea that emerged some 40 years ago in academia. The ideas originators, most famously the late Harvard professor Derek Bell, argued that "race" infuses virtually every aspect of American social reality. The idea was as debatable then as it is now. No proof was ever offered. Except now, debate is dead." The greatest proof of the fallacy of this theory is the large and growing number of inter-racial marriages. Indeed, it proves that love is the overriding human emotion. (20)

Critical Race theory rejects the principle of equality of opportunity. Its adherents insist that equality of opportunity is a myth, not a reality, in today's America and that those who pursue it are misguided. The real goal is equality of results, measured by black share of income, wealth and social standing. Critical race theorists reject the idea that sought-after goods should be distributed through systems that evaluate and reward "merit." (21) Of course, this completely made-up theory only applies to black Americans not to Chinese, Japanese, Italian, Jewish or any other of the hundred plus minorities. CRT has no scientific basis because social scientists like Ibram X. Kendi are NOT scientists at all.

"In October of 2020, Chris Wallace asked President Trump why he directed federal agencies to end racial sensitivity training that addresses white privilege or critical race theory. President Trump answered 'because it is racist. They were teaching people to hate our country.' 'Nobody is doing that', Joe Biden replied. He was wrong."(22)

Critical race theory training sessions in public agencies have pushed a deeply ideological agenda that included reducing people to a racial essence, segregating them, and judging them by their group identity rather than individual character, behavior and merit. Remember

Martin Luther King's famous "I Have a Dream" speech where he stated that he wants an America where people are not judged by the color of their skin but by their character.

Diversity trainer, Howard Ross, taught Treasury Department employees that America was built on the backs of people who were enslaved and that "all white Americans are complicit in a system of white supremacy by automatic response to the ways we're taught."

In accompanying documents, Ross argues that whites share an inborn oppressive streak. Whiteness, employees are told, includes white privilege and white supremacy. Consequently, whites struggle to own their racism. He instructs managers to conduct listening sessions in which black employees can speak about their experience and be seen in their pain while white employees are instructed to sit in the discomfort and not fill the silence with your own thoughts and feelings.

At the Sandia National Laboratory, which develops technology for Americas nuclear arsenal, executives held a racially segregated training session for white male employees. The event set the goal of examining white male culture and making employees take responsibility for their white, male and heterosexual privilege (and this was a racial sensitivity training session). In one of the opening exercises, the instructor wrote on the whiteboard that white male culture can be associated with white supremacists, KKK, Aryan Nation, Make America Great Again hat and mass killings. On the final day, the trainers asked employees to write letters to women (this was racial sensitivity training) and people of color. One participant apologized for his privilege, and another pledged to be a better ally.

"At the Department of Homeland Security, employees and diversity trainers held a session on microaggressions, based on the work of psychologist Derald Sue. In his academic work, Sue argues that white Americans have been fed a racial curriculum based on falsehoods, unwarranted fears, and the belief in their own superiority and thus have been socialized into oppressor roles. Trainers taught Homeland Security employees that the myth of meritocracy and colorblindness is a foundation of racist microaggressions and microinequities. The trainers insisted that statements, such as 'America is the Land of Opportunity,' 'Everybody can succeed in this society if they work hard enough' and 'I believe the most qualified person should get the job' are racist and harmful -- merely code for people of color are lazy and incompetent and need to work harder. If a white employee disagrees, he is dismissed as a denier of individual racism another type of microaggression."

Sue has apparently never heard of the National Basketball league nor the National Football League, sports franchises that recruit based "on merit" who are predominantly composed of black Americans. Nor has he watched the summer Olympics where the track and field events are dominated by black athletes from around the world. (Never let the facts contradict a good narrative.) Then, there are people like Damon John, CEO of FUBU, a self-made BLACK billionaire who got rich by working hard and building his businesses.

There is no doubt that these so-called training sessions are cosmetically encased indoctrination sessions and persecution of specific groups of white men. We have seen these methods used before in the Soviet Union, Communist China, Vietnam and Cambodia. Forcing people to adopt beliefs they know are lies to avoid punishment. The fact that the government has been infiltrated to this level must concern all Americans and people around the world who believe in democracy. WAKE UP AMERICA! The communists are here, among us. We are in a war to save our country.

White supremacy, critical race theory and racial superiority theories have been mostly espoused by black professors, probably to gain notoriety and separate themselves from the crowd of "average" professors. This is social science claptrap with no basis in fact whatsoever. No proof is ever submitted. No actual "science" is evident. Many of these professors "hallucinate" these theories instead of depending on concrete studies that can be documented, and the results duplicated by other professionals. What is surprising is that many of these people have gained their positions due to affirmative action programs. They were not the best qualified, but they were the people imbued with the highest level of hate for America.

Ethnic Studies

Ethnic studies, one of the new buzzwords for racism, is moving ahead in school systems across the country. Of course, the super liberal states are leading the way. In California, a new curriculum has been adopted to be taught in every high school and will most likely be required for graduation very soon. Stanford Professor Thomas Dee believes that ethnic studies "don't exclusively emphasize victimization," they stress "the considerable cultural assets" of minorities. As discussed above, everyone in America comes from a minority ethnic group. There are 100 or more. Why are they being studied at all? Because it is all about victimhood for the super minorities. California's model curriculum excludes many ethnic groups (Italians, Irish, Poles, Vietnamese, Chinese, Japanese, Filipinos, Jews and Armenians who came to America to escape persecution). It also fails to include the European persecution of the Protestants and Catholics who settled in America in the 17th century. They were the original white settlers of America. (23)

"The California ethnic studies focusing solely on blacks, Latinos, Asian-Americans and American Indians. Focusing solely on these groups and treating them as victims (of discrimination by the other ethnic groups), it fails to teach students how ethnic groups can climb the economic ladder, making use of their cultural assets and the opportunities the country affords them." This curriculum further justifies the success of Irish and Jewish immigrants as derived from securing white privilege rather than through their own hard work.

Welcome to "critical ethnic studies," California style, which boils down to vulgar Marxism, identity politics and victimology," brainwashing children to hate people of different ethnic backgrounds.

Some people are fighting back against the equity programs that are just racial preferences for the Democrats grievance groups, namely their core constituencies. Washington State passed a law preventing the government "from discriminating or granting preferential treatment based on race, sex, color, ethnicity or national origin in public employment, education and contracting." Opponents, including Asians for Equity, fought back. (24)

The very vocal minority who is leading the effort to transform America is attempting to replace parents' right to bring up their children, specifically to teach them about sex when the parent believes they should. These ideologues want the state to replace the parents and, of course, teach children their views on sex from the earliest days when the state begins to have control over children, namely kindergarten and first grade. To them, it is never too early to begin indoctrinating children to become sexual deviants, whatever deviancy they eventually choose is okay with the LGBTQIA2s+ group.

"These people seek to redefine American pluralism and what it means to be an open and tolerant society. The fact that most Americans would see people who are different then they are in a tolerant manner was the established norm. Unfortunately, this group of ideologues and sexual deviants wants the rules changed. They want to set the standard for what all children are taught. It is no longer acceptable to be tolerant, now individuals and institutions must be a participant in a campaign to reorient our culture. It is they who are now intolerant of any other viewpoint." (25)

These groups are extremely well-organized and funded. Many of them scan the Internet for impressionist children who they start a dialogue with, entice them into their "chat room" to discuss gender issues and slowly indoctrinate and coerce the children into believing they are NOT heterosexual but another "deviant." They are "told" by individuals in chat rooms they must be gender fluid and pansexual if they have any sexual identity questions. If they don't completely agree, then they are further threatened with disassociation as not truly supportive of the LGBTQ community. "You can't just say you support the LGBTQ community; you have to be in it. And if you are part of it, you have to find a very specific label and stick with it." For young impressionable children who are seeking to belong to something, this is the coercion process. Sexual deviants want to increase their power, and they need more individuals to "identify" with their perversive behavior. This is how they "enlist" children. Schools then add their "false narratives" regarding sex, gender and race and one can see how many impressionable children suddenly decide they are a deviant. (26)

The Obama Factor

While President Obama campaigned as a moderate and rarely used race as a reason to vilify whites. When elected, he completely changed. His racism became apparent in almost all domestic issues. He played the race card daily, dividing a country that had looked to a black president to bring Americans together. He repeatedly took sides in police incidents involving black suspects. He dispatched Attorney General Eric Holder to attack voter ID laws as racist (which he continues to do). He made one of the country's most polarizing figures, Al Sharpton, his point man on civil rights. Obama was a racist.

Footnotes:

1-"When Slave Traders Were African," Adaobi Tricia Nwaubani, *WSJ*, 9/21/2019

2-Frederick E. Forbes, Commander, British Royal Navy

3-"The Silk Roads," Peter Frankopan

4-"Columbus Day Stands for Diversity," Alexandra Bocchi, *WSJ*, 10/12/2020

5-"Systemic Anti-Asian Bias," William McGurn, *WSJ*, 12/7/2021

6-"McDonald's Aims to Lift Minority Ownership," Heather Haddon, *WSJ*, 12/9/2021

7-"With Justice Barrett, Is the End Near for Racial Preferences?" Jason L. Riley, *WSJ*, 10/28/2020

8-"The Predicament of Counting Americans by Race," Janet Adamy and Paul Overberg, *WSJ*, 11/28/2020

9-"Revolution Consumes New York's Elite Dalton School," Scott C. Johnson, *WSJ*, 12/20/2020

10-"The Tyranny of Diversity," Joseph Epstein, *WSJ*, 12/31/2021

11- "The Downside of Diversity," Anthony Kronman, *WSJ*, 8/3/2019

12-"Law Firms Jockey to Help Firms with Race and Diversity Audits," Erin Mulvaney, *WSJ*, 9/3/2022

13-"Board Diversity Drive Sparks New Training," Emily Glazer and Theo Francis, *WSJ*, 1/3/2022

14-"McDonald's CEO Apologizes for Telling a Simple Truth," Jason L. Riley, *WSJ*, 11/10/2021

15-"Racial Preferences Harm Beneficiaries, Too," Jason L. Riley, WSJ, 10/5/2022

16-"A Chance to Remove Race from College Admissions," Jason L. Riley, *WSJ*, 1/26/2022

17-"A Simple First Step for Youngkin to Stop Leftist Tyranny," R. R. Reno, *WSJ*, 11/8/2021

18-"What Would We Do Without the Word Racism?" Joseph Epstein, *WSJ*, 8/3/2019

19-"The Race Card Has Gone Bust," Jason L. Riley, *WSJ*, 7/17/2019

20-"Banning Critical Race Theory," Donald Henninger, *WSJ*, 6/3/2021

21-"A Deeper Look at Critical Race Theory," William A. Galston, *WSJ*, 7/21/2021

22-"The Truth About Critical Race Theory," Christopher F. Rufo, *WSJ*, 10/5/2020

23-"Critical Ethnic Studies Returns to California," Williamson M. Evers, *WSJ*, 8/28/2020

24-"Tech Workers and Asians Against Racial Preferences," John Carlson, *WSJ*, 10/26/2019

25-"Disney Decides to go for Woke," Gerard Baker, *WSJ*, 4/5/2022

26- "How Gender Forums Online Can Pose Risks," Julie Jargon, *WSJ*, 10/25/2021

Chapter 11 Reform Is Not a Dirty Word

<u>Background</u>

If you travel around the world, there are two conversations you can have with every soul, the weather and the government. Of course, the government conversation varies among countries, but there is always some grousing about politicians. Citizens complain that politicians:

- talk a lot but do little or nothing to solve problems

- promise but never deliver on the promises

- are corrupt, accepting bribes from lobbyists and big business

- place their own interests above the peoples

Some of the highest government positions are continually filled by industry veterans to protect that industry. These include the position of secretary of the treasury which is almost always filled by Wall Street bankers. These individuals' primary allegiance is to Wall Street because they know their government service will be short and they can return to Wall Street with a better paying position. This cozy relationship creates serious conflicts of interest. A case in point is the action of Secretary Hank Paulson during the initial phase of the mortgage crisis. It was his firm Goldman Sachs that was the primary villain in selling derivative investments to investors who were naïve. Many of these individuals or groups managed pension investments for cities, states and foreign governments. Not truly understanding the complex mathematics involved in the derivative, they believed the involvement of Goldman was assurance enough that the derivative was a good investment tool that would benefit their investment community. In many, many instances the leverage created by the derivative assured it would create large losses. Goldman was acting for Goldman not the investors, earning huge fees on each derivative sold. It was like selling swamp land to first graders. We learned that many of the individuals in government responsible for investing money are not too sophisticated. Maybe their pride would not allow them to "just say no" and instead signed agreements they did not fully understand. Whatever the reason, the result was a financial disaster.

As a former executive of Goldman, Paulsen has a substantial amount of money tied up in Goldman stock. His decision to force AIG, who did not sell the worthless derivatives, to cover the insurance of the derivative contracts to Goldman caused AIG to file for bankruptcy protection. Goldman made millions of dollars; the investors got screwed. Was he protecting his per-

sonal interest first and foremost? We can only spec-
ulate. The larger issue here for Americans is whether
individuals should be placed in these very responsible
and powerful positions with such obvious conflicts of
interest.

<u>Ethics</u>

Stories abound of robber barons who had suitcases
filled with cash delivered to prominent members of
Congress in return for favors. In the modern era, the
art of influence is more sophisticated. There are no
suitcases of cash (or none the public is aware of) because they are concerned about whistleblowers. That
still leaves the influence peddler a litany of options to
transfer wealth to the members of Congress, senators
or cabinet secretaries. Junkets are legal. Hosting din-
ners for donors is legal. Providing manpower for an
election is legal. Providing investment advice and the
ability to purchase hot initial public offerings (IPO)
is legal. Providing information on real estate investments that later may be rezoned or purchased for
development is also legal for members of Congress.
The use of the private jets of "friends" is legal. There
is never a clear-cut quid pro quo on any specific deal.
Lobbyists are "working with members of Congress" to
educate them regarding the complexities (why is the
legislation so complex the elected member of Congress
cannot figure it out?) of the proposed piece of legislation (which many times the lobbyists lawyers wrote).

Also, public speaking gigs are legal for themselves
and their family. Their goal is to engender goodwill
so that when they need support for legislation, yea or
nay, they can call the member and just ask for their
support, call in a favor for a favor. You know quid pro
quo. Elected officials' priority is always survival in the
<u>political space. That means getting re-elected. There
is never enough money available to win an election.
Lobbyists are the bankers of the ruling class in Washington just like the Rothschilds were the bankers of
the European monarchies.</u>

Of course, insider trading is also legal. Members of
Congress are aware earlier than anyone how a piece
of legislation will affect companies and industries.
They and their families can buy and sell depending on
the information and profit. Ask Nancy Pelosi, who has
built up the family fortune to over $200 million by do-
ing just that. Will she be investigated? Was Hillary investigated? She sold favors when she was the secretary
of State. Do you think all those foreign governments
and Communist oligarchs were interested in the work
of the Clinton Foundation? After her term as secretary of State, the Clinton Foundation could not raise
enough money for a McDonalds Happy Meal. Some
politicians reach a level where they are truly untouch-
able. These two surely have.

Congress has an ethics committee but hardly anyone
is ever chastised by it. As the previous discussion enu-

merates, there are many legal situations for Congress that would never be tolerated for employees of companies and certainly not for senior executives of public companies. Congress writes its own rules as members write their own laws. The fact is that these rules need to be tightened up considerably to assure the public that the elected official is in office, at least partially, for the interest of the people. How can we achieve this? Keep writing letters to your congressional representative. Some of them are truly honest and want to be part of a body that is perceived by the public as being honorable and NOT for sale.

The Role of Government

When you step back and consider what is happening in America, no person with basic common sense can believe the government operates for the benefit of the people.

More recently in the aftermath of the 2016 election, we are learning more every week about the gigantic, government conspiracy to accuse falsely, discredit and impeach a sitting president. The fact that this cabal was organized by government employees at the highest levels of the Justice Department, the FBI, various intelligence services and maybe with the support of, or at least the acquiescence of, the former president and the federal court is mind boggling in a country that regularly holds its justice system up to the rest of the world as the "standard of excellence."

Wake up Americans! Your Justice Department is not much different than the Russians.

These are a few of the many examples that can be outlined to demonstrate the problems that exist in the government today. Most people would agree when confronted with the fact that this behavior is unacceptable. Unfortunately, the longer it endures, the more it becomes the norm and not a behavior to be rejected, attacked and eliminated. Since the Obama administration, we have seen a steady increase in the level of political persecution of Republicans by the deep state. The Democrats and their allies, the left-wing media, propagate false narratives against their enemies, the Republicans, conservatives and the religious. Trust in the institutions that were established to protect people is at an all-time low. When the government is no longer perceived to be honest and apolitical by the people, then the degradation of society begins in earnest. Society is built on each person's belief that he or she is being treated equally under the law. This belief encourages the individual to "follow the rules."

As Liz Wheeler used to state on "One American News," America is at a tipping point. Many Americans no longer believe that the federal government operates for the benefit of the people. In fact, the institutions act for the benefit of the wealthy, well-connected private citizens, corporations and the influential members of the government.

America is a country in decline, rotting away from the inside outward. Nuclear weapons, guided missile submarines and space-launched rockets cannot save it from itself. The American government works mostly for the ruling class. Working people just pay the bills.

So, this begs the question, how would you reform government if you had the power to do so?

<u>Term Limits</u>

The very first reform that should be enacted by the federal government should be term limits. This law should cover not only the president and Congress but also for every elected and appointed official in the country. One term period, no exceptions. People like Anthony Fauci, Nancy Pelosi, Chuck Schumer and countless others need to be recycled out of government. The country needs to move beyond the era of professional politicians for life to a citizen soldier mentality. You run for office, serve your time and recycle back into private life. The present system creates power centers for certain elected officials and political parties in states that are red or blue, making it almost impossible for new candidates of either party to compete against entrenched officials. Once a person gets into Congress, it becomes almost impossible to remove them. Incumbency allows them to raise more money, call in more favors and utilize the party apparatus to power up their campaign and subsequently stay in the office. America would be better off with new people in government, regularly replacing the previous office holder. If there is only one election for each person, it becomes much more difficult to bribe them with campaign donations for favors.

Gerrymandering

When a party in power reaches a level of majority, members will redistrict the state into voting districts that allow them to win even more elections and increase their power and their ability to ward off challenges by the opposing party. In Illinois, the Democrats not only gerrymandered the legislative districts but also then redesigned the districts for the election of judges. With a majority of judges, other issues brought before the courts would be decided by Democratic judges adding to the obstacles to get any Republican representation. (1)

We must find a better way to set up voting districts.

Election Funding

The next reform is the reduction of money in politics. For many years, the orthodox thinking in the United States was that whoever raised the most money would have a significant advantage in an election. President Trump's election proved that was not always true, but still, it does not negate the need to remove money from politics. Why? Because this is the beginning of the chain of influence on candidates and political parties. Money gets you access; access gets you influence; and influence gets you favors. Favors can make a bad company profitable, at least for a period of time. Money keeps sugar prices artificially high in the United States. Money kept Solyndra afloat during the Obama years. Money is the oil that lubricates politics and has been for many years. Some votes are bought for a price, such as cash, debit card and cell phone. Only American citizens of voting age should be allowed to contribute to candidates. Limits for each should be set and enforced.

During the 2020 election, a non-profit called the Center for Technology and Civic Life (CTCL), funded by Mark Zuckerberg, gave $350 million to 2,500 election departments. "CTCL consistently gave bigger grants and more money per capita to counties that voted for Biden." Why can rich people provide millions to influence elections when the individual donation limit is $3,300 per candidate, and the party limit is $41,300? (1)

We should have no corporate contributions, no labor union contributions, no PACS and no massive contributions from the wealthy. Contributions should only come from individuals of voting age who are U. S. citizens with limits that are enforced.

<u>Transparency</u>

The very next reform is transparency. To reduce the perception that contracts are awarded to friends, donors and cronies, all government contracts should be awarded using a transparent methodology. The contract should be announced together with the requirements. Companies should be required to post a performance bond. All contracts should state the deliverables by quantity, quality and time with penalties for late performance and remedies for replacement of the vendor. All contracts, qualifications and awards should be posted on the appropriate government website so everyone can see the status of the contract bid and performance once awarded. If there are five equally qualified vendors, then draw straws in a public forum. Contract preferences for special groups must be eliminated. These are simply political preferences. As no ethnic group in the United State is a majority, then all people are minorities and should be afforded equal opportunity to federal, state and local contracts.

<u>Election Reform</u>

The election of 2020 demonstrated to Americans that political activists can change the rules midway into an election cycle, and these changes can change the election results from candidate A to candidate B. The election also demonstrated that partisanship trumps the law in every part of government, such as judges, governors, secretaries of state, senators and representatives all ignored major violations of election law in numerous states to arrive at the result the Democrats, media and big tech wanted.

The concept of, a fair and transparent election, was violated in so many places and in so many ways that any person with common sense would be completely correct in comparing elections in the United States to those in Russia, Venezuela, Cuba and totalitarian led countries across the globe.

It is so ironic that the United States, the country that preaches to other countries about election integrity, allows dishonest practices in its elections. It is also ironic that the person most connected to election integrity, namely Jimmy Carter, for his participation in election oversite around the world watched as his party violated countless election laws to win and did nothing. Hypocrisy is alive and well. This is a perfect example of why Americans have no faith in politicians. They will do whatever it takes to win -- lie, cheat, steal or defame others.

How can a political party, called the Democrats, continue to tell voters that showing a photo identification is racist and voter suppression? Is showing an ID to collect social security benefits suppression? Is showing and ID to register a child for kindergarten, denying a child the right to attend school? Is showing ID to obtain a driver's license suppressing the rights of blacks to drive? Is asking for a photo ID at a house closing intended to block minorities from purchasing houses? Of course, the answer to each of these questions is NO. The same is true for asking for an ID to vote.

These are just a few examples that illustrate the absurdity of this position. Yet, it continues. Someone once said, "if you tell a lie often enough, it becomes the truth." That may be true for weak-minded people but not for the rest of us.

America's elections and its election law in many states need to be reformed to adhere to the highest standard of transparency and integrity. (Refer to *2000 Mules*, a documentary by Dinesh DeSousa) All voters must feel assured that every election is carried out honestly. So, what exactly does this rhetoric mean when it is transformed into policy?

First, elections in a democracy must be strictly about the will of the people, human beings, not corporations. Athenian Democracy required voters to meet in the city center and vote on issues. That is precisely what needs to take place in a country that defines itself as democratic. This requires the country to conform completely to the concept of "one man one vote." Wealthy individuals should not be allowed to contribute unlimited amounts of money to elections. Corporations and unions should be completely barred from participation in elections in any manner including financial contributions, offering manpower to candidates or using their influence or their power to aid one candidate over another. Contributions by candidate and party must be limited to each voter. Strict records must be kept of each election. Cash in and cash out must be controlled with an audit after the election has been concluded and before the electee assumes office. Violators must be sentenced to long prison terms and in elections with severe violations the results should be summarily invalidated, and the election rescheduled. A standard must be set to test against to determine whether an election result must be nullified, and the election redone.

Voting needs to be tightly controlled from registration to the counting of ballots and to the storage for recounts. Long voting periods should be rejected in favor of a one-day election as stated in the Constitution. Mail-in voting should be restricted to individuals who cannot be present, invalids, people confined to nursing homes, and those travelling or living outside of the country. Nursing home patients must be transported to the voting site. All voting facilities must be under 24-hour video surveillance inside, outside and throughout all hallways. All boxes and cartons moving in and out of the facility where votes are being counted must be examined by representatives of both parties and checked. None of the workers should leave unless they ALL leave, and the facility is locked and guarded. All police are to be neutral and not take sides as they are employed by the party in power in that jurisdiction. If representatives from one party complain about voting procedures, the police should NOT be empowered to remove them under any circumstances. All disagreements should be resolved by the two senior party members present. If they cannot be resolved, the facility should immediately be vacated, locked down and a state judge should be called to hear the dispute and rule according to state law.

One week before the election, registration should be closed, and the computerized voter rolls in each state run against every other state to determine if voters are registered to vote in more than one state or if they live in a cemetery.

As voters vote, they should be required to dip a finger into a long-lasting liquid dye to identify them as having voted already. Voters that show up at a polling location must all show their hands have no traces of the dye.

Registering to vote should require several forms of identification including 1) a photo ID with the full name and address and 2) a recent utility bill to demonstrate that the voter does live currently at the address and 3) a birth certificate or other document proving the voter is a U. S. citizen. If these do not match, the voter registration must be rejected.

France manages to have all citizens vote, count and announce winners the same day year after year. America can do it but will not, leaving room for nefarious practices in some states and cities.

Entitlements Reform

Social Security, Medicare and Medicaid are the three largest entitlement programs in the United States. The government provides updates on the funding of these programs occasionally as they monitor when they will run out of funds.

Medicare

Medicare collections per person are estimated as follows: (USAfacts.org)

1.45 percent of payroll paid by the employee and a matching 1.45 percent paid by the employer, for a total of 2.9 percent of payroll. The average salary of an American worker in 2019 was $56,000. Therefore, the Medicare premium per worker was $56,000 times 2.9 percent or $1,624.

Assuming the average worker works 40 years, (26 to 66), then they will have paid into Medicare (40 years times $1,624) or $64,960 over their working life.

In 2019, the average Medicare payout per client was $14,150 per year. Assuming the average individual receives benefits for 15 years (from 66 to 81) the total amount paid out for each individual care over their retirement is $212,250 (15 years times $14,150 per year). *(All calculations are in constant dollars.)*

Therefore, the net deficit for each retiree is $147,290 ($212,250-$64,960). Where does this money come from? Taxes and borrowing.

It is no wonder that the Congress reports the Medicare fund is running out of money. It was a Ponzi scheme from its inception, sold to the American people with blatantly false assumptions. If this were a private pension scheme the executives would be in prison. Politicians, however, shower in Teflon.

To make Medicare solvent and self-supporting, the premiums would need to be increased by two to three hundred percent, which is not politically feasible. Thus, the continual calls for national health insurance that Democrats claim would keep a lid on the costs. Sold as a program that would cover all Americans, it would ration care operating as it does in other countries.

Another solution suggested is to make three changes to Medicare:

First, increase the age at which people become Medicare eligible. It is presently at 65 where it was when the program was first enacted in 1967. In 1967, the life expectancy was 79.8 or 14.8 years past 65. In 2019, seniors aged 65 were expected to live an additional 19.3 years to 84.3 or longer, thus draining Medicare for an additional 4.5 years or 30 percent longer. Many people are in their 90s and still on Medicare. In fact, three generations of Americans are on Medicare right now. The solution is to increase the eligibility age until it matches the social security age of 67. Then the ages for both programs should be increased to 72. (3)

Second, reassert the standard for disability benefits to "unable to work any job in the economy," the original standard. Additionally, reformers can require the applicant to complete a rehabilitation program before assessing their ability to perform a job. New technology should enable almost all people, handicapped or not, to find a job they can perform. Both Medicare and social security have lowered the standard for benefits allowing people who just do not want to work to live off the government programs. (3)

Third, adjust deductibles and coinsurance discounts to levels like private insurance programs. (3)

These three changes will make Medicare solvent again. Will Congress step up to the plate? Don't bet your lunch money. (3)

Medicaid

Another federal program that needs oversight is Medicaid. The federal government used to verify the income of applicants for Medicaid. However, new rules that were supposed to "streamline the process" were apparently a ruse by the Obama administration to transition to no verification of applicants' income. Just apply and the government will pay you. (You know like getting a mortgage with unverified income) This complete scam of the program began with President Obama's Medicaid expansion. It required no verification of income. Anyone who applied could just declare their income and receive benefits. In one Medicaid audit in Louisiana, it was found that in a sample of 100 Medicaid recipients, 82 did not qualify for the benefit. These changes to loosen the eligibility are done purposefully to encourage more people to get on the government dole and result in less work and more sloth. They also result in lifetime loyal Democratic voters. Government cares little about spending the taxpayers' money wisely. (4)

Social Security

Established In 1933, Social Security has been a very popular program with American seniors and for the most part, it has been successful. Prior to its creation, seniors were the group with the highest poverty rates in America. Social Security has provided a minimum income level for seniors who have worked during their lifetime and paid into the fund.

To assess the financial viability of the program, we have used several of the same assumptions as in the example above for Medicare. The average income in 2019, was $56,000. The average working life for a recipient is 40 years.

The Social Security tax for an employee is 6.2 percent, which is matched by the employer for a total of 12.4 percent of the individual's payroll. At $56,000, the annual tax collected is $3,472 times two or $6,944 per year. Multiply this by 40 years (26-66 years of age) of earnings and the total contributions for employee and employer are $277,760.

According to CNBC.COM, the average Social Security benefit check is $1,543 per month or $18,516 per year. Using the same assumption as the Medicare example, that benefits will be paid for 15 years (66 to 81 years of age), the total benefits paid are $277,740, or almost an exact match of the benefits collected of $277,760. This begs the question, why are alarms sounded approximately every 10 years that the fund is going broke?

The major reason is that there are fewer workers working and contributing to the fund now, compared to past years.

The second reason is the ever-increasing number of claims for disability that are filed against the Social Security fund. For many years, the number of these claims was extremely small, and most were rejected, but in the past 10 years, the new age attorneys have prosecuted these claims more aggressively, the bureaucrats caved in, and many more claims have been approved. This section of the Social Security Act has been politicized to award benefits to people who persist in claiming some type of disability even though they cannot, in most cases, be proven. They are mostly soft tissue or headaches, which only the applicant can verify. The proof that many are false is that the number of claims rises when the economy is bad and then falls off again when the job market improves. The Social Security fund was never designed to support disability claims. Taxes were never collected to support these claims. Thus, a shortfall in funding is real for Social Security beneficiaries.

Third, in 1972, Congress under the direction of President Nixon raised Social Security payments by 20 percent and added a cost-of-living adjustment for payments. Due to these changes, the fund was almost immediately unsustainable.

In 1933, when the Social Security Act was passed by Congress, the average life expectancy was 65 years. Now it is 81 years. Life expectancy has increased by 16 years, but the age that full benefits can be applied for has only risen by one year. To be fair, the government has raised the contribution percentage and that has offset some of the increase in benefit costs. However, the system is badly in need of "serious" reform. Several reforms that would increase the solvency of this program are:

1. Extend the age at which full benefits can applied for to 72 on a graduated basis over five years and raise the age for early benefits to 69 on the same

five-year schedule.

2. Remove the tax penalty for Social Security recipients who work and earn money over the limit for Social Security. This is a stupid disincentive and must be changed to encourage older people to work as long as they are able and wish to work. Working adds funding to the Social Security program, which, in turn, makes it financially stronger. Common sense. Right? Not to politicians.

3. Change the awarding of Social Security disability benefits to temporary awards of two years and require the recipients to reapply after the benefit period expires. The bar to receive Social Security disability must be raised to prevent the fund from becoming insolvent.

4. Raise the salary limit to $300,000 for collection of Social Security taxes and adjust the limit at the inflation rate. A small tax on high earners to help the solvency of the fund.

If long-term funding is not addressed, then the Social Security fund will become insolvent and then there will be no benefits for the many who have paid in over their lifetime of work. (4)

Economists have learned from watching Western European countries that expanded entitlements reduce incentives to work and invest and lead to slower economic growth, lower living standards and less room in the budget for other essential funding, such as infrastructure and national defense. This was evident during the Obama presidency when social programs were expanded and the defense budget cut to a point where the military had no ammunition and no funds to purchase aviation fuel.

Voters may have turned to the Republicans to stop the tax, spend and regulation assault by the Democrats, but once established, entitlement programs are impossible to reduce. Don't even dream about eliminating any of them. Argentina is the proof. Argentina was once one of the world's most prosperous nations. Following a military coup in 1930, the country renounced its original constitution and began its journey toward socialism. Hyperinflation and debt defaults have not changed the policies. Their legislature is full of socialists, elected by people who support these policies. It seems that unless there is a civil war, the policies will never change. The people believe that if they change the government, the results will be different, but until the policies are changed, the economy cannot. America is on this path. (6)

Venezuela is another example of how socialism destroyed a prosperous country. The discovery of oil in

Venezuela in 1914 made it one of the world's wealthiest countries. By 1950, its per capita income was fourth behind only the United States, New Zealand and Switzerland. In 2001, it was the wealthiest country in Latin America. However, socialism was on the rise. Price and foreign exchange controls were enacted together with tax increases and property rights restrictions. When Hugo Chavez was elected in 1999, he enacted large social programs to secure voter support. The result was hyperinflation and a collapse of the economy. Now, it suffers from a contracting economy, mass emigration, hunger, starvation and lawlessness. If it sounds like New York City, you are correct. Is this the future of the United States? (7)

Some European governments have seen the error of their expanding social welfare state and tried to rein it in with some success. Germany's labor participation rate rose from 58.1 to 61.3 from 2000 to 2019. Sweden's tax and spending reform of the early 1990s resulted in increased labor productivity, and a 400 percent growth in disposable income. France and Greece have both reduced corporate tax rates. Unfortunately, as Europe learns from their mistakes and moves away from the welfare state, America under the Democrats continues to increase taxes and spend money on faux social programs. (8)

"Congress increased food-stamp benefits by 27 percent in 2021 to improve the diet of Americans. The benefit increased to $835 for a family of four, even though a family of four only spent $537 per month on food in 2019. The justification for this increase is to ensure people eat a better diet. According to government data, 20 percent of food stamps are spent on sweetened beverages, desserts, salty candy and snacks. Like other Great Society programs, food stamps have done nothing to reduce poverty and little to improve public health. They continue to encourage government dependency as evidenced by the continued decline in the nation's labor participation rate. (9)

Throughout our history entitlements have continued to expand. The first entitlement was a pension for the Continental Army soldiers who were wounded. This was later expanded to include state militia and finally to all veterans regardless of how they became disabled.

The Civil War pensions were initially restricted to U. S. servicemen who incurred wartime injuries and survivors of those killed in battle. This was later expanded to all U. S. veterans with any disability and finally to some Confederate widows. Civil war pension costs kept rising until they accounted for 40 percent of the federal budget in 1921.

Congress continued to expand entitlements. In 1956, the Social Security disability program was restricted to permanently disabled workers aged 50 and older. In 1966, this was expanded to temporarily disabled and partly disabled workers. The cost estimate was $1.1 billion in 2000. The actual cost was $56 billion.

There are many, many more examples of entitlements that were expanded to cover other groups. The real question is WHY? **The equally worthy claim is the answer**. A group gets something from the government, so another group lobbies for the benefit because they are "equally worthy." Congress ALWAYS accedes. It's just good politics. Thus, the continued expansion of entitlements happens. No one in Washington has the courage to say NO. (10)

Entitlements are the biggest long-term threat to America and the Democrats conjure up a never-ending stream of new entitlement ideas for each new administration. Slowly but surely, the entitlement nation is taking over the country's "land of opportunity" roots and replacing it with the "land of government entitlements." This transformation is on purpose to create a giant munificent government with free programs for most everything a person needs; food, clothing, housing, education, medical care and transportation. The goal is complete dependency on the government, and, of course, lifelong voter loyalty. Even the implied threat to reduce or repeal the benefit will result in a storm of protests and riots. The result is a continued expansion of the welfare state, requiring ever increasing taxes. It is these taxes that choke off money for investment in productivity improvements and new technologies, both of which are necessary for increased wages and a higher standard of living. The Democrats are wed to their communist ideology and the Republicans are out-to-lunch. The future of America for our children and grandchildren does not look too promising. The results of these programs are evident in democratic-controlled cities like Baltimore; Hartford, Conn.; Memphis, Tenn.; Newark, N.J.; Philadelphia; San Francisco; and Washington. Detroit is the poster child for degradation and despair. In the European welfare states of France, Greece and Italy, this is evident too. There are high taxes, no growth, high unemployment, limited opportunities for the young and a hostile business climate. Wonder why everything is made in China? (11) Entitlements also lead to what is happening now. Many people do not have any interest in working.

Tort Reform

Changes to the rules for tort lawsuits in the 1960s have opened the way for a new business model for lawyers to prosecute claims in the United States. Once a company files for bankruptcy, the tort attorneys vie to become the firm with the largest number of claims so that they can become the firm of record in the case and control it through the bankruptcy proceedings. This has led to the introduction of all sorts of nefarious legal practices, some of which are shady and some of which are illegal but are pursued until the judge ends them. In a *Wall Street Journal* editorial entitled,

"Looting the Boy Scouts," on March 3, 2021, the editorial board describes the practices used in this tort case. "Insurer court filings note that when Scouting of America (BSA) filed for bankruptcy, it was the defendant in 275 cases and been notified of the potential of 1,400 more, BSA now faces 95,000 claims. Behind this assault is a sophisticated new tort machine that leverages Wall Street Litigation funding, third-party brokers to collect and commoditize claims and sweeping online marketing that recruits and coaches' claimants. This is the new mass tort industry." The Coalition of Abused Scouts for Justice is a group coordinating these efforts. "In one email presented to the court. Their strategy was "to keep focused on our marketing and media efforts" so that we "control 80 percent of the claims and we control the case" (and of course the fees).

A preliminary investigation by the two BSA insurers has found that out of the 95,000 cases:

1. 11,676 appear to be duplicates

2. More than 7,000 do not identify a perpetrator

3. 4,700 do not identify any connection to scouting

4. 54,000 appear to be time-barred

"It seems that the attorneys hired claims aggregators, which are private companies that employ call centers and advertising to produce claims. These processors then sell the claims. Plaintiff attorneys use hedge fund money to finance these operations."

These types of practices make a mockery of the intent of bankruptcy law and reward unethical legal practices with large fees for attorneys and payouts to many who were not damaged. These outcomes reduce the funds available for the real victims.

Have you heard of the Camp Lejeune Justice Act? Carcinogenic chemicals leaked into the water supply at the camp. Congress established a multibillion-dollar fund to help the victims. As a gift to the tort lawyers lobby, victims need to be represented by an attorney. Why can't the Judge Advocate General (JAG) corps process these claims?

<u>The Roundup Settlement</u>

In June 2020, Bayer agreed to settle the claims by two different groups of tort lawyers for $10.9 billion even though regulators in the United States, European Union, Australia, Japan and other countries agree that glyphosate (the active ingredient in Roundup) isn't a likely carcinogen. The EPA refused to approve a product warning label claiming the weedkiller causes cancer because it would be "false and misleading." In fact, only the World Health Organization continues to assert that glyphosate is "probably carcinogenic."

In the first three cases to be tried in California courts,

several judges allowed testimony that supported the plaintiffs' assertion that glyphosate "could" cause cancer while, at the same time, disallowing all evidence by other organizations including the EPA that Roundup does not cause cancer. One wonders whether California is still part of the United States and adheres to its federal rules of evidence. The company has now been forced to settle a never-ending string of lawsuits by consortiums of attorneys for damages that have never been proved by science. This amounts to the legal extortion of corporations by the legal profession, aided and abetted by federal Judges. This extortion racket raises insurance rates for companies and the cost of products and services. (12)

Tort lawyers are a loyal group of financial supporters to the Democratic Party. No changes to these laws are likely.

<u>Federal Reserve</u>

There are literally hundreds of federal agencies that operate under the auspices of the legislative branch of government. The one that was set up to be independent and non-political is the Federal Reserve. Its independence was justified by their management of monetary policy, whose goals are full employment and stable pricing. Unfortunately, Congress has begun to use the Fed more often for political and more recently social objectives. During the housing crisis of 2008, the Fed was called upon to back up one specific industry, housing, and a group of non-bank financial institutions. Neither part of its mandate.

During the advent of COVID-19, the Fed has expanded its role in fiscal policy by becoming the buyer of trillions of dollars of government and corporate debt to maintain low interest rates. This is not part of its mandate. Congress is now discussing bills to expand the Fed's role to fund government programs for transportation, public arts, border security and racial inequity. These are not part of its mandate.

It is easier to use Fed funds than to go through the legislative process of having bills passed by both houses of Congress. More members seem willing to expand the Fed's role if they can get funds for their pet projects. Of course, the Fed is not an innocent victim here. It loves the additional power these expansions give it and cooperates with the political party in power. Congress must tighten up the Fed's powers to keep it focused on the narrow responsibility it has. (13)

The federal government is again pursuing policies that work in opposition to each other and do not help the economy grow nor help minorities that they expressly tell everyone they wish to help. A case in point is the Fed's limitless financing of massive government spending. This massive increase in spending and concurrent increase in the money supply is the fuel for inflation and its progeny, price stability.

While the Fed has been busy over-regulating banks to ensure they have "ample reserves," it has created a climate wherein the banks are making conscious decisions every day to buy Treasury debt and reduce the size of their commercial lending portfolio. Their lending is mostly to small businesses that drive the economy and employ the largest percentage of people, many of whom are minorities.

The Fed defends its actions based on its belief that the high joblessness in the economy is the higher priority, but while inflation hurts everyone, it particularly strikes the poorest Americans the worst.

The truth here is that the best way for any economy to grow is through solid business development and expansion that produces a continuous supply of goods and services to customers. Over-expansion of the money supply is a financial "trick" that accelerates economic growth, akin to drinking more Red Bull instead of doing the appropriate training for a marathon.

All capitalist endeavors carry with them a certain level of risk and that risk is better managed by your local lender not the federal government.

"The Fed must avoid turning banks into government utilities through its carrot and stick approach of providing incentives for the accumulation of reserve balances while enforcing compliance parameters that discourage risk taking," such as lending to their local business community. (14)

Price stability is the primary mission of the Federal Reserve. Unfortunately, it has not taken this responsibility seriously. The failure to maintain price stability always results in a financially unstable economy. During the past year, prices increased at three times the Fed's 2 percent target level. This trend was dismissed by both Secretary of Treasury Janet Yellen and Federal Reserve Chairman Jerome Powell. History tells us that "inflation is a choice, a choice which the Fed is responsible." The Fed has been the enabler of the Biden administration in printing excess amounts of money and continuing the expansionary policies when the economy was already growing rapidly." The Fed has continued to deflect responsibility for the ensuing inflationary spiral that is now embedded in the economy. A recession appears to be the result. (15) Congress has the power to rein in the Federal Reserve and have it refocus on its mission of price stability. Again, Democrats want easy money and massive federal spending. The Fed operates as an arm of the administration in power, not independently as it should.

<u>Government Spending</u>

One of the great things about the United States is that there are 50 different models of government to examine. One can choose to follow the path of the lower taxed or the opposite and follow the spend-thrift example. The 41 states with an income tax spent 55 percent more per resident in 2018 than the nine states without an income tax. Florida, which does not have an income tax, spent the least at $2,327 per resident. Texas and New Hampshire, both without income taxes, spent $2,585 and $2,773 respectively. Many of the high tax states run up debt and then seek a bailout from the federal government, threatening a severe cut in service without federal aid. In most states, the appropriation process is more like a negotiation between the legislature and the various agencies on how much to increase their budget for the new year. This failed system should be replaced with one that identifies the priorities and then addresses how to meet them in the most efficient and economical way.

In 2001, Washington State adopted this approach and used a priority-based (businesses refer to it as zero-based budgeting) budget system and erased a 2 billion budget deficit without resorting to tax increases. This approach takes REAL leadership and much more work, something most politicians are averse to doing. (16)

Unfortunately, during the past 20 years the federal government has forgotten its important role in the long- term financial prosperity of the American people. The cornerstones of this prosperity include: 1. A Sound Currency -- not too strong to make exports uncompetitive but not weak so that imports are expensive; 2. Low Federal Debt -- while some debt is necessary for investors to purchase no-risk Treasury debt, large debt loads systematically shut down the economic growth prospects as the rising interest rates and Treasury bond sales soak up an overly large percentage of the available capital; 3. Low Federal Tax rates -- again the government competes for capital with the private sector. History has repeatedly shown us that the private sector is the engine driving economic growth and prosperity, not the government. Presently, the federal government is spending like teenagers with their parents' credit cards. Waste in programs that disburse funds continues to grow and fraud continues to rise in federal programs like Medicare, Medicaid and COVID-19 relief. What is so distressing is that the federal government is both unable and uninterested in stopping fraud and waste. It has no respect for the hardworking taxpayers who toil day after day to earn the money the government steals.

"Washington's reckless spending is completely out of control." "Too many in Washington have accepted deficit spending, blank checks, tax hikes and skyrocketing inflation as the status quo," said Sen. Rick Scott. The nation's debt load has reached $33 trillion, and there is not even a conversation in Washington about a plan to reduce it. No country in history has survived massive debt for very long. The interest payments alone suck a larger and larger portion of the available capital from the economy, which reduces growth and results in long-term stagflation. Low growth with inflation reduces the purchasing power of the dollar and increases the level of poverty. (17)

The Republican-majority house is finally confronting this crisis. As mentioned earlier, the present path of reckless spending leads to becoming Argentina.

<u>Excessive Licensing</u>

"Craft and professional guilds that push licensing requirements often claim they are protecting the public. But typically, they're protecting themselves from competition. How was Florida protecting people by requiring licenses for boxing announcers and boxing timekeepers? Most of the people affected by these overreaching laws are people who either run their own small operation or who work for a small business. Hefty license requirements including fees, educational requirements and governmental paperwork, including licenses and permits keep people from earning a living. Licensing reform across the country is necessary to help people at the bottom of the employment ladder earn a living doing what they know best. (18)

Gov. Ron DeSantis has led a reform of these policies. The Occupational Freedom and Opportunity Act is the largest deregulation in the state's history. Included in this legislation are landscape architects, cosmetologists, hair braiders and barbers. The bill reduces training hours, duplicative business licenses and increases license reciprocation from other states. It is estimated this legislation will free up 130,000 jobs. Other states should follow Florida's lead to help small businesspeople work. (18)

<u>The Green New Deal</u>

The Green New Deal has the immense goal of eliminating fossil fuels in 10 years. To do this, it wants to retrofit every building in America, guaranteeing high paying jobs to everyone working on the project. However, as we all know the devil is in the details for all these massive government initiatives. The New York City Housing Authority housing projects near Rep. Alexandria Ocasio-Cortez's office have a limited goal of a 30 percent reduction in greenhouse gas emissions by 2027. One of their initiatives is to switch to LED lighting systems, which use less electricity and last longer. One recent project was completed at a cost of $33.2 million or $1,973 per unit. Electricians for this project were paid $81 per hour base, plus $54 in fringe benefits. That computes to 15 hours of work for each apartment unit. She was correct about paying high wages, but can we afford these exorbitant costs? The squad believes that the government can just print more money when it runs out, so spend, spend, spend on their projects. (19)

Part-time "Professional" State Legislators

There is a growing movement across the United States to convert all state legislators to full-time "professional" bodies. The proponents assert well-paid "professionals" are less susceptible to corruption, are more responsive and give citizens better government. This is part of the movement away from citizen legislators, the part-time, non-professional lawmakers who have populated state legislatures since the early days of the republic." Of course, the facts do not support the theory. Voters in the states that pay legislators the most are the most dissatisfied. The major job of the state legislature is to spend the taxpayer's money "wisely." A Pew study found the correlation between high pay and responsible state budgets was almost exactly inverse, meaning the less the legislators were paid, the more responsible they were with the taxpayers' money. (20)

Public Employee Unions

President Franklin Roosevelt wrote that the process of collective bargaining has "insurmountable limitations when applied to public personnel management." He believed that the employer of government workers was the people and Congress represented the people in determining government employees' pay. In practice, the insurmountable problem with government unions is that there is no effective representative of the people in the negotiations." The effects President Roosevelt warned us about are present in New York State. Every government employee is represented by a union that works overtime to stymie innovation, drive up costs and taxes. The unions and the Democratic Party are merged at the hip. They are arms of the same beast and have no regard for the public. The entire concept of arms-length negotiations between two parties with different objectives does not exist. They have the same objectives, higher pay and benefits for their workers and screw the taxpayers. (21) President Kennedy signed the bill allowing government workers the right to collective bargaining. This unleased the genie, and the results have been catastrophic for state and city budgets. Good luck ever getting the genie back in the bottle.

The Housing Crisis

Welcome to Oregon where the population grew by 400,000 from 2010 to 2019. Unfortunately, due to restrictive land-use rules, rent control laws and other barriers to building, the construction of only 148,000 housing units was allowed. The state and local governments operate in a kind of intellectual dreamland where they work hard to attract new business and just as hard to prevent builders from accommodating the employees of these businesses with places to live. Residents do not like multi-family housing and do not want their pristine vistas spoiled with housing and shopping centers, so the cost of housing continues to rise, impacting low and middle earners the most. Home prices rise, rents rise, and the dumb politicians increase rent control laws. High rents are a symptom of the problem, not the cause. (22)

These same practices are in force in many affluent Democratic communities, mostly along both coasts. They prevent housing from being built because they believe multi-family housing attracts a lower class of people into the community. These are the same people who repair and clean their homes, wait on them in restaurants, work in retail stores and provide other services to them. Where multi-family housing is constructed, they make war on the landlords by enacting rent control laws to starve them into abandoning the building because they are unable to generate enough cash to pay for repairs. These forms of persecution result in an inadequate level of investment in housing for the working class.

<u>Student Loans</u>

With the government "takeover" of the student loan industry under the Obama administration to "save money," the historical relationship between debtor and creditor has now become a political relationship between lender and voter. Since Democrats will do anything (and have) to entice life-long voter loyalty with "special preferences," the government-funded student loan industry is just one additional group to eat at the government's hog trough. This special is doubly beneficial to Democrats because it rewards two groups at the same time. The first of course is the colleges, whose tuitions have risen at 4.6 times the rate of inflation for the past 50 years. Student debt is now a staggering $1.7 trillion. The changes incorporated into the 2010 government takeover allowed students to borrow much higher amounts of money for college, in effect giving a teenager an unlimited credit card with someone else paying the bill. The fact that changes to the Federal Bankruptcy Law in 2005 excluded the discharge of student debt is the reason the federal government now has to pass another law to cancel this debt. At the time, private lenders were the only ones involved. What did colleges promise to obtain this special consideration from Congress? They must have paid plenty because that is how things get done in Washington. Or, it may have been part of a longer-term plan by the Democrats to create an additional reason for the eventual cancelling of student debt. (23)

The cancelling then begets the question of whether future debt will be cancelled as well. Because the same forces are at work, outrageous tuition that continues to rise, the inability of many students to pay off the loans due to their poor choice of majors and the desire for Democrats to offer special considerations for voter support, it leads directly to free college for all.

Free college for all sends many messages to the country: 1) to colleges, you can continue to raise your tuition and the federal government will pay the bill (similar message to health care providers from Medicare and Medicaid); 2)to students, spend whatever you want, wherever you want 3) study anything regardless of whether it leads to a real job 4) for non-college graduates, pay the bill and shut up ;5) for those who paid their own tuition, tough luck, now pay for these other people.

This is another example of the Democrats at work. They create a problem, the massive student debt and then their solution is to make it free to "solve" the problem they created. In fact, students were paying their college loan debt very well with private loans, scholarships, grants and work programs offered by the colleges themselves.

The goal by the Obama administration was to change the relationship from lender/borrower to lender/voter, thus an opportunity for special treatment for the borrower and their conversion into a lifelong Democratic voter. Student loan programs must be returned to the private sector.

<u>Special Districts</u>

Until the recent blow-up between Disney and DeSantis, the Reedy Creek Improvement District was virtually unknown inside Florida. However, once the story broke and questions were asked, the mysterious and virtually invisible world of "special districts" became a topic for further investigation. Special districts were championed by FDR as a way to apply for and obtain federal funds for special projects without going through voters and local politicians. Presently, there are more than 38,000 special districts nationwide (No surprise FDR always acted as if he was above the law) with 1,800 in Florida. They operate completely independent of local government, making it impossible for taxpayers and politicians to have any oversight of their spending. The special district makes its own decisions, and the taxpayers get the bill. This lack of oversight has contributed to corruption and even debt defaults at five times the rate of other municipal debt. (24) We hope that more state governors will step up and kill these special districts.

Bureaucratic Tyranny

The COVID-19 crisis was an unfortunate episode in history. If there was one good thing that came from the pandemic, it was the ability of the American people to see the government bureaucracy in action, the half-truths, outright lies, the contempt for the people and the use of its power to deny citizens' rights enshrined in the Constitution. It was nothing short of startling. Many people were continually asking whether they lived in Russia or the United States. The policies of both became so similar no one could distinguish between the two of them. Mayors and governors behaved like the banana republic dictators we have always been told to view with disdain. Perhaps, the most egregious of all was the federal government's medical leadership, specifically, Fauci and Collins. These two became addicted to their sudden rise to power and continued to collude with the media and the Democratic Party to cancel and denigrate anyone who disagreed with their policies, including several well-respected epidemiologists. *The Great Barrington Declaration* was "a statement signed by Harvard's Martin Kulldorf, Oxford's Sunetra Gupta and Stanford's Jay Bhattacharya against blanket pandemic lockdowns. They favored a policy of what they called "focused protection" of high-risk populations, such as the elderly or those with co-morbidity conditions. Thousands of scientists signed the declaration." Instead of an open forum for ideas to find the very best solutions, we experienced the tyranny of these petty bureaucrats whose policies killed thousands unnecessarily, caused thousands of Americans to go bankrupt and millions of children to suffer from being locked up for years away from their friends. (25)

The Poverty Delusion

"Since the War on Poverty started in 1965, the labor force participation rate of the bottom-quintile of earners, who now receive more than 90 percent of their $50,000 average income from government transfer payments, has fallen from almost 70 percent to 36 percent. How long will it take for the national labor force participation rate of 61.6 percent to fall to 55 percent as it is in France or 50 percent as it is in Italy." The Democrats are doing to the United States what they have done to our European friends, destroying their economies. This is the first step toward their march to full Communism. A smaller and smaller percentage of the population who work supports an increasing percentage of the population who do not work. It seems doable until it all falls apart because the productive group can no longer carry the financial burden. What specifically drives Democratic governments to believe that it must place a person on welfare to help them? Governments have developed a whole body of rationale for helping people and conversely a menu of programs for every possible contingency of life. Helping people is complicated according to them. Maybe the old and very simple question is a guide: Do you give a man a fish? Or do you teach him to fish? (26)

The American welfare system provides its recipients $65,300 in benefits, including food, housing and medical assistance, all for NOT working.

The Census Bureau purposely does not count as income numerous social program transfer payments including refundable tax credits, food stamps, Medicaid, the Children's Health Insurance Program, rent subsidies, energy subsidies, and health insurance subsidies under the Affordable Care Act. In total, more than 100 other federal, state and local transfer payments aren't counted by the Census Bureau as income to the recipients. (27)

If the Census Bureau would have included the missing $1.9 trillion in transfer payments, child poverty would have been only 3.2 percent in 2017 compared with the official rate of 17.5 percent. In 2020, if all the transfer payments were recorded, the poverty rate would have been 2 percent. (27)

This is the biggest fraud in the country perpetrated on the American taxpayers. The government must continue the "war on poverty" by increasing the amount of money spent on poverty-reduction programs. The Democrats purposely instruct the Census Bureau to lie about the poverty rate so they can continue to justify large increases in spending. This money is directed to blue cities and states that use it to hire more and more people (overseers) to "administer" the ever-increasing social programs. The number of overseers increases and the number of people who receive benefits increases, and more of them decide not to work. This also creates an army of loyal Democrat supporters and party workers whose livelihood depends on these programs.

Department of Injustice

On July 1, 1870, Congress created the Department of Justice to "handle all criminal prosecutions and civil suits in which the United States had an interest." Unfortunately, in recent years, Americans have seen the department frequently weaponized by the Democrats to prosecute any group who dared to fight Democrat policies. The most recent incursion has been using the Patriot Act to prosecute parents who are fighting school boards who insist on teaching their children racially divisive theologies. The department mobilized their "counterterrorism" agents to monitor parents at school board meetings. Parents have every right to protest school board officials' decisions regarding the school curriculum. None other than the United Nations in its *Declaration of Universal Human Rights* states "parents have the primary right to choose the kind of education that shall be given to their children." It is only in totalitarian countries that the State believes all children are wards of the state and will be taught what the State decides. (28)

The FBI needs a complete overhaul of its management and procedures. "Former FBI special agent Thomas J. Baker has made a compelling case that the bureau's post 9-11 focus on 'intelligence' and subsequent centralization of case management are part of the problem. This plus the clique of insiders who have abandoned the ethos of fairness and impartiality have converted the FBI into a purely political police force working for the Democrats. (29)

FBI agents were caught making highly unflattering

remarks about President Trump and his supporters while pursuing a case against him based on a fake dossier fed to them by the Hillary Clinton campaign. (30)

Merrick Garland is using his office to persecute President Trump. The raid on Mar-A-Largo was clearly an effort to discredit Trump and to get this charge into the media headlines before the November election. "Lawyers David Rivkin and Lee Casey made a compelling case that President Trump has every right to hold the documents for a time at his home under the 1978 Presidential Records Act." Disputes are a matter of negotiation with the National Archives.

Inspector General Michael Horowitz Report on the FBI's surveillance abuses is evidence of its belief that it is "above the law" and not in any manner accountable to Congress for its illegal activities. "The FBI must abide by the Woods procedures that include a file supporting every factual assertion in a warrant application." The *Inspector General's Report* found numerous errors and omissions, including some that were material enough to change the FISA courts determination to issue a warrant. "Congress should abolish the FISA court as there are too many opportunities for the Justice Department to request unsubstantiated FISA warrants. It must return authority to law enforcement for surveillance decisions, then hold DOJ accountable for abuses, including jail time." (30)

Congress must increase its regular oversite of the FBI and Justice Department and pass legislation to tighten up and clarify penalties for violations.

<u>Weaponizing the Government</u>

The Biden administration is requesting an increase in the IRS budget of $80 billion to collect the estimated $600 billion to $1 trillion the administration "claims" is unpaid each year. Thousands of additional agents and of course a plethora of new rules and reporting requirements to "catch" people avoiding the payment of their "fair share" of taxes. The U. S. Federal Income tax system is not the greatest, but it does work fairly well to collect taxes from individuals and businesses. The main question is whether adding more people and more regulation is the best method to achieve a higher level of adherence to the law. Milton Freidman believed that the lower the tax and regulation burden, the higher the adherence and the greater the sums collected. Of course, the difference in ideology is the difference between the two political parties' philosophy. The concern taxpayers have about the IRS hiring more staff is that it will increase its persecution of taxpayers who the Democrats do not like. Lois Lerner, an IRS Director, singled out conservative non-profits for special scrutiny and harassment. Will the IRS identify Republican donors for special scrutiny, Right to Life activists or Parents Who Protest Critical Race Theory teaching at their local school? No one knows until it becomes a *fait accompli.* (31) The IRS operates under the philosophy that everyone is guilty until proven innocent. It also is the agency that most Americans hate.

The IRS has so many different missions besides collecting taxes with its numerous credits, refunds and deductions. Can it do it more effectively? The better way forward is not MORE regulation but to cut the tax code by 50 percent. It presently costs American taxpayers $304 Billion to comply each year with the numerous tax regulations. The U. S. tax code is one of the most complex in the world. Simplification will allow taxpayers to better understand the compliance requirements. Eliminating social missions and credits will reduce complexity. A simpler code requires fewer people to administer. Democrats always want more government employees. (31)

<u>Over-Regulation</u>

The most insidious form of taxation of the American people is the continued addition of new regulations and new regulatory agencies. In 1950, the Code of Federal Regulation consisted of 13 books, each approximately 750 pages in length. By 2013, the code was comprised of 235 books of the same size, an 1,800 percent increase. According to the *Journal of Economic Growth*, if the regulatory burden was maintained at 1950 levels, by 2011, the Gross Domestic Product (GDP), the size of the U. S. economy, would have been three and half times larger. Instead of being $23 trillion, it would be

$80 trillion. Instead of generating $4 trillion in tax revenues for the government, they would be $14 trillion.

What is happening is that the stupid, feckless policies of the Washington lawmakers and bureaucrats are actually killing the economy. Instead of being $32 trillion in debt and unable to buy enough fuel and spare parts for the Air Force to train our pilots, the country would have a sizable excess of cash and be able to reduce taxes. It seems ridiculous for them to continue along this path. However, if you understand their goal is to transition the U. S. to a communist society, destroying the economy and hiring more disciples makes perfect sense.

One solution would be a congressional bipartisan task force, like the Base Closure Task Force, who reviews regulations and their impact on the country and recommends their elimination. Lump them together in a group so that the individual beneficiaries of the regulations are unable to lobby for the exemption of their favorites for a straight up or down vote. This should be an ongoing task force with a new list each year, trying to reduce the overwhelming tide of new regulations that strangle the country. The goal should be a 50 percent reduction in regulation. If that sounds severe, think about the always reliable 80/20 rule of thumb. It postulates that 20 percent of the regulations would cover 80 percent of the situations. At 50 percent of

the regulations, they must cover well over 90 percent
of the situations. The addition of more and more regulation in most cases just adds more complexity and
confusion. New regulations conflict with others. More
lawsuits are a direct result.   (32)

Footnotes:

1-"Democracy Dies in Illinois," Review and Outlook, *WSJ*, 11/17/2012

2-"Zuckerbucks Shouldn't Pay for Elections," Review and Outlook, *WSJ*, 1/4/2022q

3-"Modest Cuts Could Save Medicare from Disaster," John F. Early, *WSJ*, 6/11/2019

4-"Means Tested Welfare Means Nothing in Practice," Robert Doar, *WSJ*, 12/12/2019

5-"Why Bernie Sanders Is Wrong About Sweden," The Weekend Interview, Adam O'Neal, *WSJ*, 8/24/2019

6-"Argentina's Welfare Warning to America," Mary Anastasia O'Grady, *WSJ*, 11/8/2021

7-"Venezuela's Tyranny of Bad Ideas, Daniel Pipes," *WSJ*, 8/27/2018

8-"The Entitlements of U. S. Decline," Review and Outlook, *WSJ*, 10/7/2021

9-"The Democratic Food Stamp Boom," Review and Outlook, *WSJ*, 8/18/2021

10-"Entitlements Always Grow and Grow," John F. Cagan, *WSJ*, 1/4/2022

11- "It's The Entitlements Stupid," Review and Outlook, *WSJ*, 6/29/2021

12-Review and Outlook, *WSJ*, 6/29/2020

13- "A Politicized Fed Endangers the Economy," Jeb Hensarling, *WSJ*, 1/18/2022

14-"Fed Policy is Smothering Private Lending," Judy Shelton, *WSJ*, 3/9/2021

15- "The Fed Is the Main Inflation Culprit," Kevin Warsh, *WSJ*, 12/13/2021

16-"The Alternative to a Bailout for Fiscally Mismanaged States," Jonathan Williams and David Trabert, *WSJ*, 10/17/2020

17-"How the Fed Finances U. S. Debt," Judy Shelton, *WSJ*, 10/14/2021

18-"Florida's Licensing Breakthrough," Review and Outlook, *WSJ*, 7/27/2020

19- "$1973 LEDs and the Green New Deal," Review and Outlook, *WSJ*, 2/16/2019

20-"Lawmakers Are Doing a Bad Job, So Give Them a Raise," Steven Malanga, *WSJ*, 1/12/2019

21-"FDR Was Right on Public-Employee Unions," Letters to the Editor, Greg Brown, *WSJ*, 3/3/2020

22-"The Housing Shortage in Profile," Review and Outlook, *WSJ*, 1/6/2020

23-"Student Loan Relief Should Come in Bankruptcy Court," Richard J. Shinder, *WSJ*, 5/11/2022

24- "Special Districts, Where Dreams of Unaccountable Power Come True," Judge Glock, *WSJ*, 4/26/2022

25-"How Fauci and Collins Shut Down Debate," Review and Outlook, *WSJ*, 12/22/2021

26-"The Democrats Tax the Rich Ruse," Phil Gramm and Mike Salon, *WSJ*, 10/15/2021

27-"What the Child Poverty Rate is Missing," Phil Gramm and John Early, *WSJ*, 9/21/2022

28-"The Patriot Act Wasn't Meant to Target Parents," F. James Sensenbrenner, *WSJ*, 10/13/2021

29-"Garland Goes Solo at Mar-A-Largo," William McGurn, *WSJ*, 8/16/2022

30-"The FBI's Other Warrant Abuses," Review and Outlook, *WSJ*, 10/6/2021

31- "Defund Joe Biden's IRS," William McGurn, *WSJ*, 7/6/2021

32-Patrick McLaughlin and Robert Greene, Mercatos Center, George Mason University

Final Thoughts

After three years of research and writing, I have decided to conclude the book and publish what has been written thus far. More subjects could be researched and added, but it is time to let the work that has been written speak for itself. Research is hard work. Writing is hard work. The combination of the two is doubly difficult. However, once completed there is a sense of achievement and satisfaction. The goal has always been to uncover the truth and bring it to the reader in an easy-to-understand prose style. Examples have been added where it was believed they could further clarify the content.

This is an unusual book in that it encompasses many subjects. Most authors in this genre limit their writing to one or a few topics. This book covers at least 10. Notwithstanding the breath of topics, there are two themes that are constant throughout the various chapters and subjects.

First, government interference, while well-intentioned, does not always result in benefits for many people. A current example is the present Biden economic policy that has resulted in stagflation, low economic growth and persistent high inflation. The Biden economic team was warned about this possibility, but the administration disregarded the warnings and plowed ahead to inject over $8 trillion into the economy. Demand accelerated while supply was still recovering from worldwide COVID-19 lockdowns. Unable to satisfy the rapidly increasing demand, the result was, as expected, higher prices and shortages. The economy would have recovered on its own. There was no need for the massive injection of cash by the government. It was an opportunity by the Biden administration to distribute money to blue states and pet projects. Now Americans are stuck with the problem of systemic inflation. The Federal Reserve's poor prescription for a solution has only created other problems, such as bank failures. The bank failures were due to changes in the banking laws requiring current valuations of all assets.

Medicare is a prime example of government intrusion that has had unintended consequences for American citizens. The small payroll deductions, even over many years, are insufficient to cover the medical expenses of the elderly. Congress knew this when it enacted the law. The construction of the policies forced the non-Medicare patients to pay most of the bill in the form of inflated prices for medical care to cover their care, plus the care of the Medicare patients, who receive care at subsidized prices. The government is picking winners and losers.

Welfare is probably the most pervasive example of government policy gone wrong. Originally intended to help poor blacks improve their economic condition, it has, in fact, destroyed millions of black families and consigned them to perpetual poverty by destroying family structures. Although the evidence is overwhelming that welfare and the attendant poverty programs are destroying the lives of the poor, government refuses to correct or eliminate the programs because it would change the political landscape and expose protected Democratic legislative representatives to challenges and possible loss of their seat.

The rules and regulations concerning climate change are damaging. In this instance, the government has cowed scientists to adopt the narrative that climate change is due to human causes, and it can only be controlled if everyone will do exactly as they say. This means transforming the entire economy. This transformation will take place according to the edicts of mostly unelected government bureaucrats. All opposition is to be attacked, censored and shut down. This transformation will cost more than $100 trillion, which will be largely borrowed and added to the national debt without discussion or debate. Climate science is unsettled but disregard that fact and instead accept the fallacious storyline of the federal government. Fossil fuels are the perpetrators, and they must be eliminated, whatever the cost. So shut up and do what the bureaucrats tell you.

Throughout the United States, private elementary, high schools and colleges are the highest-rated educational institutions. With some exceptions, public educational institutions are second class. If this is the reality, then why do politicians fight to maintain children in public schools where they receive a second-class education? Politics and money are the reasons. Teachers' unions run public K-12 education and they are the major donors to Democratic candidates. Nothing can interfere with this cozy relationship, certainly not something as unimportant as children's education. There has been some recent pushback with parents fighting for school choice. Red states will change, but blue state children will continue with the poor union education and woke sexual indoctrination. America's students are continuing to fall in international ratings. We cannot maintain our economic leadership with students whose educational attainment is 30th worldwide.

The second theme that continually arises as we traverse through the various topics is the inability of government to improve. This is manifest in every state and federal election cycle where several states take days and even weeks to count ballots. Many of these elections are so fraught with violations and fraud charges that the final vote takes months for the courts to certify. France has 47 million voters and same day in-person voting. They count all the votes before midnight on Election Day. Many states encourage weak election rules that foster cheating of all types. This is all done under the false umbrella of voter suppression. Democrats continue to complain that requiring any ID is a suppression of the right to vote. They should know. It was the southern Democrats who passed the laws that prevented blacks from voting in southern states for almost 100 years. While they cry foul at any suggestion of reform, it is the same blue states year after year that compile the most voting irregularities and have the most difficulty delivering a certifiable tabulation of the votes.

The Social Security program was initially enacted to provide a source of funds for the elderly when they retired. Actuaries were hired by Social Security Administration to forecast the life spans of Americans and calculate the benefits based on age, years worked and amount contributed to the Social Security fund. Life spans increased. President Nixon gave Social Security recipients a 20 percent increase. Claims for disabilities exploded as attorneys solicited those denied benefits sued and the Social Security Administration caved into their threats. The result is that the fund is going bankrupt. Several administrations have allowed the situation to deteriorate instead of making the changes necessary to strengthen the reserves. Extending the age is the best remedy, yet it is politically unpopular and so nothing is done. Waiting for financial collapse? It seems the answer is yes.

The Biden administration has continued to ignore the southern border crisis. The mainstream media cooperate by reporting nothing about the southern border. That leaves a few conservative media organizations and Republicans in Congress to focus a spotlight on the problem. Unfortunately, there is not enough attention to get any action from the federal government. Included in the mass of humanity crossing the border illegally each day are drug mules carrying all types of illegal narcotics and human traffickers of women and children. Biden tells us there is no problem. His lackeys have explained they wish to help those fleeing persecution. Fentanyl is killing 100,000 a year, the Democrats are benefiting from an open border. Others are not.

President Reagan was right when he stated that the nine worst words any American should ever hear are, "I'm from the government and I'm here to help."

Politicians have deluded themselves into believing they can enact laws to "fix" what they perceive as social inequities. But their so called "fixes" have unintended consequences and create other problems that, in turn, require a new "fix." The cycle continues and the distortions in the social fabric of the country continue to drain the economic vitality and faith in government. The very best solution is for government to exercise a light hand over the economy and the American people. A free people and free open market can do a much better job of allocating resources and addressing problems.

In this book, I have endeavored to propose better solutions to persistent problems. None were politically motivated. Businesspeople see problems and fix them. Many politicians like to keep the problem static as it is a perpetual campaign theme. It is unlikely that any of these proposals will ever be adopted on a federal level. States, however, are more practical, less political and open to different ideas.

To each of the readers, thank you for joining me on this journey. I hope I have helped to enlighten you on a few topics. I have certainly learned a great deal.

On to the next book.

James Razzino

Bibliography

Charter Schools and Their Enemies, Thomas Sowell

Drug Use for Grown-Ups, Chasing Liberty in the Land of Fear, Dr. Carl L. Hart

The Diversity Illusion, How Race and Pandering Corrupt the University and Undermine Our Culture, Heather MacDonald

Death of a Nation, Plantation Politics and the Making of the Democratic Party, Dinesh D'Souza

False Alarm, How Climate Change Panic Costs Us Trillions, Hurts the Poor, and Fails to Fix the Planet, Bjorn Lomborg

Unsettled, What Climate Science Tells Us, What It Doesn't, and Why It Matters, Steven E. Koonin

An American Sickness, How Healthcare Became Big Business and How You Can Take It Back, Elisabeth Rosenthal

The Silk Roads, A New History of the World, Peter Frankopan

The Intelligence Trap, Why Smart People Make Dumb Mistakes David Robson

January 6, How Democrats Used the Capitol Protest to

Launch a War on Terror Against the Political Right, Julie Kelly

Overcharged, Why Americans Pay Too Much for Health Care, Charles Silver and David A. Hyman

The Russia Hoax, The Illicit Scheme to Clear Hillary Clinton and Frame Donald Trump, Greg Jarrett

American Marxism, Mark R. Levin

Great Society, A New History, Amity Shlaes

Cobalt Red, Siddharth Kara

Harnessing the Intellectuals, Carlos Ripoll

The Plot to Change America: How Identity Politics is Dividing the Land of the Free, Mike Gonzalez

Winning the Race, John McWhorter

In Defense of German Colonialism, Bruce Gilley

The Upswing, Shayla Romney Garrett

The Routledge History of Italian Americans, William Connell

The Declining Significance of Race, William Julius

The Smartest Kids in the World and How They Got That Way, Amanda Ripley

Thank you for purchasing this book.
Please leave a review on Amazon.

www.ingramcontent.com/pod-product-compliance
Lightning Source LLC
Chambersburg PA
CBHW071353150726
48000CB00001B/4